William Brown
and the
LOUTH PANORAMA

William Brown
and the
LOUTH PANORAMA

David Robinson OBE
and
Christopher Sturman

Published in association with the Society for Lincolnshire History & Archaeology by

Louth Naturalists', Antiquarian and Literary Society

The Museum, 4 Broadbank, Louth, Lincs LN11 0EQ
(Tel: 01507 601211)
2001

ISBN 0 9539533 0 0

Text set in Baskerville BT
Colour scans by Gordon Graphics
Book design by David Robinson

Printed in Great Britain by Allinson & Wilcox Ltd.
Queen Street, Louth, Lincolnshire LN11 9BN. Tel: 01507 606661.

Contents

Panorama panels and transparent keys –
in pocket inside back cover

Foreword

THIS BOOK is a tribute to both the painter William Brown, and to that scholar of Lincolnshire, Christopher Sturman, whose last years in a short life were spent with David Robinson unravelling the life of Brown of the great Louth Panorama.

The *Panorama* would have featured in all histories of Panoramania had it not disappeared. I saw it first when in the county that hot summer of 1959: no rain for a month and Lincolnshire lying somnolent. For me this heightened the sense of rurality across this most rural of English counties. I had a rendezvous in Louth with Jack Yates. He enthused, 'You must see Brown's Panorama', explaining how it had been discovered in a cottage in 1948. 'Quite marvellous, a national treasure'.

I don't know what I expected. Certainly not the two canvasses, each measuring six feet by nine feet. I was confronted by a miracle, but one jewel-like, glowing among the detritus of the Town Hall's Council Chamber. What a mess: chairs piled up, paper cups lying about, a folding table propped against one end, shabbiness overall. To many it might have been two pieces of decorative wallpaper. John Betjeman had tried to see it and failed, and only succeeded when Henry Thorold drove him across the county in his stately Bentley. I truly gasped. Jack was right, 'Nothing like it'. Indeed, nor anywhere in Europe, and here I was in the remote Wolds.

What a fascinating tale David Robinson tells. As much as anything it is about education and the dissemination of learning in a remote market town in the first half of Victoria's reign. We read of the *London Panorama from Primrose Hill* exhibited in the Louth Theatre in 1823, and speculation as to whether the young Brown could have seen it. What he did see for certainty were exhibitions in the Louth Mechanics' Institution, which he joined in 1834, where in the following year he exhibited his own *Peripatetic Diorama*. In the Institution's reading room he would have eagerly studied in the *Illustrated London News*, on 7 January 1843, the *London Colosseum Panorama*. One year later the spire of St James's church was scaffolded, and Brown was up there, making his preliminary drawings. He exhibited his final work in the Louth Mansion House in 1847.

Among European panoramas, Brown's can hold its own with the best, but in many ways it is better than the best. He saw it as a personal challenge, one with as much intensity as his own Dissenting Methodism. What raises his *Panorama* to a unique position in the history of panoramas, is that Brown as a Ludensian knows everyone and sees all, intimate with the evolving social and architectural history of the town. We can recognize people, daily incidents, and even the correct prevailing wind. When the *Panorama* was exhibited again in 1848 and 1856, Brown had incorporated the East Lincolnshire Railway opened in 1848. Had it been engraved as intended in 1844, Brown would have long secured a place in the Pantheon of British artists and artists of panoramas.

I remember the crowds who came in 1988 to Colnaghi in Bond Street, London, to marvel at the Panorama exhibited there. I recollect, too, many astonished comments such as, 'but it's in Louth, in the Town Hall', marvelling that such a treasure could be found in a town hall. When I returned to Jack Yates that day in sultry 1959, he said of the Panorama, 'It really is Lincolnshire's most precious possession' – referring to the Magna Carta in Lincoln Cathedral. To which I replied, 'But there is more than one copy of the Magna Carta'.

John Harris
London
February 2001

Introduction and Acknowledgements

CHRISTOPHER STURMAN's mother and my father were cousins. I knew Christopher from the time he was a pupil at King Edward VI School, Louth. Our common ground was historical geography, particularly of Louth and north-east Lincolnshire, in which we collaborated through his university and schoolteaching years. Our interest in the Panorama of Louth and its painter William Brown was long-standing, and many were the hours we spent discussing it and him, and avenues of research. In the early 1990s we conceived the idea of an illustrated book on Brown and the Panorama. In October 1997 he was to have delivered the annual Wallis Lecture on the subject to the Louth Naturalists', Antiquarian & Literary Society in the Council Chamber of the Town Hall where the Panorama hangs. Sadly his cancer was more advanced than we thought, and I gave the lecture, using his notes. He was still dictating outline sections for the book when he died on 3 November, aged only 47.

I took up the daunting task of completing the research and writing, a more complex and detailed process than I and, I suspect, he had anticipated. Christopher had written an introduction, and this I felt should be included in near entirety. It was written in October 1997.

Christopher Sturman takes a Brown's eye view of the town from the lower vantage of the tower gallery of St James's church. (Photo: Valerie Purton)

"As a native Ludensian I seem to have been always aware of the existence of the Panorama: there it was, in the Council Chamber, part of the day-to-day life of a vigorous market town in the decades after the Second World War, hidden behind piles of chairs, stampeded around by doughty local ladies during coffee mornings and sales of work, or by uniformed pupils of King Edward's School at our speech days, an old friend, never consciously thought about, an angel entertained for years unawares.

"It was not until the 1960s, as I entered my teens, that the Panorama achieved greater visibility when it appeared in black and white (and somewhat imperfect reproduction) on the dustjacket and end papers of *The Story of Claribel* (the Louth Victorian ballad writer) by Phyllis Smith and Margaret Godsmark (1965), and the left panel as an end paper in David Robinson's *Book of Louth* (1979). After these brief flirtations with fame, it remained as before in the Council Chamber, uncelebrated until the 1980s.

"I was asked to give a talk on local artists to the Ant and Nats (Louth Naturalists', Antiquarian & Literary Society). This took place in the Council Chamber, and the Panorama was therefore, possibly for the first time, examined critically by an informed and enthusiastic audience. I went to work on the files of the *Stamford Mercury*, the newspaper for which William Brown, in his other role as reporter, worked for many years, and became increasingly absorbed in and impressed by the life and work of this eccentric and undervalued man.

"In 1988 came the important exhibition in the Colnaghi Gallery in London to celebrate the work of the National Art Collections Fund. I was delighted to be asked to write the catalogue entry for the Panorama, and then approached one of the commissioning editors of *Country Life* to propose a full-scale article on Brown's Panorama. The editor agreed, not realising that a different commissioning editor had assigned John Harris, the eminent architectural historian, to the same task. John was Director of the Colnaghi Gallery, joint author with Nikolaus Pevsner of *The Buildings of Lincolnshire* and a frequent contributor to *Country Life*. We turned up in Louth on the same day, with the same brief, and encountered one another on the steps of the District Library, then housed in the old drill hall on Victoria Road. The rather delicate situation was resolved by our joining forces, John's more general interest in architecture and especially in the history of gardens combining with my local historian's focus to produce, we both felt, a richer piece of writing.

"I continued to gather material during the 1990s, and used details of the Panorama in other published work. My interest was sharpened in 1996 by the discovery of Brown's original preparatory sketches for the Panorama, and other watercolours, which were in the possession of his descendant Anthony Jarvis who had kindly loaned them to Louth Museum to be copied. The opportunity to compare the painting exhibited in 1856 with the sketches of 1844 increased my sense of the work's importance as a piece of three-dimensional history – enabling twentieth century eyes to reconstruct the crucial years of the Railway Boom which so decisively changed the face of our country. I had worked reasonably through the *Stamford Mercury* files and intended to move on to explore further the *Lincolnshire Chronicle* when illness in summer 1997 made further library research impossible."

Had Christopher been able to complete the research and to write it up in the detail it deserved, he wished to dedicate it to three people. To Alex Slack, through whom the Panorama was rediscovered during his term as Mayor of Louth (he also died in 1997); to the late Gill Foot (who painted under her maiden name Nadin), from whom he learned much of his understanding of and approach to the study of environment; and to Pat Salton, who retired from librarian of Louth Library in 1997, and who for over twenty years had helped and encouraged his enquiries.

In the event, I feel that the book should be dedicated to Christopher himself. Without his polymath passion for research into neglected aspects of Lincolnshire people and history, the study of William Brown and his Panorama might never have been started, let alone pursued to such depth of detail. Certainly Christopher's notes on newspaper reports and constant questioning of events in Brown's lifetime stimulated me to leave no page unturned or lead neglected until I had found an acceptable interpretation. In fact the research broadened beyond the bounds he had reached, particularly about Brown's family and his life as a Methodist. The result is a more substantial work than either of us had envisaged.

It seems appropriate therefore, bearing in mind Christopher's interest in meteorological events and particularly his affection for the rainbow, to include here a piece of Brown's newspaper reporting. It does not fit easily elsewhere in the book, but was written in language Christopher appreciated – which is no doubt why he made a note of it. It is from the *Stamford Mercury* 31 December 1841.

That rare spectacle, a lunar rainbow, caused by the refraction of the moon's rays on drops of rain in the night-time, was witnessed by the inhabitants of Louth last Sunday evening as they were leaving their respective places of worship. The rainbow was extremely beautiful, though much less than those which appear in day-time; and although a yellow or rather straw colour chiefly prevailed, yet the prismatic colours were well defined. The spectacle was supported by a beautiful arrangement of the *cirro cumuli* or Leader clouds, a series of small well-defined roundish masses which floated around like so many satellites in stately attendance on the 'Queen of Heaven'. The whole suggested the idea of a beautiful piece of damask tapestry, with a splendid centrepiece.

Louth, from an old picture

We warmly acknowledge the support and assistance of the following. Louth Town Council for permission to reproduce the Panorama and details from it, and for providing a generous interest-free loan for printing; Dr Valerie Purton for taking and transcribing Christopher's dictation, for collecting together the mass of research material and for reading and commenting on the final manuscript; Jean Howard, honorary curator of Louth Museum, for researching the 1850s *Stamford Mercury* and other newspapers, for checking other research leads, for identifying items in the Museum collections for illustration, and for proof-reading and compiling the index; Anthony Jarvis, Ann Cramphorn and John Baxter, descendants of William Brown, for the loan of Brown's panorama sketches and other paintings, with permission to reproduce them in this book, and a small leather-bound volume of data about Brown's family; Bill Painter for family history research on Brown's descendants; Mervyn Heard, magic lantern historian, for insight into Brown's polyopticorama when he gave a show in Louth in September 2000; and John Harris for kindly contributing the Foreword.

Unless acknowledged in a caption, all other illustrations are from Louth Museum, to which Christopher bequeathed his collection, or from the David Robinson collection. Additional information on Louth inhabitants and their occupations were sourced in county directories for 1826, 1830, 1842, 1849, 1856 and 1861.

The Society also gratefully acknowledges financial assistance in the publication of this book from the estate of Christopher Sturman, from the Society for Lincolnshire History & Archaeology, and from the Marc Fitch Fund.

David Robinson
February 2001

William Brown

Chapter 1
Panoramania and the Louth Eye

WILLIAM BROWN'S PANORAMA OF LOUTH is a major work of nineteenth century provincial art. It is a unique record of the town 'set in the aspic, or time-warp'[1] of the middle of that century. And yet its value as a piece of three-dimensional history has only fleetingly been recognized. When first exhibited to the public in Louth Mansion House in 1847, it was described as 'very ingenious, interesting and accurate'[2] and 'an admirable work of art'.[3] At the second and last public exhibition in the painter's lifetime, in Louth Corn Exchange in 1856, it was viewed as a 'source of ... instruction to the rising generation',[4] and as affording 'much rational amusement'.[5] Even when it was rescued from potential oblivion in 1948, restored and hung in the Council Chamber in the Town Hall, it was never promoted as an attraction for townspeople and tourists.

Not until 1988 did the Panorama receive eulogistic recognition from the wider world when it was the star of the show in a London exhibition at Colnaghi's: 'a brilliant achievement',[6] 'an extraordinary time capsule of an expanding Victorian town surrounded by rolling farmland',[7] 'a pair of landscapes with a message'.[8] In fact the Panorama, 'limned in such astonishing detail',[9] is full of messages. That is perhaps the major reason why we, as historical geographers, became so fascinated and engrossed by it and the man who painted it. 'Any sign of human action in a landscape implies a culture, recalls a history and demands an ... explanation'[10] is the dictum which applies and which we have followed. The culture of a mid-Victorian provincial town is set out before us as a freeze-frame record of a point in history, a window in time: there is the culture of dress, of occupation, of transport and even of gardening. And almost everything you spy tells a history and demands an explanation – which we have attempted to give.

We have no doubt that William Brown was a proud man when he exhibited his masterpiece in Louth. We hope that his eccentric spirit was at the London exhibition 'to see the surprised and delighted reactions of all who [were] confronted by the panels, from art and architectural experts to whom they [were] a revelation, and casual visitors peering along the streets of the town to spot all the bustling activity he ... so lovingly recorded'.[11] That record and his copious and detailed newspaper reporting on building developments in the town should help us to understand and better appreciate today's townscape.

Brown was born in 1788 in Malton in Yorkshire, and lived in Hull and Grimsby. When he came to Louth in 1818, it was a town just coming out of the post-Napoleonic wars depression.

Activity in Bridge Street (left), Upgate (right) and Chequergate (in front).

A conversation piece in front of The Limes, and the gardener rolls the gravel.

... Brown the miniaturist ...

A groom prepares a horse for his master in Westgate.

He lived through momentous years of growth and change in population, agriculture, industry and transport, to see it burgeon into the third largest town in Lincolnshire. He was an active member of that changing community, faithfully recording those changes as the local reporter for the *Lincoln, Rutland & Stamford Mercury*. By the time of his death in 1859, the newspaper was the principal one in the East Midlands, with a circulation of around twelve thousand. Brown's trade, however, was a housepainter, which no doubt took him to different parts of the expanding town.

He was a family man, married three times, fathering fourteen children, all by his first wife, of whom only five grew into adulthood and only two outlived him. For most of his life he was a Methodist, and always a staunch teetotaller. He held firm views, not always expressed in terms to endear him to his opponents, but he was always prepared to stand up for the principles in which he believed. The way in which he did that show him to have been a man of considerable learning, particularly of the Bible, and to have a good command of language. More than that, we believe him to have been a visionary with a sense of the vastness of the world, and in particular the battle of Good and Evil within it – a perspective which was inextricably linked with his powerful Christian convictions.

Those convictions, and his commitment to education through Sunday School, the Mutual Instruction Society, and particularly to the Louth Mechanics' Institute, we believe were key to his development as an artist. Just when Brown first developed an interest in painting as an art form is unclear, but the evidence points to it not being until the 1830s. Thereafter he produced drawings of chapels for engraving, religious drawings, the most notable being The Pictorial Pilgrim's Progress, and watercolours of nature and art (and inventions). In these he developed the skill of the miniaturist, demonstrated so well in both architectural detail and the Lowry-like figures in the Panorama. The skill was also employed in painting lantern slides for his polyopticorama – a word he coined for 'many optical views'. However, Brown might have remained obscure to all but local worthies had it not been for his ambitious and successful project to paint the two great panoramas – to the east and north, and to the west and south – as seen from the top of the spire of St James's church. What prompted him to undertake the project?

The term 'panorama', from the Greek and meaning 'all embracing view', was invented about 1785 by Robert Barker, an Irish-born artist working in Edinburgh. He created a 360 degrees circular vista, painted with tempera on linen, to be exhibited inside a cylinder, which required a special building, a rotunda. Barker moved to London and he and his son Henry painted a number of panoramas which were exhibited in his permanent rotunda, the Leicester Square Panorama. As entertainment, going to the Panorama was all the rage, a time of 'see-fever', almost panoramania. And then in 1829 the circular Regent's Park Colosseum was built, the brainchild of Thomas Hornor, son of a Hull grocer, where opera glasses were provided as an aid to viewing. The panorama was also an instrument of instruction, and in John Ruskin's view it was 'one of the most beneficial school instruments'.[12]

In 1842, Herbert Ingram from Boston launched the *Illustrated London News*. The first issue on 14 May promised subscribers a wood-engraved Colosseum View [Panorama] of London. In fact it was two prospects, to the north and to the south, from the top of the Duke of York's Column. First Antoine Claudet, then the sole British licencee for the daguerreotype process (see Chapter 6), made a series of images on silver plates; an artist copied the topographical details and another transferred them to box-wood which were then

THE ILLUSTRATED LONDON NEWS

No. 1.]   FOR THE WEEK ENDING SATURDAY, MAY 14, 1842.   [SIXPENCE.

engraved by a team of eighteen engravers for printing. The two views were printed on a single sheet (to the north above and south below) and given with the magazine issue of 7 January 1843.[13]

Brown would have seen the London Panorama in the Mechanics' Institute reading room. He could perhaps have known of the commercial exhibitions of panoramas, including moving panoramas – a long roll of painted canvas on two spools.[14] He certainly knew about dioramas, invented by Louis Daguerre in 1822, where transparent canvas was painted on both sides with say a summer scene on one side and an equivalent winter scene on the other, the differing effects achieved by alternate illumination of each. Some form of this must have been what Brown exhibited as a peripatetic diorama at the Mechanics' Institute in 1835[15] (see Chapter 6). However, here was a double panorama in print for him to study in detail at leisure, a new way of viewing one's surroundings (or environment in today's terminology).

A strangely selective view of Louth buildings from Grimsby Hill. The spire before repair (1844) but with the Corn Exchange (1837) beyond the church chancel. Workhouse (1837) left. Artist unknown. Not Brown's accuracy. For what happened to the post-mill, see Chapter 7 under Industries.

Was it then that the seed of the idea for a panorama of Louth took root? Could it be done from the gallery of St James's tower (as we photograph now)? There is certainly the compulsion to reach the highest point in the landscape, to obtain, as it were, a 'God's eye view of creation as modified by man'.[16] It is highly unlikely that Brown would have read Louis-Antoine de Bouganville: 'Nothing is more precious than the view of a landscape that is open on every side',[17] or Goethe: 'How lofty and broad, how splendid the prospect of life spread out below',[18] but surely he must have been stimulated by the panoramas in the *Illustrated London News*. Within little more than a year there was the opportunity to ascend to a new highest point in the landscape, the scaffolding encasing the church spire, to have an unbroken view in all directions. Brown seized it.

Once up there, he had to plan carefully how to delineate correctly and connectedly every object in view as he turned round. He could have marked sectors on the wooden platform to ensure continuity of accuracy on his many ascents. Sectors of 45 degrees would have required eight sketch panels, but in fact he used seven, each about 51 degrees. Somewhat surprisingly the two painted panels are not orientated exactly to north and south (as in the published London panoramas). They are ten degrees out, the divide being 100 degrees and 280 degrees from north, that is looking north and east, and south and west. It seems that the reason for this was to avoid an awkward division of the town between the two panels. Also he just did not have the working space for a single canvas 18 feet long. Which also means that it was his intention to exhibit the two paintings flat and not curved.

... the prospect of life spread out below ...

Did Brown use the artist's aid, Alberti's veil, a frame with a string grid over the sketch panels, with a proportionally enlarged grid on the painting panels? Whatever the system, he was a one-man operation, and it is little wonder that it took him nearly three years to complete the painting itself, at the same time as preparing lantern slides for his polyopticorama shows – and earning a living painting houses. Imagine two canvasses, each six feet high and nine feet long in his shop in Vicker's Lane, braced and hung on a wall, with the trestles and planks of his trade to reach the upper parts. The detail, as you will see, is truly obsessive, and the quality of perspective impressive.

Whether Brown just wanted to fulfil a personal ambition in creating the Panorama, or whether also he had in mind its potential use as an educational experience, we don't know, but certainly he met the requirement of the latter in its accuracy of visual information about the real world. Today, of course, the Louth Panorama is of immense value in the information it conveys.

No comparable panorama of any English town executed with such detail and felicity existed when William Brown made his Panorama, and for this alone he deserved a place in the annals of English art. His two panel painting of town and country is one of the great works of the nineteenth century, not simply a local curiosity, a freak of naive art, but a paean to one 'dear familiar place'. In an age rapidly losing its sense of locality, Brown's Panorama is a unique monument to the British provincial tradition. We hope that this book will, after a century and a half, mark the full acceptance and appreciation of his masterpiece. London now has its Eye; William Brown was the 'Louth Eye'.

... a landscape open on every side ...

Brown's drawing of the scaffolded spire which appeared in the *Illustrated London News* in March 1845. Was the man on the scaffold meant to represent John Dales the builder?

Chapter 2
Genesis – the opportunity of the broken spire

EARLY in 1844, increasing concern was being expressed about the state of repair of the fine spire and tower of the parish church of St James. However, at the Easter Vestry Meeting on 11 April, chaired by the vicar, Rev Edward Reginald Mantell, other matters had to be dealt with first – the accounts, tuning of the organ and distribution of charities. No mention of the tower until the election of churchwardens, when Thomas Fuller (porter merchant) and Thomas Phillips Waite (solicitor) were 're-chosen as being the most eligible to see the contemplated repairs of the tower completed which they had already got so very efficiently surveyed.'[1]

The first survey had been by the respected Louth architect Charles John Carter.[2] Evidently it was a complex problem, and the London architect Lewis Nockalls Cottingham[3] was called in to provide additional expertise. In response to a comment from surgeon Samuel Trought that the churchwardens were 'censurable for neglecting to lay a report before the parish at an earlier meeting', the vicar said he had postponed the matter to the present meeting, that 'the parishioners might not be inconvenienced by an unnecessary meeting'(!). His imprudence was soon revealed by the seriousness of the reports (complete with coloured repair plans) which showed that 'it was absolutely necessary ... to take immediate steps to render the tower and spire ... stable'.

The *Lincoln, Rutland & Stamford Mercury* gave a graphic account of the extent of the damage to the fabric and the causes, not least the lack of a lightning conductor. Repeated strokes of lightning had created a 'fissure extending nearly from the top to the bottom, in some places wide enough to admit a man's arm'. Attention was drawn to the 'numerous doorways and apertures in the structure, and the ill-judged reparations it had undergone', but the main cause of damage was 'the extravagant height at which the bells were suspended, the ringing of which had caused such a vibration as had made it surprising no accident had already occurred'. The combination of lightning and the 'rich-toned' peal of bells had thrown the tower 'slightly out of perpendicular, the building inclining to the S.W. and having several fissures through the entire thickness of the walls on the four sides of the tower, through which the country might be seen'.[4]

The bells had not been rung since the delapidations had been discovered (the previous August!), and it was Cottingham's opinion 'if proper measure be taken immediately the Spire may be effectively secured by a comparatively moderate outlay, but that, if now neglected, or only *partially* repaired, it must either be supported, at no distant date, at an immensely increased cost, or fall into utter ruin!'

The new finial and vane, drawn by Brown for the *Illustrated London News*.

The old top stones from the spire which were placed in the rectory garden.

A steeplejack job in the 1920s shows the different shade of the new stonework of 1844.

The full scaffolding of 1936-37 gives an idea of the kind of wooden platform that would have been used at the top in 1844.

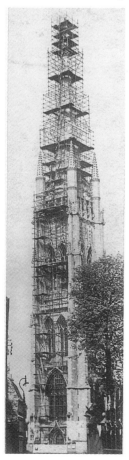

The proposed solution was to 'build up with solid masonry several of the apertures, to replace the dislodged stones, to insert several strong curved cast-iron bars (covered with a resinous substance to obviate the effects of lightning), to replace with sound wood the rotten timbers, and to affix to the building a lightning conductor (these rods being purely of a passive kind, and not as is imagined, inviting the lightning) to ward off the electric fluid from the building'.

The estimated cost, excluding the lightning conductor, was £580. This would be in addition, the Vestry Meeting was told, to current expenses and paying off an Exchequer Loan, giving a total requirement of £1,000. The Meeting agreed that, 10d in the pound being required, a 6d rate should be levied on ratepayers, the remaining 4d to be obtained by voluntary subscriptions 'with the honourable understanding that the work contemplated should be forthwith done'. And the inevitable committee was formed to supervise the work – the vicar, the two churchwardens and six leading citizens.[5]

A confident notice was prepared for circulation and insertion in the *Stamford Mercury*, stating that 'the parishioners had cheerfully submitted to the financial burden under the hope, and not unreasonable expectation, that the *entire restoration* of so beautiful a specimen of British Ecclesiastical Architecture would be regarded as an object of County and even of National Interest, and that the further sum required ... would be readily contributed by public subscription'. Within a few weeks £429 had been raised, increasing to £740 by early July (and reaching £1,273 by the end of the year). This was just as well, because the contractor's estimate was £975.[6] (It may be noted that the contractor's final account was £1,207 of the total cost of £1,746, which was met in full from subscriptions.)

The successful competitor for the contract was 23-year old builder John Dales. He was also a brick and tile maker, employed 20 men, and lived on Westgate. His father Benjamin was a joiner and cabinet maker on Broadbank, and his brother, also Benjamin, was a carpenter and joiner. John's future father-in-law, Thomas Ablewhite of Gospelgate, was the master mason for the repairs.[8] Work began on 8 July with erection of wooden scaffolding around the 140-feet spire. A series of ladders were lashed together to form a spiral round the spire inside the scaffolding to get to the summit. Just below would be a platform for the workmen and for the shearlegs[9] used for lowering damaged stone and raising new blocks.

Repair to the stonework of the spire included removal of the top 4ft 7inches (which was put in the rectory garden), and replacing it with a crocketed finial of 10ft 9inches, weighing seven tons, to carry the new weathercock. This would increase the height from 288ft to just over 294ft.

With some fifteen feet of damaged stonework removed, a number of townspeople (only those with a head for heights) were allowed to climb the ladders to the top. One was 23-year old woodcarver Thomas Wilkinson Wallis, who took measurements of the upper crockets on the spire. 'We had a splendid view of the country for many miles inland, and several miles on the German Ocean beyond the marsh, being about 380 feet above the mean level of the sea', he wrote.[10] On 26 August 'the broach of St James was ascended with right good courage' by Sarah Mantell, wife of the vicar, to see the removal of the last stone. Courage indeed, in the voluminous dress of the day, the changing view of the countryside through the rungs of the ladders, and the difficult descent backwards.

The newspapers reported that 'the view from the top is very beautiful and extremely novel: the gardens appear like little green plots on a topographical map; the hay stacks like beehives, the mansions of the gentry like robin houses, the carriages and homes like dutch toys, and the inhabitants, walking hither and thither in the streets, neither exactly like human beings nor quite like the industrious ants of which they are atypical'.[11]

This sparkling account could only have been written by 56-year old William Brown himself, probably engaged in sketching when Mrs Mantell joined him. He was at that time a local correspondent for the *Lincoln, Rutland & Stamford Mercury*, and his hand was undoubtedly behind much of the copious journalism about the repairs to the tower and spire.

It was certainly during those late summer days that the main sketching for the Panorama was done – trees in full foliage, hay stacks, cornfields, and strong shadows from an afternoon sun. The feel he gave to the final painting was as though it had all been done at 2 o'clock on a balmy summer's day. In fact there was a happy coincidence about the weather in summer 1844. There was a period of drought from mid-April to mid-June, broken by a lightning storm, and then showery until mid-August. September and October were warm months with occasional thunderstorms. The hay harvest had been generally poor, but the grain harvest was quite good.[12]

Perhaps it was Brown himself who was responsible for the report in September: 'If anything has shared the attention of the inhabitants in this time of beautiful harvest, it is the interest taken in the reparation of the church ... We are glad to state that no accident has occurred hitherto, to either the workmen, or the numerous visitors who ascend the spire to gaze on the natural phenomena beneath (second perhaps to none in the kingdom), and to witness the almost unceasing industry of our reporter who, with an artistic skill appropriate to the subject, is almost daily to be seen perched upon the summit of the spire, sketching the beautiful town and neighbourhood'.[13]

The stonemason's yard of Thomas Ablewhite in Gospelgate.

Louth from Hubbard's Hills in 1840, by artist and solicitor James W Wilson.

Sailing ships off Mablethorpe.

In October he reported that about noon on the 2nd 'the Royal Squadron was seen on its southern course considerably off Spurn point, and upwards of twenty miles from Louth. The fleet appeared to be making as short a leg as possible to the Norfolk coast (which accounted for their not leaving the Lincolnshire coast) and stretching away homeward as fast as tide and streams and a remarkably brisk northwester would carry them'.[14] These are not the ships he included on the painting, most of which are sailing towards the Humber estuary.

Even the approaching Municipal Election was seen in terms of the town's current obsession with the spire: '... we advise the present contending individuals, to both of whom we are friendly, that if the pistol is to decide the precise amount of honour due to each, no better course can be taken than that they cast lots for the following positions: The one party to be pitched on the highest apex of the finial of Louth spire (in passing, we would advise the masons to hasten fixing the same) and to turn his face to the sun rising; his antagonist to foist himself in the north-west angle of Elkington cow pasture, and look to the sun setting; and when we give the word "fire", blow away pistol and all; and may the cephalic treasure of both our friends have a happy escape'.[15]

A north-west prospect of Louth from rural St Mary's Lane, before the repair of the spire. Artist unknown.

Brown continued to chart the day-to-day progress of the work during his sketching trips to the top platform of the scaffold. Being a house painter, he would be used to ladders. Access to the top platform was through what sailors called the 'lubber's hole'. Work days would be dictated by weather conditions, and one wonders how many times he ascended and descended, carrying his sketching equipment in a satchel over his shoulder. And did he also carry a telescope for discerning details in the distant views? He must have done in order to be able to paint distant features so accurately.

Rebuilding the top of the spire began on Thursday 26 September when the old 'wild mare' (treadwheel windlass) in the tower was put back into use.[16] The foundation stone for the new work, weighing three quarters of a ton, was first lifted to the scaffold above the pinnacles. 'The next morning a rope communicating with the wild mare was passed through the spire, and running through tackle fastened to the shear erected above the summit, was made to pass down the west side of the broach to where the stone rested, to which it was securely attached, and then hoisted up between the scaffolding and the spire to its place ... At 5 minutes before 12 on Friday it was safely embedded in the mortar'. Credit was given to the clerk of works, Benjamin Bowden, and 'the sober workmen engaged in so ... hazardous an enterprise'.[17]

The repair to the spire was completed in December. The top stone, millstone grit from Calverley Wood quarry near Leeds,[18] was transported by rail to Hull and then in one of William Nell's vessels via the Navigation Canal to the Riverhead. It was taken into the church to be carved by masons William Wilson and Henry Jewitt; this took nearly six days. On Tuesday 10th, it was cradled in matting and the wild mare began operations at 2.30pm. 'In ten minutes it was safely landed as high as the pinnacles, on to the third scaffold of the spire, ... after a quarter of an hour's rest [for the men working the treadwheel] resumed its travels: in another half-hour it was seen ... poised over the centre of the spire, whence it was speedily lodged on the four copper dowels ... to the great satisfaction of the workmen and the numerous spectators. ... The event was commemorated by merry peals from the bells, which had lain dormant for over a twelvemonth'. In the evening the vicar provided a supper in the Masons Arms for the workmen.[19]

Ten days later, at 1.30pm, the new cross and weathercock was placed by George Laver and Henry Mills of London, 'on which occasion the workmen gave a hearty cheer, which was responded to by those below who witnessed the final adjustment'. The trebly-gilt copper weathervane was designed by Cottingham and made at Kepp's factory in London. The cross is 3ft broad and the cock 2ft 2inches, and 2ft from talons to crest. The copper lightning conductor, 350ft long and weighing over two tons, was fixed on 2nd January 1845. It ran down the south side of the spire and tower, ending in a broad sheet of copper in a well 25ft deep and immersed in water 'for the more ready diffusion of the electric fluid'.[20]

Brown's last chance to check any details of his sketches for the Panorama (at least from the correct perspective) was in December, as at the beginning of January the scaffolding round the spire was taken down to be re-erected around the tower. Nearly seven tons of stone had been used in repairs to the spire, and workmen were cutting and carving large quantities of stone in the west end of the church to repair the tower. Details of the restoration were supplied by Brown to the *Illustrated London News*, along with a view of the tower and scaffolded spire, and a drawing of the new weathervane, and appeared in March 1845.[21]

HULL AND LOUTH
TRADING VESSELS.

WILLIAM NELL

BEGS respectfully to announce to his friends and the public in general, that he has determined on sailing one of his Vessels from SMITHSON'S WHARF, HIGH-STREET, HULL, EVERY SATURDAY, and also to assure them that no attention shall be wanting, or expense spared, to accomplish this desirable object. Dispatch being his aim, he trusts that all goods will be promptly ordered down in time.

Louth, March 27, 1837.

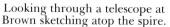

Looking through a telescope at Brown sketching atop the spire.

A family watching work on the spire.

He had expanded his drawing of the scaffolded spire into what might be called a precursor of the Panorama, or more properly a prospect. It was drawn in Indian ink, and is a view from the north-west from high ground above St Mary's burial ground (the Old Cem) and what is now St Mary's Lane. It shows the nave and chancel of the church, with a sweep of houses from the Bridge Street terrace on the left to Westgate Place on the right. It bears an interesting resemblance to the north-west view of Louth drawn by Thomas Espin and engraved by Bartholomew Howlett in 1793, an engraving Brown would have known. Brown's 'New Picture of Louth ... taken on the day John Dales finished the scaffolding ... July 27th 1844' (and before the working platform was built) was exhibited in the shopwindow of William Davis in Eastgate.[22] (One might even imagine that it was John Dales himself who Brown saw on the scaffolding as he completed the drawing that day.) It was accompanied by a key to sixty buildings (with names of occupants) and other features. Among them were Jackson's Printing Office in the Market Place (now Oxfam), the British Schools (Kidgate), the Boar's Head inn, the Catholic Chapel, and Muckton church (now demolished) on the horizon.

Brown's 'New Picture of Louth' with key (opposite).

Stone by Wm Walton, from a Sketch by W. Brown.   Hullmandel & Walton Lithographers.

A North West View of Louth Church taken on the day Mr John Dales finished the Scaffolding preparatory to the Tower & Spire being repaired, under the Superintendence of Mr Cottingham & the Chief Clerk Mr Bowden; Mr Ablewhite, Stone Mason, Rev. E.R. Mantell, Vicar July 27th 1844. Messrs T.P. Waite and T. Fuller, Church Wardens. Joseph Larder Esq Mayor.

Church Spire 288 Feet from the Ground

1. St James's Church
2. The Spire scaffolded
3. Mr Rylay's Stone Mason
4. Wes. Preachers Houses & Chapel
5. New St Mr Habbard &c
6. Mr Pearson's Graham's Mitchell's
7. Mrs Jackson's Printing Offices
8. Crown & Woolpack's Inn
9. Mr Sharpleys Mr G Foster's &c
10. Mr Hudson's Residence
11. Mr Harold's Rev. Dale's St Geo Gee Esq.
12. J Wilson Esq. Mr Philbrick Surgeon
13. Mr Standalands E Gate
14. Mr Pearson's baker D
15. The Guild Hall
16. Mr Edwards, Anderson's, Philipson's
17. Mr Hallams Premises
18. Mr Tate's Masons Arms Inn Yard
19. Mr Coulters Ironmonger
20. Mr Robeons Druggist

21. Mr Achtons Ironmonger
22. Mr Brada's Lees Mr Swaby's &c
23. J. Wright Esq. Residence
24. Mr Pool's Property Paradise
25. The British Schools
26. Corporation Prop. Robinson
27. Mr Hurst's Jacksons, Hockford's Ockings
28. Mr Jones Gardener Paradise
29. Messrs Edwards S Ingoldby's Prop
30. Mr Sam. Hempstock's Bretts Long Acre
31. The Albion Rooms
32. Mr Markham's Rosemary Lane
33. Lindsey Bank Butcher Market
34. Mr Wait's Mr Birketts
35. Messrs Allison's & Hardys Stamp Office
36. Mechanic's Institution
37. Dog & Duck Tavern
38. J Bogg Esq. Surgeon
39. Rev. G W Brameld's
40. Mr Habbard's, W Dales &c

41. R. Hoyle's Esq. 2d Bridge St.
42. Muckton Church
43. Mr Coultman's, Duty's &c Property New Mkt
44. New King's Head Inn
45. Mr Allison's Warehouse Kidgate
46. Mr Poters D. Mr J Smith's D.
47. Mr Simpson's &c Lee Street
48. Mr Ingoldby's Property Quarry
49. Bears Head Inn
50. N Entrance to St Marys Burying Ground
51. Vicarage Rev. E.R. Mantell's
52. Mr Grants Scarle's Ditchett's Lee St
53. Pipe Manufactory Thompson's
54. The Quarry Pits
55. J. Johnson Esq. Prop. 5th Parade
56. The Catholic Chapel
57. Mr Boothby's Resid. &c Parade
58. Mr Ablewhite's Mason
59. Miss Grey's Sem. West Gate
60. West Gate Place Wheat Sheaf Inn

Town Crier James Wakelin
(also a housepainter).

The newspaper was flattering in comment on the quality of the drawing, and continued: 'We hope the draughtsman (Mr Brown) will be encouraged to get his picture engraved and sold at a reasonable price: We trust also the rare opportunity of securing "a bird's eye view" of the town and its enchanting vicinity, from the top of the spire, will not be suffered to pass away unimproved by the gentlemen who form the committee for superintending the repairs'.[23] By the end of the year a lithograph had indeed been made, by W L Walton (of Hullmandel & Walton), and was on sale, and received a ringing recommendation in the press. 'As a specimen of lithography it has rarely been equalled: the richness of the sky and the general effect of the picture is very pleasing; and we doubt not that Mr Brown's skill will be amply remunerated by his townsmen in a speedy purchase of his rich little work of art'.[24]

In July 1845 the scaffolding was removed from the tower of the church, and Brown reported that 'a week or two more will be required to finish the work'. That included repair to the turret steps which must have been subject to excessive wear. However, he also sounded what was to become a characteristic note of vociferous complaint, in this case about features of other parts of the church. 'Before the workmen leave the building ... it is exceedingly desirable that a trifle of the funds should be employed in replacing with more chaste design the supporting crockets or brackets on the more conspicuous parts of the church.' He was presumably referring to some of the medieval gargoyles – 'the *ugly, abominable and superlatively obscene* figures which by a strange perversity of taste have been thought to ornament this church'. He further contended that 'free as are some of the pictorial illustrations of the day, no Ecclesiastical Architectural Society could be prevailed on to publish drawings from some of the offensive brackets'.[25] Clearly his nonconformist beliefs were offended, but it was probably this strain of querulousness which later blighted his career and damaged the prospects of his masterpiece, the Panorama.

Louth in 1839.

EAST GATE, LOUTH, *Drawn from Nature by W. Brown. 1852.*

25

North

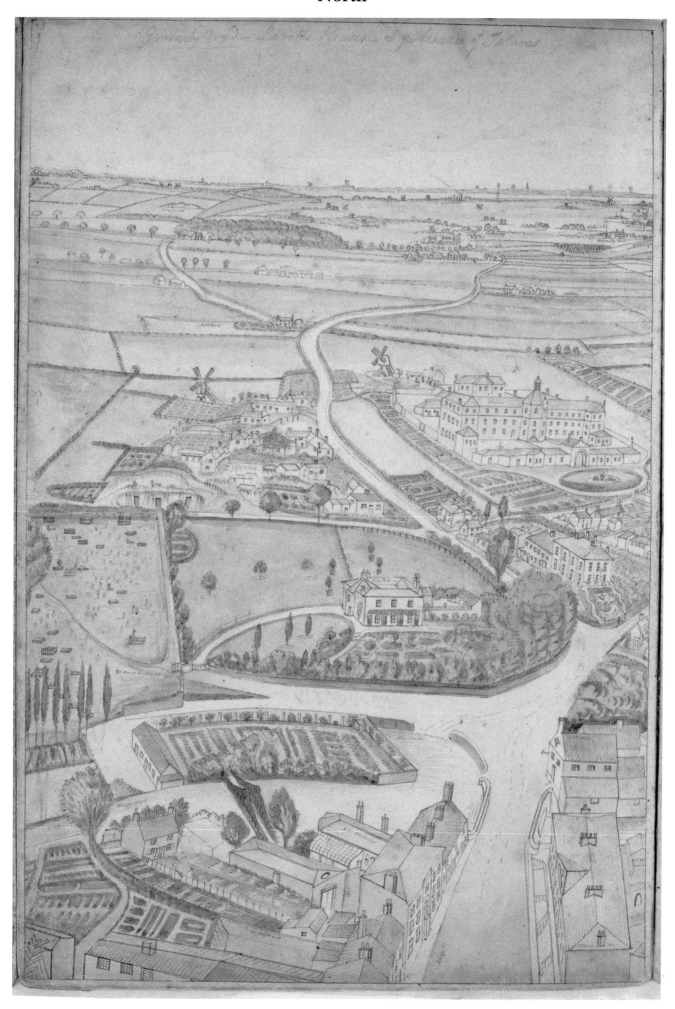

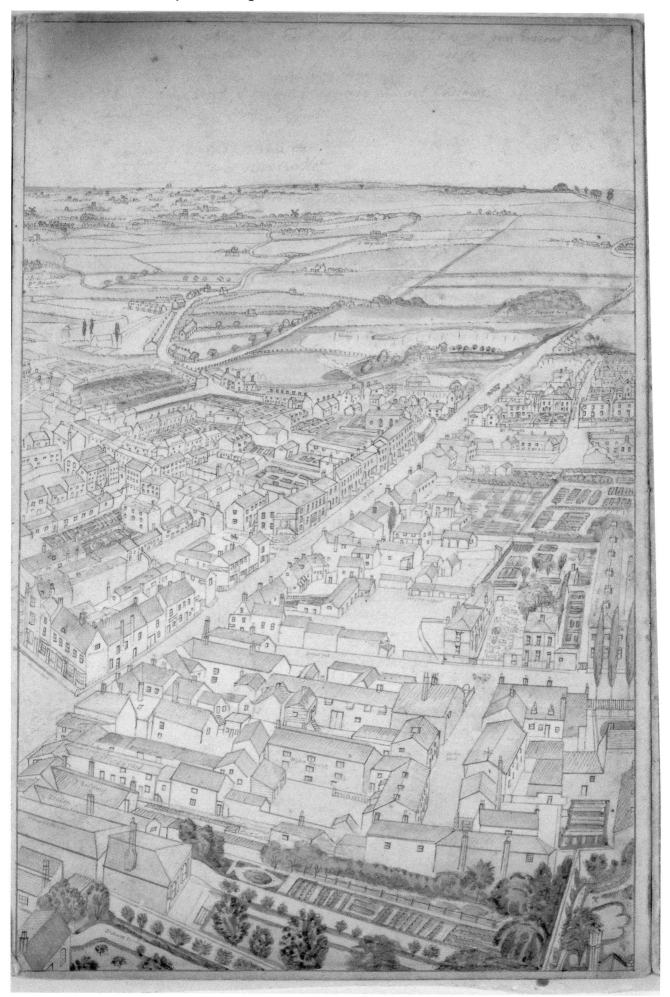

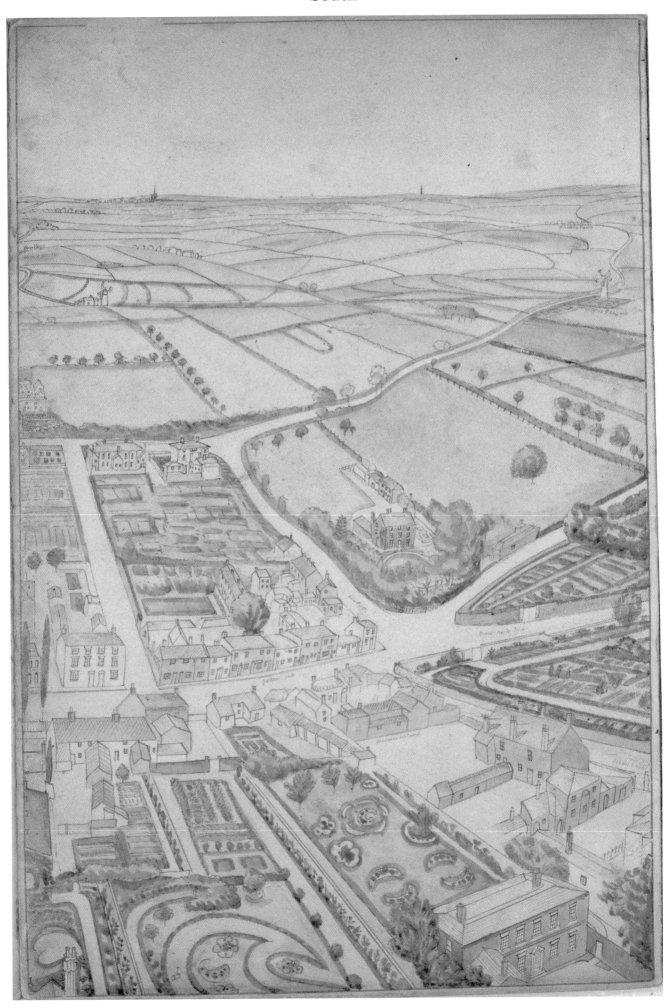

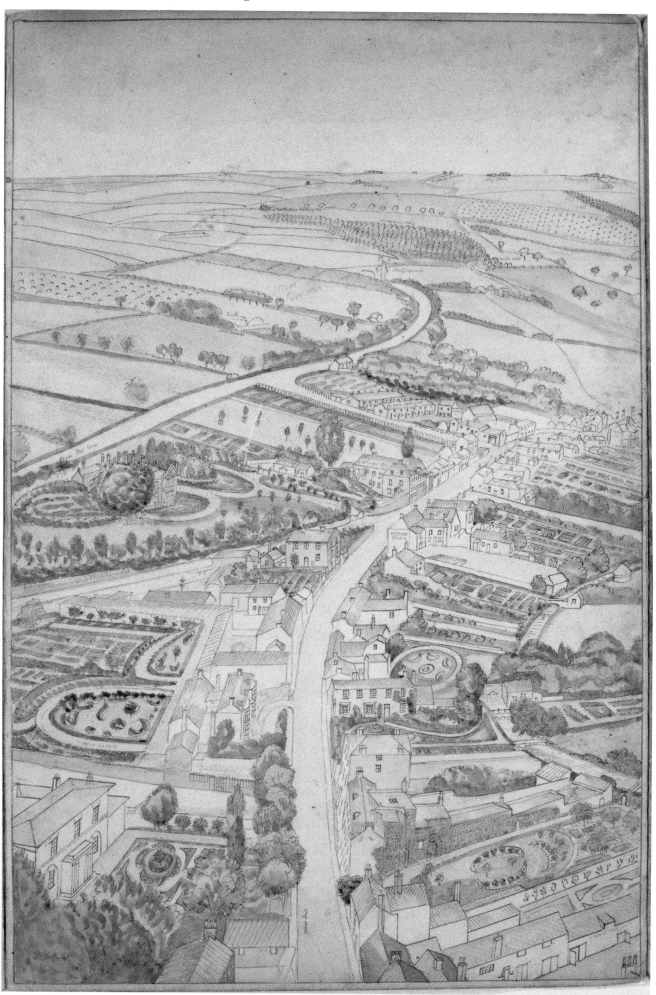

Bridge Street, the mill dam
and St. Mary's Mount.

Chapter 3
From Sketchbook to Canvas

WILLIAM BROWN made his sketches on seven panels, $7\frac{1}{4}$ inches wide and $11\frac{3}{4}$ inches deep. These were pasted onto a backing sheet so that they could be folded into an artist's satchel. On the back he made notes, now somewhat faded, and some other preliminary sketches. One is of Louth railway station, another is what appears to be farm buildings with figures; there are sketches of chimney stacks and pots (from ground level) and, most intriguingly, what seems to be the preliminary idea for his unfinished *Last Day*, 'in which are grouped about 200 portraits of the good and wise of all generations, as about to ascend to glory, and personifications of the Vices, under the ban of the "Destroying Angel" '.[1] There is also a clear pencil note: Painted 1847. Finished 1853.

Of the seven sketch panels, one is divided in two, one part fitting the other end of the panorama. In other words, the continuous scene could be confirmed. Therefore each of the final panels of the painting are made up from $3\frac{1}{2}$ of the sketch panels. However, a closer comparison between the sketch panels and the final panorama reveals that a continuous strip of the foreground, including the rectory for example, is not on the surviving sketches. This strip of about 3 inches has been lost. Also there is more sky on the finished painting.

But there are crucially important pieces of information on the sketches – buildings and other features are named. In the town streets are named, house occupiers' names are added, as are those of pubs and chapels, and the names of public buildings are inscribed on the roof, for example the Union (Workhouse) and the Mansion House (on Upgate). Even names of owners of some of the fabulously designed gardens are given, and we discover where the foundry was on Westgate – at the bottom of Irish Hill. There are other clues of changes to come – no Town Hall, no Corn Exchange (but the previous Guildhall is shown – now the site of the Halifax Building Society), no public cemetery on the London Road, virtually no houses on George Street, and no railway.

Out in the country, villages are named, there are some thirty windmills, mainly in the Marsh, and church towers and Spurn Lighthouse are shown in Yorkshire. On the skyline of the Lincolnshire Wolds the roads to Market Stainton and Donington (the latter through the trees at North Farm as now) are labelled. And to the south-west of Haugham is a tall, slender tower named as the Government Observatory. This was a temporary structure built by the Ordnance Survey as part of re-triangulation of the country for mapping on the scale of six inches to one mile.[2] It stood on the site of the present trigonometrical point for 489 feet on the road from Maidenwell to Scamblesby. The preliminary work had begun in 1840, and

Government Observatory
on the south sketch panel.

John Sanderson's Ironworks

... on the Panorama

The Railway Station

... drawn on stone by T W Wallis

two years later Brown had reported that 'considerable alarm is being excited among the rural population about Louth, particularly those inhabiting the hilly districts, by the peremptory, suspicious, and to the mass unintelligible erection by certain soldiers of poles ... on the summits of the rising ground stretching across the county'.[3] Apparently the media had not been told of the purpose of the poles for surveying base lines. There is also a white triangular structure at Donna Nook, and similar ones on the Yorkshire coast, but those were navigation beacons.[4]

Such is the fascination of Brown's sketches and Panorama that there is still much history to be teased from it. The sketches were given a simple and light watercolour wash to identify major features in green, brown, pink and blue. The area of sky contains more written reminder notes, for example about Saunderson's works and steam chimney between Charles Street and Holmes Lane (High Holme Road) which he had not included in that sketch panel.

So, how did Brown progress from sketch to canvas? Work on the painting was to occupy him for several years. In September 1846 the *Stamford Mercury* was able to report that he had 'resumed the painting of his panorama view of Louth ... and corrected by later inspections, on 160 square feet of canvas (an over-estimate; the reality now is 108 square feet) ... so far as we are able to judge from a single private inspection ... it will make a beautiful picture when finished, and that the minuteness and accuracy with which the many hundreds of objects of local interest which it contains are delineated, will render it a most valuable record to future generations of what Louth was like in 1846'[5]. Prophetic indeed, although the Panorama's real value as an historical document has only begun to be properly appreciated in the last two decades.

In 1847 work had already started on the East Lincolnshire Railway, and in June the Panorama was linked with the railway boom – quite appropriately since together they embodied the economic and creative energy of the times. The press reported that a 'drawing of the elevation of the intended [railway] station may be seen in the window' of William Davis, gilder, in Eastgate, together with 'a couple of outline drawings of Louth as taken from the church spire in summer 1844, and which present miniature outlines of Mr Brown's large oil painting panorama ... now nearly complete for public exhibition'.[6] The elevation of the station was by the architects Weightman & Hadfield of Sheffield (to be lithographed by T W Wallis in 1848), and the two outline drawings would have been taken from the sketches.

The Panorama was finally exhibited to the public in July and August 1847 in the Mansion House (the mid-18th century Assembly Rooms then in the ownership of the Borough Council) on Upgate. 'This very ingenious, interesting and accurate painting, which reflects great credit upon Mr Brown', reported the *Louth Herald*, 'takes within its view the town of Louth and upwards of 30 towns and villages in the surrounding neighbourhood, and furnishes a pleasing occupation to all who visit it, especially those conversant with the country'.[7] As, indeed, it still does.

The *Stamford Mercury* was more florid: 'If we are to judge upon the testimony and encomiums [high commendations] of the gentry who have inspected it, it is not only an admirable work of art, but an accurate delineation of the objects which it portrays'. Did any of the gentry use an opera glass as an aid to 'descrying the distant scenery' (as Brown later suggested in his 1849 advertisement)?

The paper also expressed the hope that lithographed copies of convenient size of the pair of prints could be produced, as they would become highly prized as a memorial of Louth.[8] Whether or not the recommendation that for the price of one admission ticket, people should be able to visit the exhibition as often as they chose was taken up is not known. However the *Lincolnshire Chronicle* expressed the hope that 'Mr Brown will receive a satisfactory remuneration for his great ingenuity and talent'.[9] It should be noted that for the exhibition, Brown had anticipated the completion of the railway and included it in the painting, along with the station (from the architect's drawing) which had begun to be built the same month. The two paintings were on rollers, and after the exhibition they were rolled up and taken back to Brown's premises on Vicker's Lane.

Within a few weeks of the closing of the exhibition, Brown's second wife, Letitia, died aged 68. He was then 59. Ten months later, in July 1848, he married his third wife, 41-year old Ann Donner of Alford, in Louth Wesleyan Chapel. In December 1848 there was a special showing of the Panorama to 'some hundreds of juvenile teetotallers (male and female) ... in the Wesleyan schoolroom, Lee Street' together with moral pictures of The Bottle 'elucidating the evils of intemperance'. Brown was a strong supporter of teetotalism, on which he had spoken earlier in the month at a public meeting called by the Abstinence Committee in the Temperance Hotel.[10]

In April 1849, Brown published an engraving of the Wesleyan Chapel on Eastgate, together with the small newly-built chapels at the Riverhead and on Newmarket, 'the whole forming a pleasing memorial of Methodism in Louth', as a companion to the lithographed prospect of St James and part of the town of 1844. The *Stamford Mercury* again recommended that their weekly correspondent should 'bring out and get engraved (on copper) in a pair of pictures of convenient size and moderate price his splendid Panorama of Louth'; he had, of course, written it all himself.[11] Bearing in mind the size of each painting, 6ft by 9ft, it would have been a considerable undertaking to redraw to near the size of the original sketches, from which an engraver could work. However, Brown did in fact respond to the recommendation, and in August placed an advertisement in the *Stamford Mercury*.[12]

The size he proposed was almost exactly that of the original sketches (including the bottom strip now missing). He also responded to the suggestion in the April review that the nobility and gentry would liberally patronise an example of accurate delineation in which estates and properties would be 'occularly identified, and legally vouched for', by stating that the engraving would be a 'voucher for the Estates and Properties' in the town. Moreover he proposed a key, probably as an outline, similar in style to that which he did for the prospect in 1844.

... an accurate delineation. The grey-roofed building left, with people in the garden, is the Mansion House on Upgate where the Panorama was first exhibited to the public.

... a voucher for estates and properties – on Westgate and Crowtree Lane.

Looking over the Cornmarket, town centre, along Monks Dyke and towards Mablethorpe.

The road to Horncastle snakes over the Wolds past the five-sailed mill. Note the boys flying a kite in the field behind The Lodge, the home of the flogging headmaster of the Grammar School, Rev John Waite.

PANORAMIC VIEWS of LOUTH, Lincolnshire
Dedicated to the Nobility, Gentry and Clergy
of the County of Lincoln.

Preparing for Publication in Two handsome Engravings,
size of each Two Feet Two Inches by One Foot Four Inches,

Mr WM BROWN'S PANORAMIC VIEWS of LOUTH and its VICINITY, as taken from the summit of the Spire of St James' Church in MDCCCXLIV, accurately drawn from the original Oil Paintings subsequently completed by the same Artist in 1847, on 120 square feet of canvas, and exhibited in the Mansion House, Louth &c, – The above Pictures to be engraved on Copper, and to include a delineation of every Edifice raised in the Town and Neighbourhood up to the time of publication, so as to render the pair of Engravings not only a handsome appendage to the Parlour or Drawing-room, but a voucher for the Estates and Properties in the Town, and a faithful Memorial of Louth in MDCCCL.

The price of a Pair of Engravings will be One Guinea;
or with Key, One Pound Five Shillings.

Subscribers' names will be received at Messrs JACKSON'S, Booksellers, Louth where the Outline Copies of the Originals, the size of the intended Engravings, may be seen; also at Mr BROWN, the Artist, Vicker's Lane, Louth, who will show the Original Paintings.

In the above Pictures, the great features of Louth – Queen of the Towns of Lincolnshire – are so placed before the eye at a glance, as if the spectator had the flight of an eagle – was suspended over the beautiful spire of the parish church of Louth – and could pause over the multitudinous objects of interest below him, which are so correctly delineated, that the inhabitant will easily thread his way from street to street to his own dwelling; or, if he choose, he may in fancy perambulate the beautiful environs to any village he may select. Indeed, the pictorial illusion, in the large painting especially, is so complete, that as in nature the telescope is necessary to view remote objects, so in the Panorama a small opera glass was found a pleasing aid in descrying the distant scenery – the shipping on the German Ocean and River Humber, the Yorkshire and Lincolnshire coasts, the Queen's Return from Scotland, the East Lincolnshire Line of Railway, and the fifty Towns and Villages – in so extensive and multifarious views of Louth.

– Those who may kindly honor [sic] the Artist with their patronage, will please to send to either of the above addresses, stating name, residence, and the number of copies they may wish to have sent.

Despite the dedication and the descriptive hype, the scheme came to nothing. Had the novelty worn off or was the cost too high? Or was it a combination of Brown's reputation for awkwardness and that people in the establishment to whom he referred in his newspaper articles felt unable to subscribe to the work of such a religious independent, not least one who had just published engravings of three Wesleyan Methodist chapels? Perhaps it was just that in rural Lincolnshire there was simply not the demand for engraved pictures (in black and white) that to many must have seemed just curiosities.

However, this setback did not deter Brown; it perhaps even spurred him to complete an engraving of the Baptist Chapel, and by 1850 he had sold over two hundred copies. His next engraving was to be the enlarged Primitive Methodist chapel on Northgate,[13] and this duly appeared after the opening in November 1850. His obsession however remained the Panorama. As the town changed with rebuilding and new buildings, the pigment on the paintings suggests that he altered or added to the original. Preparatory to making the changes, he had to ascend the church tower to see them. Although this did not give the same angle as from the top of the spire, the perspective of the additions fits well with the earlier painting.

There was in fact much change in the 1850s, as a result of population growth and the burgeoning confidence of the Victorians. The population had more than doubled since the beginning of the century – 4,236 to 10,467, increasing by 2,000 in the 1830s (with the building of 425 new houses) and by nearly the same again in the 1840s. In 1850 and 1851 there were new villa residences to be added on George Street, and new houses on Gospelgate, Lee Street and Broadbank, and the Primitive Methodist chapel on Northgate was substantially enlarged (the site of the present Library). In 1852 Brown added the Grimsby Dock Tower.

1854 was a particularly significant year for new public buildings and developments. The Corn Exchange replaced the Guildhall in the Cornmarket, the Town Hall was built on the site of dwellings between the Marquis of Granby inn and Cannon Street, the Free Methodist chapel was erected on Eastgate (now a car park, next to the Woodman inn), and the ground for the public cemetery at Julian Bower was cleared. All were incorporated in the Panorama although the Free Methodist chapel is rather surprisingly slightly misplaced. 1854 was also the year when Brown's third wife, Ann, died in February, aged 46.

On the occasion of the stonelaying for the new Town Hall, on 16 June 1853, there was a festive programme in the grounds of the Priory on Eastgate. Brown exhibited a150-feet panoramic painting of scenic and historical subjects including Holbein's *Imagen Mortis* or 'Dance of Death', Bunyan's *Pilgrim's Progress* and some 'spirited illustrations' from 'Mrs B. Stowe's celebrated book *Uncle Tom's Cabin*'.[14] The next time his Gallery of Illustration – Historical, Scenic and Allegorical appeared was for the peace celebrations to mark the end of the Crimean War in May 1856, when it was described in more detail: 25 scenes from the Dance of Death, 40 scenes from *Pilgrim's Progress* and 16 sketches from *Uncle Tom's Cabin*.[15]

Brown was now living on his own in Walkergate (Queen Street) and described in the directory as artist and reporter. For him the peace celebration was a golden opportunity to show the updated Panorama with the Gallery of Illustration, to provide a pictorial promenade of nearly 200 feet of canvas. He booked the Corn Exchange for three days, Thursday 29th to Saturday 31st May. The *Lincolnshire Chronicle* was delighted with the educational aspect, with children being admitted for a penny: it would add 'another source of amusement and instruction to the rising generation'. Moreover, the newspaper pontificated, 'the exhibition is an attempt to improve the working classes, and thus further the aim of the philanthropist in promoting that sympathy which shall mingle class with class, to the refinement of the character of those by whom the higher classes are surrounded'.[15] The *Stamford Mercury* expressed a simpler sentiment, that it 'afforded much rational amusement'.[16]

It seemed at last as if the Panorama was to take its place as a treasured feature in the life of the town. In fact it was shortly to disappear, after his death in 1859, not to be seen by the public again for 92 years.

The grounds of The Priory on Eastgate, where Brown exhibited his other panoramic paintings in 1853. (Drawn by J W Best).

The new Corn Exchange where the Panorama was exhibited in 1856, the last time in Brown's lifetime.

Louth, looking down the London Road (the Dexthorpe Turnpike) from Julian Bower in the early 19th century. The Catholic 'chapel' on the right was rebuilt in 1833 and the priest's house added in 1839. Brown was to report on the improvement of the road by making a cutting through Julian Bower Hill, and the entrance through the side of the cutting to the new public cemetery. Artist unknown.

Chapter 4

Recording Public Improvements

THE PANORAMA as we now have it, when compared with the preliminary sketches, provides a fine record of building developments in the town over the period 1844 to 1856. Brown's copious journalism supplements the visual by vividly conveying the texture of improvements to the urban environment. Thanks to his attention to detail, we can also discover who were the agents of change, the architects, contractors and builders. We find, for example, how Lincoln architect Pearson Bellamy and Louth builder John Dales prospered out of improvements to the town. He not only commented on general improvements, but also charted specific campaigns, in particular the agitation for a new public cemetery.

The Old Corporation[1] had obtained the Act for Paving, Lighting, Watching, Cleansing, Regulating and otherwise Improving the Town in 1825. The following year the gasworks were built. When the Municipal Borough was established in 1836, following the Municipal Reform Act of 1835, it took over the powers of the Act and formed an Improvement Committee in 1837. Early that year there were plans to make a new street, 30 feet wide, from the Market Place to Eastgate (the present New Street). Included in the plan were shops and covered markets for butter, poultry and vegetables, and on the north side of Eastgate a public hall.[2]

In June 1837 the Commissioners for Paving the streets advertised for experienced paviours for taking up nearly 1,500 yards of carriage ways in Westgate (west from the church) and about 1,250 yards in Mercer Row (from Upgate) and repaving with pebbles at least five inches in depth. Channels by the side of the 'foot pavements' were to be included in the contract, and it was estimated that 400-500 tons of good pebbles would be required.[3]

Streets

BROWN began his twenty years as Louth correspondent for the *Lincoln, Rutland & Stamford Mercury* in March 1839, and immediately went on the attack about the state of the streets: 'The streets of Louth are in a most deplorable state at present: Bunyan himself, if he could behold the fair Christians of the town wading through such a slough of despond, would pity their miry pilgrimage'.[4] This was typical of Brown's style of reporting, mixing the realistic, the literary and the allegorical with energetic abandon.

As the streets became dry and dusty in May, he took a different tack. 'The town of Louth is most delightfully situated, and the air is salubrious: it possesses two episcopal churches, one Roman Catholic church, and five dissenting places of worship: it has a Mansion House or Guildhall, a spirited Mayor, a zealous Vicar, a parish church with a beautiful spire, a wide-awake police force; it is a sessions town, and possesses numerous advantages, including a good supply of beautiful water; its buildings are compact, and admired by strangers; in fact, Louth is considered the pet borough of Lincolnshire, yet with all its possessions and all its advantages it does not possess one *watering cart*'.[5] However, in July the next year he was able to report 'cooling of streets with a watering cart'.[6]

The town watercart filling up in the mill dam on Bridge Street.

He was on the attack again in June 1839, under the heading HINT. 'Bunting-lane (Burnthill Lane) ... in the winter time is a complete slough, almost impassable for mud; and at this season of the year it is a complete annoyance from the stench arising from stagnant water and filth. Very few of the Commissioners, we think, pass that way'.[7] The next week he had another go at the Commissioners: 'It was decreed some time ago at the Board of Paving Commissioners that the south side of Eastgate, from Mr Morton's shop downwards, should be re-paved. There is no sign of any commencement of the work. It is supposed by the inhabitants thereabouts, [who included Brown himself] that when the summer is over, and the opportunity gone by, the "authorities" will begin to talk about it again, as they possess more *talking* than *doing* properties'.[8]

Whether or not this had any effect, we don't know, but in August he reported that 'the long talked of corn-punishing pavement on the south side of Eastgate has undergone improvement by means of a curb and pebbles'.[9] He also detailed other improvements, some of which would eventually show up on his Panorama – widening of the road from Enginegate to the Union (hence the name Broadbank?), and the cutting of the London road through Virginia (Julian) Bower Hill, with the embankment beyond. The latter was engineered by Robert Cropper, the surveyor of roads, it having been three years since the mail coaches had used that steep section of the road, and was opened in August 1839.[10] A year later however Brown reported that the carriage road on Upgate-London Road was in need of a sewer as during heavy rains the water ran down in torrents and washed off the gravel.[11]

Two other improvements Brown noted were the 'Mansion-house heretofore famed for its Tory feasting, though its culinary utentils now lack employment, still maintains its dignity, now boasts a double coat of corporate paint', and that 'the Old King's Head inn glories in a new face, and smiles elegantly on the inhabitants in the Gothic order'.[9] The frontage of the King's Head in Mercer Row was the work of George Rivis Willoughby, a trained architect, and is an example of his exuberant and eclectic style.[12]

Workmen repairing, and discussing repairing, Westgate.

In September 1839, Brown turned his attention to the Fish Shambles which he wrote, 'are in a most disgraceful condition: there is no accommodation whatever for fishermen who stand their own market, or those who deal in fish and have no shop; Louth fish market is a mere burlesque on the name'.[13] Again he

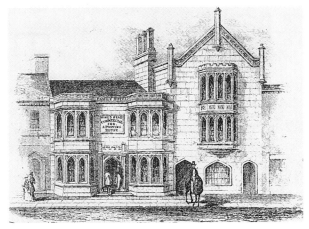 

The King's Head Hotel then .... and now

seems to have anticipated change, because in July 1840 he reported that part of the fish market was being 'Macadamised'.[6]

However there were still complaints six years later about the dilapidated state of the area and of 'the nuisance and pestilential effects of the fishmongers offering their commodities on the ground without the boundaries of the shambles'.[14] And again in 1856: benches and slabbing had been supplied for the fish trade but 'the offal is slovenly cast upon the cobbles, where it often remains, infecting the air in the vicinity, to the detriment of the neighbours, and disagreeable to the olfactory nerves of all having occasion to pass through the narrow defile of the fish shambles'.[15]

The Market Place was no better. 'We have been more than once reminded of the filthy condition of Louth market-place and adjacent streets on the sabbath', he reported. 'Were a rake summarily used on a Saturday night (if men and brooms are so scarce), it would be the means of lessening in some tolerable degree the heaps of garbage and litter which now accumulate from one market-day to another'.[16]

There were other improvements which took his attention in 1840. As a result of the increased congregation, he noted the intended enlargement of the General Baptist Chapel (in Cannon Street) by 'adding considerably to its length'.[17] Referring to the former 'lamentable' state of the ground in front of Holy Trinity church, he reported it to be 'much improved with a lawn and semi-circular gravel walk and gates to the road'[18] (achieved by public subscription). Might it have been Brown who then made the drawing of those improvements?

Trinity Church, erected 1834.
Improved by public subscription 1840.

The British (Kidgate) School.
The painting was damaged – in the area of the playground – because it is on the edge of the right panel.

Writing about the site of the proposed British School (Kidgate), he commented that the 'place called Paradise is anything but an Elysium', but went on to say that the new building 'will no doubt work a perfect rejuvenation in these blighted regions'.[19] Perhaps it was a crack against the Tory Council who owned the land and gave part of it for the building of the school. It began building in September and opened in March 1841, and is clearly shown on the Panorama.[20]

Shops

LATER in 1841 Brown sent in this glowing account of the improved buildings on the south side of Mercer Row, little realising that he would be portraying them on his Panorama. Moreover, it is interesting to stand in the Market Place and compare what Brown described with what you see now: the shop fronts have changed but not the upper storeys.

'A laudable rivalry has existed during the past summer among the tradesmen ... in regard to decorative shops, which has occasioned the entire rebuilding of some of them, and the erection of several imposing and attractive structures, to the general improvement and beautifying of the town. This has been particularly the case in ... Mercer-row. Taking the point of view from the town pump in the Market-place, or from the angle of the house of Mr [William] Ashton, ironmonger, and running the eye down the south side of the street westward, the spectator will be pleased with the *coup d'oeil* of the perspective. The foreground of the picture is composed of the handsome range of buildings, with the stuccoed fronts and richly crowned pilasters bisecting into several elegant compartments the entire front, belonging to Mr Joseph Larder, and occupied respectively by Messrs [John] Hurst [druggist], ... [Henry Jackson] Pearson [tailor & draper], Miss Hackford, and Mr [Thomas] Cocking [nurseryman & seedsman], and built by Mr William Colam, doing infinite credit to his constant personal superintendence and eminent skill.

'The next is the splendid establishment of Messrs Strawson and Young, chemists, with its fluted columns, Corinthian capitals, and colossal glass panes. Passing the old branch Boston banking house of William Allison Esq [now Lloyds TSB Bank], the many storied, light and elegant printing establishment of Mr Henry Hurton, the extensive linen-drapery emporium of Messrs Sutton and Pettinger, the ample oriental spicery depot of Mr Isaac Smith, and the mansion of Samuel Trought Esq [surgeon], the eye naturally stretches on to Mr [Michael] Longbottom's [druggist] in the extreme limit of the prospect, but instinctively returns and dwells with pleasurable emotion on the renewed face of the New King's Head Hotel, and its recently-completed rich abbey-like wing in the Elizabethan style, the pediment, panels, mouldings etc being illustrative of the taste prevailing at that period of our history.'

The article ends with a flourish, combining the worldly, the religious and the patriotic in a crescendo typical both of Brown and of his age: 'Should the town progress in improvement for a few years longer, as it has done during the last two or three, and in morals too (thanks to the clergy of the different religious denominations, and to that grand moral movement, the Temperance cause), it will be entitled to be considered by all, without dispute, what its respectable, loyal and high-spirited inhabitants believe it now to be – one of the neatest little towns in Victoria's dominions, and worthy of the visit of a Queen.'[21] The nearest to a visit by the Queen was in fact in October 1854 when the royal train passed through Louth at 60 mph, on the way to Grimsby for the official opening of the Royal Dock.[22]

The coach in the yard of the King's Head Hotel.

Mercer Row in 1905, virtually unchanged since
Brown's description sixty years before.

The Market Place Brown wrote about, drawn on stone by T W Wallis.
For details about the shops, see Chapter 7.

Freeze-frame

ASIDE from noting houses building in Trinity Lane in 1842, and dealing with the saga of the stricken spire, it was not until the beginning of 1845 that Brown wrote at length about changes in the town. He provided in effect a wonderfully evocative companion-piece to his Panorama, detailing improvements to date, and then fulminating with his usual energy against those which had not yet taken place. It moved from a eulogy on noble facades and imposing frontages in the town centre to a blistering attack on the unsymmetrical and chaotic cluster of buildings on the north side of St James's. Part of the latter appeared on the Panorama, although we suspect that the lower edges of both panels were lost where they had been attached to wooden rollers. Brown also had specific ideas for improvements, including signposting, and railings round the church. This article provides a word 'freeze-frame' of a thriving market town amid the rush and energy and optimism of the mid-19th century.

'A very few years last past have witnessed considerable and extensive improvements of the town ... Not to mention the entire districts ... of Byron's hill [Broadbank], Spittle hill, the Boar's head, the River head, and London road, the gentry have enlivened the outskirts of the town by several handsome villas, as that of Henry Pye Esq [The Cedars], Miss Emeris [The Hill, Crowtree Lane], Benjamin Hyde Esq [Southfield House], and the beautiful splendour of Elizabethan architecture which characterises the vicarage, ... Besides them, the erections for business, improved and rebuilt, have been frequent, as may be witnessed in the noble facade of the drapery establishment of Messrs Campbell, Bowmar and Ranshaw [now Eve & Ranshaw[23]]; the Lindsey bank [later Midland, now HSBC]; the range of shops nobly supporting the stuccoed and pilastered pile of buildings in the butcher-market, belonging to Joseph Larder Esq; the imposing frontage in Mercer-row, including the nonpareil drug establishment of Mr John Hurst; the handsome gothic front of the New King's Head inn; the Savings Bank buildings [later TSB, Eastgate]; and ... the remarkably high, elegant and substantial printing premises of Messrs J and T Jackson [now Oxfam], opened a twelvemonth since on new year's day. Moreover, we have had erected one new church [Holy Trinity], a Catholic chapel, an Association chapel [Warrenite, now Masonic Hall, Queen Street], a Primitive Methodist chapel, and a large Wesleyan chapel, all for the service of Almighty God. And now we have being completed the extensive repairs of the magnificent church of St James – which building, without hyperbole, may be designated "perfection completed", in the beautiful elongation of the spire, and "beauty embellished" in the handsome finial, cross, and weather vane, which crowns the whole.

'There are two or three other points of improvement ... we would venture to suggest as necessary, and which we do not entertain a doubt will ere long be attended to, if only from a regard to the comfort of the inhabitants and the maintenance of the credit which the town has already gained among strangers for its neatness and compactness. We advert, first, to the necessity of the removal of the entire batch of unsymmetrical and chaotic buildings, with their *disgusting appendages* called the Feoffee houses, on the north side of St James', and impinging so closely on the road as to render it at times dangerous in the passage of carriages to and fro. Why such a reproach to public decency should have been so long permitted is wonderful, obtruding as the mounds of bricks and mortar do on two or three of the most populous thoroughfares and entrances into the town, and being in close contiguity to the principal sacred edifice, and to Westgate, a department which may be called the Louth court-end: the senses of both

The *Forester* coach leaves Louth along Bridge Street, bound for Grimsby.

The Feoffee houses, with their disgusting appendages, in Bridge Street.
Brown strongly advocated their demolition. They were finally removed – but not until 1888.

sight and smell are violated on every occasion of passing. The space occupied by these obnoxious buildings should by all means be cleared, so as to present an unobstructed view to the traveller entering the town from the north, of the entire outline of the church, now without controversy ... designated the finest structure of its kind in the world; or, if the locality be occupied at all, there might be a circular grass plot, in the centre of which a gas lamp like that in the market-place might be erected, on a square base, on which should be inscribed the names and distances of the nearest towns, and of the metropolis, so that the numerous travellers may not (as is of daily occurrence) have to enquire which of the two contiguous streets, Westgate or Bridge-street, leads to Lincoln or Hull. This would be a real improvement ....

'We think the good work (of repairs to the church) should be completed by the erection of a substantial iron balustrade, with suitable entrance gates, east and west, so that the edifice might be preserved from the filthiness to which it is occasionally liable'.[24]

Town improvements continued through the 1840s and 1850s. Yorkshire stone was used to repair the greater part of Eastgate, Maiden Row (Church Street) and Walkergate (Queen Street) and the entire length of Ramsgate[25] because it led to the railway station. Three years later Brown was keeping a close eye on footpaths, particularly in Eastgate, welcoming their slabbing and asphalting. He averred that 'neither appearance nor utility has been kept in view on the south side of Eastgate opposite Thomas Forman's [baker, confectioner and dining rooms, No 45], where a considerable eyesore ... would vanish if the flagging was neatly continued'. He was also concerned that 'the west side of Vicker's Lane (since the opening of the railway a direct route for passengers) should be flagged in similar fashion to the east side: this would most likely prevent the casualty of broken limbs in time of frost and snow'.[26] The limbs at risk, of course, included Brown's own, since he lived at the time in Vicker's Lane.

Work elsewhere in the town continued over the next two years. In August 1852 Brown noted with pleasure the 'vigorous prosecution, under the skill of William Elliott (stonemason, Enginegate) of the slabbing, curbing and asphalting ... of Walker-gate, Engine-gate and the road leading to the Union-house, usually called Byron's-hill – will soon afford a pleasant footpath to pedestrians, particularly those afflicted with pulmonic complaints, who have not infrequently found it a task to rise the acclivity ...'[27]

In March and May 1849 Brown had reported on other improvements including the church railings which he had suggested two years earlier.[28] Later that year he delighted in the improvements to shops in Eastgate near the Fish Shambles, one of which was that of his friend William Armitage (operative chemist), the others being George West, gunmaker and James Adlard, watchmaker. 'These (shops) afford a capital specimen of acumen in the architect (Pearson Bellamy of Lincoln, who later designed the Corn Exchange, Town Hall, extension to the Baptist chapel, Free Methodist chapel and the layout of the public cemetery), considering the difficulties he evidently had to contend with in the attempt to retain so large a portion of the old premises, and yet to produce so elegant and even classical an appearance ...'[29]

He also wrote approvingly of the Mansion House which had been 'entirely new-faced, and in a style of ornament and execution which certainly reflects the highest credit of the repairer ... John Dales'. He went on: 'The present lightness and inviting appearance of this building, constituting as it does both as a prison and an assembly-room, renders it a suitable object to contemplate ...'[29] The present glass lantern in the roof was installed in 1853, but Brown did not alter the Panorama.[30] He also noted the construction of a new sessions house on Ramsgate 'in close contiguity to the gaol', that is the House of

In the garden behind the Mansion House.

The Mansion House eighty years later when it was the Mechanics' Institute (see under Town Hall below). Standing outside is librarian Miss G E Brain.
The Mansion House is owned by the Louth Naturalists', Antiquarian & Literary Society.

Correction which is quite prominent on the Panorama. 'So simple, neat and comfortable' is the sessions house, he enthused, 'that it is considered to be as unique in the county as it is a necessary ornament'.[31] It was designed by the county architect, James Sandby Padley of Lincoln, and the builder was James Hunter Ryley, stone and marble mason and brickmaker of Chequergate; his brickworks were on the other side of Eastgate, now Orme Lane, and are also clearly seen on the Panorama.

In 1850 Brown reported a proposal to improve property on the north side of the Cornmarket by building three shops for £3,000, with architect C J Carter and builder John Dales. When excavating for the purpose of making cellars, the builders unearthed an area of about 400 square yards which formed one of the principal grain stores in the town before the opening of the navigation canal.

Dwelling-houses

A PROSPECTUS was also issued for the erection of '12 superior modern dwelling-houses, or villa residences, on the east side of George Street, to form a square'. The architect was Samuel S Markham of London, and they were to be built on a shareholding system, the funds necessary, £6,000, to be vested in trustees. Brown believed that 'the increasing demand for family residences ranging from £50 rental to little more than 60s will soon be fairly met by spirited proprietors and owners ...'[31]

September 1851 saw Brown again full of the pride and optimism of the time: 'Strangers are struck with the improvements made in the cheerful borough ... which is not without reason styled the "Queen of the towns of Lincolnshire".' He referred to the 'pleasant country boxes built by "well-to-do" tradesmen on the delightful Alford [Legbourne] road; the classic buildings belonging to Christopher Ingoldby jun Esq [solicitor] erecting in Lee-street; the filling up of the chasms in Aswell-lane with substantial houses; the real building embellishments in the poor locality of Walker-gate [south side of Queen Street between the Turks Head and Burnthill Lane] graced with Edwin Squire's literary emporium' [he was a bookseller, stationer and bookbinder]. The building development on the east side of George Street advertised the previous year had been completed by John Dales – 'tasteful piles of edifices crowned with elegant turreted look-outs'.

Brown saved his crowning comment for the extraordinary transformation of Batterhams' former linen and woollen draper premises [now 61 Eastgate] into a 'lofty and capacious building 40 feet high, costing several thousand pounds' and opened as a drapery depot by Anselm Odling. Brown also provides evidence of other unimproved properties: 'We trust the remaining few thatched premises still occupying niches in our more public streets will give way to the spirit of the age.'[32] That imposing new shop frontage does not feature on the Panorama, because of the angle of view from the spire; nor can we find convincing evidence of thatched roofs remaining.

However, Brown did report in 1857 a mud and stud, thatched building still remaining on Upgate: 'Amidst all the improvements ... there is one spot which contributes to the whole area of a very *marplot*. We allude to the remains of what was some short time ago a shop ... in Upgate opposite the Blue Stone tavern [just below the junction with Mercer Row]. In addition to its great unsightliness, being composed principally of mud and stud, and thatched with straw, a thing to be laughed and jeered at by the passers by, it must be highly dangerous, the whole of the upper part of the building (ruins) bulging over the causeway ... Whose duty is it to remove the unsightly dangerous mass of crumbling fragments?'[33] We

Housing develoment on George Street happened between the sketch (1844) and the final painting (1856).

The upper storeys of Anselm Odling's drapery depot have not changed since 1851. Now Argos.

believe it to be a two-storey building on the right hand edge of the left Panorama panel.

In 1852 Brown had noted the erection of a bath house in Spa-lane. 'The baths consist of cold, tepid, vapour, shower, and warm, containing 60 to 70 tons of water of the finest quality, apparently of a chalybeate nature, flowing from the spa spring ... which ... 40 years ago, before the Woodhall spa ... was much frequented by the inhabitants of the town and neighbouring villages.' The bath proprietor was John Harrison.[34]

New buildings contemplated in 1853 were a new grammar school and bedehouses (on Schoolhouse Lane), but these would have to wait until 1869 and designs by James Fowler. The Panorama is particularly useful therefore in showing the earlier school building and playground.

Changes and improvements continued to be reported by Brown in 1857 and 1858, after he had completed the Panorama. As an example of extraordinary change, he cited Broadbank. 'Within our recollection right and left was to be seen nought but fields and trees: now these have given way to the habitations of men, which thickly stud the road on either side. Within a short time the old residence and interesting orchards, lawns and gardens of the Byron family have given way to the elegant mansion, greenhouses, gardens and terraces belonging to the present tenant W Tate Esq.'[35] Broadbank House and gardens on the Panorama was where Mrs Mary Byron lived.[36]

The same report goes on to mention a building being erected just east of the Tate property, 'which many have puzzled to guess its purpose'. Brown said he had been given to understand that Mr H F Kemp [son of Samuel Robert Kemp, farmer at The Grange, South Elkington] and another gentleman were about to try 'an experiment on a large scale ... to produce spirits from beet root and mangold wurtzel'. If successful, it was claimed, it would 'most undoubtedly prove most important both agriculturally and commercially'.[35] What became of it, we don't know, except that the following year (1858) Brown noted that the 'beetroot distillery has had a good season'.[37]

Improvements in the Cornmarket and Market Place which had 'long been out of repair' involved repaving and levelling. 'The repeated tearing up of the pavement by bazaar and show-keepers and partial replacing of the same, had in course of time rendered the ... thoroughfare anything but agreeable for the occupants of vehicles to pass over.'[38] Brown would have revelled in reporting the town centre improvements of 1999!

His style of 1858, about improvements 'steadily and satisfactorily progressing', maintained his usual combination of praise and prodding: 'The sanitary authorities are indefatigable in their exertions to prevent diseases spreading by attending to the cleansing of common lodging houses ... The Commissioners under the Paving, Lighting and Improvement Act are "mending their ways", and still keep up the high character of the town for cleanliness of the streets. A little more [gas] light would be acceptable at night in some locations, which will no doubt be attended to in due course. A great improvement has been effected by the surveyor in lighting the gas every Sunday night during the winter season, thus enabling persons attending divine worship to go to and from their several places of worship with comfort and safety.'[39]

And a 'noble' improvement in Eastgate was the erection of yet two more 'elegant' shops (probably rebuilt or refronted), by George Swaby, tailor (No 63), one for himself and the other occupied by Richard Snowden, draper. They were designed by architects Bellamy & Hardy of Lincoln 'to whose talents and correct architectural taste ... the town ... [is] indebted for so many fine buildings'.[39]

Broadbank House.

A laden harvest waggon on
St Mary's Lane.

Street Names

ONE of Brown's successful minor campaigns (or would the Commissioners have done it anyway?) was about the street name plates. He started in July 1850: 'It would be to the public convenience if the streets were named, the doors of houses numbered, and postboxes fitted by the inhabitants for facilitating the delivery of letters'.[40] No action for two years, and then a humorous piece appeared in the paper from *Correspondent*. It bears his quirky hallmark.

'Louth is a highly respectable, wealthy and improving town. No gentleman of capital or influence need hesitate to locate in such a worthy borough, provided he possesses some fair knowledge of geography, without which it is a hundred to one that he finds his road home again in any reasonable time. Here there are streets of all sizes and dimensions, neat and otherwise, wide and narrow, up-hill and down dale, riding in circuitous and majestic gradation; but how dismayed is the unsuspecting traveller when, searching for his customers, he is told by a green-grocer's boy (who seems as "green" as himself) that such a one lives either in East-gate, West-gate or No-gate, and finally, like a wandering goose running hither and thither, finds himself comfortably in the centre of "Quarry-hill or Quarry-hole", or in the more significantly termed "Goose-pool", without a drop of water to swim in. To the wise nondescripts of Louth who have had those names handed down from generation to generation as a kind of heir-loom to be possessed by nobody but themselves, this preamble may appear somewhat strange; but let them for once "transmogrify" themselves into a commercial traveller, a stranger just stepped in to make the most of his time, gaping at every corner for the wonderful names of the streets, and, still more wonderful, finding none, – left then to the caprice of any wag who may choose to play a prank by misdirecting him, – and it will soon be acknowledged that the antiquated but loyal little town of Louth, with all its wealth and intelligence, is in this respect at least 50 years behind hand.'[41]

He followed this up four months later with a more straightforward item. 'We hope the Commissioners for lighting and paving the town will see the reasonableness of supplying another public convenience we have before respectfully urged upon their attention, and which is being daily more and more felt necessary: we allude to the naming of the streets – strangers and new residents being at a loss to determine the address of the inhabitants when they wish to communicate with them personally or by letter. There are a few streets named: all, however, should be uniformly done, and those of the greatest extent should have the name written up at each extremity.'[42]

Two months later, in October 1852, ninety street name plates were delivered, and Brown reported that 'the corners of the streets ... have been furnished with cast-iron plates inscribed with the names of the various thoroughfares', but he still couldn't resist a humorous twist: 'some of them are novel – Thames-street, Commercial-road and Ludgate ... *a la* London'.[43] However, within a fortnight they had been taken down as they were not correct in either lettering or general appearance![44] So it was not until January 1853 that the 'new issue of painted cast-iron tablets' were put up. On these, Brown noted, the 'letters are better formed' and 'instead of former dingy drab and black, they are painted with a full-bodied white ground and black letters'.[45] Today, it would appear that they are collectors' items from the number stolen, and the District Council faces the same problem of a century and a half ago in getting the correct design.

Chapels

AS MIGHT be expected, Brown took an interest in building works affecting nonconformist chapels. In June 1850 the Primitive Methodists 'seriously decided on enlarging the chapel in Pade-hole' (Northgate; site of the Library). The 1836 chapel held only about 500, and 'it not infrequently happens that one or two hundred persons have to return home from evening services, not being able to obtain accommodation'. The chapel was to be extended to 60 feet; in fact it was a complete rebuild, necessitating the demolition of adjacent houses (that was done in August). The front was fenced from the street with a 'neat dwarf wall and iron pallisades'.[46] The chapel re-opened at the end of November 1850.

Brown had a particular interest in the General Baptist chapel on the corner of Cannon Street and Northgate. Within six months of publishing his engraved drawing of the chapel, with the graveyard in front (in June 1850), he learned that the yard was to be taken up with 'a commodious Sunday School-room ... to hold 400-500 persons (and available also as a public room) ... to be erected on pillars, forming open arcades'.[47] It was designed by Pearson Bellamy and opened in autumn 1851. It is now Cannon Street House, occupied by offices.

Following the breakaway of the reformers from the Wesleyan chapel in December 1853, the Louth Free Methodist Church was formed. On 6 July the following year the foundation stone of their chapel in Eastgate was laid by John Booth Sharpley (corn and coal merchant and three times Mayor). With the stone was a memorial setting out the origin of the Free Methodist Church.[48] The 1,200-seater pillared chapel – eight Corinthian columns supporting a full width pediment – (with railings in front, which would have pleased Brown), was designed by Pearson Bellamy and built by Clark & Crow.[49] It cost £2,360, and opened on 31 December 1854, even though the chapel was not quite finished. The site is now a car park.

Brown's drawing of the Primitive Methodist chapel (1850) on Northgate, with children leaving Sunday School by the side entrance.

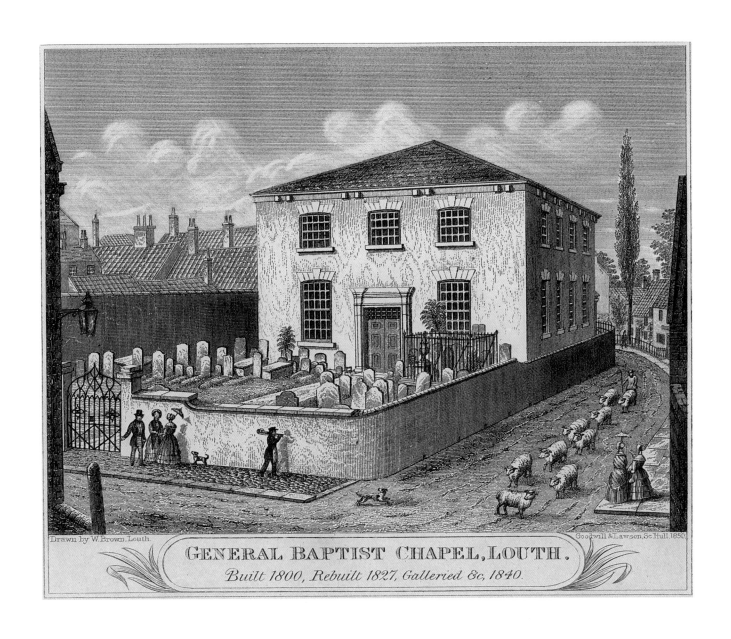

GENERAL BAPTIST CHAPEL, LOUTH.

Built 1800, Rebuilt 1827, Galleried &c, 1840.

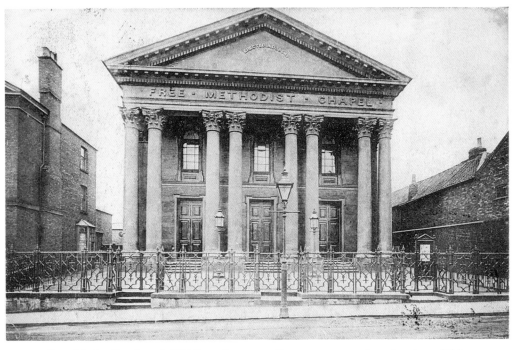

Free Methodist chapel (1854) on Eastgate. Brown never made a drawing of this.

Wesleyan Chapel & Town Hall, Louth.

Town Hall

BY 1852 the Town Council realised that the facilities of the Mansion House for meetings and as the police-station house were inadequate for a town growing in the ways Brown was chronicling. They took the usual step of appointing a committee – the Public Improvement Committee, on 14 May. It worked with commendable speed, and on 2 July presented a report recommending a new police-office and lock-up, superintendent's residence, magistrates court and offices, Council chamber, committee room, muniment room, municipal offices, and a large public room. Moreover, ground plans and elevations of the new Town Hall in the Italian style by Pearson Bellamy were inspected and approved as providing 'all the requisites of a public building'. The site was the Corporation property called the Stall-yard on Eastgate and Cannon Street. The very narrow entrance to Cannon Street from Eastgate would also need to be widened. (This explains why the Cannon Street corner of the Town Hall is not a right angle.)

Brown's report was welcoming: 'A large public room has long been felt necessary to meet the increased wants of the parish.' The probable cost was £4,000. To meet this the Council would need to sell corporate properties, particularly the Guildhall, the Mansion House and pasture land known as Factory Close on James Street.[50]

The sale took place in November, and in fact included five plots near the Union-house and 26 lots near the railway. The Guildhall was sold to Messrs Lucas of the Phoenix wine and spirit vaults for £2,400.[51] The Mansion House failed to reach its reserve of £1,000. It was eventually sold for £830 to the Louth Mechanics' Institution, who held a mammoth three-day bazaar, organised by gold medal woodcarver Thomas Wilkinson Wallis, which helped to raise £1,071, sufficient to pay for purchase and alterations.

Tenders for building the Town Hall were considered by the quarterly meeting of the Council in the Mansion House in May 1853: Charles Ward, Lincoln £7,910, Charles Clark, Louth £6,583, John Levitt, Louth £6,575 and John Dales, Louth £5,927. After 'a long, most animated, and good mannered conversation (extending the meeting to 10 o'clock),' they adjourned the meeting to the next week.[52] Present then were

MESSRS. J. AND B. DALES,

BUILDERS, CONTRACTORS

Bricklayers, Plasterers,

JOINERS, CABINET MAKERS, UPHOLSTERERS, AND HOUSE DECORATERS, ETC., ETC.,

WEST GATE AND EAST GATE,

LOUTH,

Tender their grateful acknowledgments to the Nobility, Clergy, Gentry, and the Public, for the liberal favours conferred upon them, and hope by punctuality in the execution of all orders entrusted to their care, and using the best materials, to ensure a continuance of their confidence and esteem.

JOHN DALES

Begs to inform the Public that in addition to the above, he has commenced an

EXTENSIVE BRICK YARD,

NEAR THE RAILWAY STATION,

Where he intends carrying on the above Business in all its various branches, thereby enabling him to complete all Orders at the most reduced rates.— BRICKS of every description for Building purposes. DRAINING TILES for Agricultural and other uses, RIDGE AND ROOFING TILES, WALL COPINGS, GARDEN EDGE TILES, FLOOR PAVINGS.

J. D. begs also further to state, that he has always on hand a large assortment of ORNAMENTAL PLASTER and DECORATIVE CEMENT CASTINGS, also CEMENT CHIMNEY TOPS, which are made to order after any style that may be ordered; also always on hand an extensive assortment of ORNAMENTAL FIRE CLAY CHIMNEY TOPS, FIRE BRICKS, QUARRIES, &c.; also TERRA COTTO WORK, adapted to any style of Architecture, and for all kinds of Ornamental Buildings—*wholesale and retail.*

R. DALES, JUN.,

Having removed to very eligible and extensive premises situated in EASTGATE, intends carrying on in addition to the business of Builders, &c., that of

Cabinet Maker, Upholsterer, and House Decorator;

He therefore solicits an early inspection of the very valuable Furniture Decorations and Paper Hangings selected from the first Houses in London, which for taste, quality and cheapness, will not be surpassed by any house in the trade.—All kinds of Jobbing Work, of Wood, Brick, and Stone, punctually attended to; and Paper hung by the piece or day.

N.B. FUNERALS FURNISHED

ON THE MOST REASONABLE TERMS IN TOWN OR COUNTRY.

Advertisement in Hagar's Directory 1849.

the Mayor, Samuel Trought and fourteen Aldermen and Councillors, including John Booth Sharpley, chairman of the Estate Committee, who had reached the conclusion that 'they might accept the ... plans without injury to the borough' (financially). James William Wilson (solicitor) on the other hand considered that 'they might well have all they needed in a building of lesser dimensions, and with a less proportion of ornaments for £4,600 instead of £6,000'. The motion to proceed with Bellamy's plans was carried nine to five, and the tender of John Dales was accepted.[53]

The foundation stone, in fact two blocks of Houlton stone, was laid on Thursday 16 June 1853. It is in the north-east corner, that is at the rear of the building. One stone had a hole in which to place two bottles, one with coins and the other with a parchment. The latter listed the Mayor, Samuel Trought, the High Steward, Rt Hon Charles Tennyson d'Eyncourt, Town Clerk Christopher Ingoldby jun; Aldermen: Field Flowers Goe, John Booth Sharpley, John Bogg, Thomas Overton, John Allenby; Councillors: William Henry Gray, Thomas Grant, Jonathan Birkett, Henry Boothby jun, John Henry Simpson, William Newman, James William Wilson, Thomas Philbrick, Charles Bowman, John Hurst, William Allison Dunn, Thomas Jackson, Christopher Ingoldby, Michael Plaskitt, William Ashton, Thomas Young, Charles Goodwin Smith, and William Shepherd. The stonelaying was by the Earl of Yarborough, with full Masonic honours. It was a happy coincidence, Brown did not fail to note, that the same day the Lincolnshire Association for the Promotion of Temperance held their grand annual Gala in Louth.

His very lengthy report detailed every step of the processions, words of speeches, feastings, concert and ball (to 3am) and the pyrotechnic display in the Priory grounds, witnessed, he estimated, by more than 6,000 people. The Earl visited the teetotallers' gala at the Priory, made a speech and visited Brown's 'Gallery of Pictorial Illustration'. Brown was perhaps disappointed that 'his Lordship regretted his numerous engagements that day prevented a more minute inspection' (as he discreetly reported).[54]

In August the builder, John Dales, was 'charged before the magistrates with a breach of the Local Improvement Act, in not having sufficient lights at each end of the hoard-fence ... on Eastgate'. Apparently by 'some mishap one of them went out at an early hour in the morning'. Brown did not record any fine, but noted that Dales had engaged the gas company to supply lights at night.[55] By the end of the year the building was up to 20 feet, the stonework was complete on the west front, and six columns of Caen stone were in place for the carved capitals and moulded arch of the main Eastgate entrance.[56] To undertake so large a contract, Dales had to open a new brickpit, off Brackenborough Road (now Willow Drive); it is shown on the Panorama. He also made arrangements with the Council for payments on account. The building was reported to be in an 'advanced state' in May 1854, but it would appear that Brown did not report the official opening.

Part of the preliminary sketches. The grey roof building centre left is the Wesleyan chapel, with minister's house attached. The rear extension housed the vestries where Brown showed his polyopticorama to the Juvenile Tea Meeting (see Chapter 6). The small buildings beyond the chapel were demolished to make way for the Town Hall.

The grey roof building in the near left corner of the Cornmarket was the Guildhall, which was demolished to accommodate the Corn Exchange.

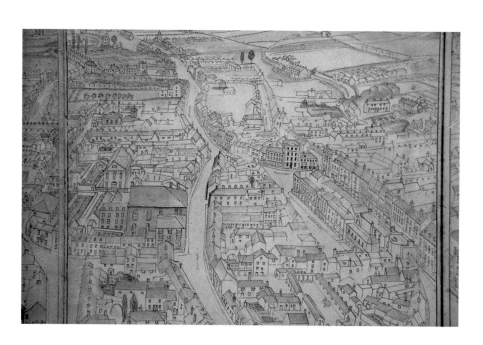

The new Town Hall and Police Station.

The new Corn Exchange with four pitched roofs of plate glass.

BOROUGH OF LOUTH.

Laying of the Foundation=Stone of the
NEW TOWN-HALL,

On THURSDAY, JUNE the 16th, M.DCCC.LIII.

Programme of the Proceedings.

At 8 o'clock in the Morning, the TEA, SUGAR, &c., will be given to the 1000 Holders of the Tickets for the same, at the British School-Room, in Kidgate.

On the arrival of the North and South Morning Trains, the TEMPERANCE SOCIETIES, with their Brass Bands, will proceed to the Priory Grounds to hold their Morning Meeting.

At 11 o'clock, the Rev. C. Badham, D.D., Head Master of the Grammar-School, has announced " that the LOUTH SCHOOL SPEECHES will be delivered in the School-Room."

At 12 o'clock precisely, the 1000 POOR AND WORKING CLASSES, holding Tickets, will sit down to THE DINNER, provided for them in the Corn-Market.

At 1 o'clock, the various SOCIETIES OF THE TOWN, headed by the MAYOR AND CORPORATION, will leave the Mansion-House, and proceed along Mercer-Row—Market-Place—Eastgate—and Ramsgate, to the Railway Station, to meet the RIGHT HON. EARL YARBOROUGH, whom they will escort, by the same route, to the King's Head Hotel, where the ADJOURNED PROVINCIAL GRAND LODGE OF FREEMASONS is appointed to be held.

At Half-past 1, the Worshipful the Mayor entertains the Corporation, the Masonic Body, and a distinguished circle, at a *Déjeûner*, at the Mansion-House, during which the various Societies will proceed through the Town by the following route :—along Gospelgate—George-Street—South-Street—Upgate—Chequergate—Northgate—James-Street—Ramsgate—Maiden-Row—Walkergate—Aswell-Lane—Kidgate—Lee-Street—South-Street—Edward-Street—Breakneck-Lane—Westgate—Bridge-Street—to the Mansion-House.

THE GRAND PROCESSION
Will be formed AT THREE O'CLOCK, in the following order :—

A Platform for viewing the Ceremony of laying the Stone has been erected on the site of the intended New Town-Hall;

POLICE.
MILITARY.
SUPERINTENDENT OF POLICE ON HORSEBACK.
CORPORATION BANNERS.
BAND.
JUDGE OF COUNTY COURT. THE MAYOR. HIGH STEWARD OF BOROUGH.
TOWN CLERK.
THE BOROUGH MAGISTRATES.
ALDERMEN AND TOWN COUNCILLORS, THREE ABREAST.
BOROUGH TREASURER. CONTRACTOR FOR WORKS.
WARDEN AND ASSISTANTS AND HEAD MASTER OF GRAMMAR SCHOOL.
COUNTY MAGISTRATES.
GOVERNOR OF PRISON.
OVERSEERS OF THE POOR.
ASSISTANT OVERSEER. MASTER OF WORKHOUSE.
BAND.
GRAND MASONIC PROCESSION.
CLERGY, AND INVITED GUESTS.
FRIENDLY SOCIETY.
LOUTH GENERAL FRIENDLY SOCIETY.
MECHANIC AND AGRICULTURAL FRIENDLY SOCIETY.
RECHABITE TENT AND TEMPERANCE SOCIETY.
GOOD SAMARITAN LODGE OF ODD FELLOWS, M. U.
ANCIENT FORESTERS { COURT MORPETH. COURT CHAPLIN.
IMPERIAL LODGE OF ODD FELLOWS, N. U.
INHABITANTS OF THE BOROUGH WHO CHOOSE TO JOIN THE PROCESSION.
POLICE.

POLICE. POLICE. POLICE. POLICE.

Tickets of admission to be had of Messrs. JACKSON, Booksellers : Reserved Seats, 2s.; Back Seats, 1s.; Standing Room, 6d.

The Procession will leave the Mansion-House at 3 p.m., and proceed along Mercer-Row—Walkergate—Maiden-Row—Eastgate—to the site of the Building ; and, after the Stone has been laid, will re-form, in the same order, and proceed up Eastgate—past the Mansion-House—to the Market-Place, where the NATIONAL ANTHEM will be sung.

☞ *The Friendly Societies, Odd Fellows, Foresters, &c., will then proceed to their respective Inns to Dinner.*

At 4 o'clock, the TEMPERANCE SOCIETIES have announced another Meeting at the Priory Grounds, and during the Evening a DISPLAY OF FIREWORKS, &c.

At 6 o'clock, the Mayor presides at a PUBLIC DINNER at the KING'S HEAD HOTEL.

At 8 o'clock, there will be a FULL-DRESS CONCERT AND BALL at the MANSION-HOUSE.

By Order,
CHRIS. INGOLDBY, Jun.,

MANSION-HOUSE, June 14th, 1853.   TOWN-CLERK.

☞ **Persons** desirous of procuring admission to the **Platform, Dinner,** or **Concert and Ball,** are requested to apply for **Tickets,** in order to prevent disappointment and confusion.

J. AND T. JACKSON, PRINTERS, LOUTH.

A section of Brown's 'Gallery of Illustration' which he exhibited in the grounds of
The Priory on the day of the laying of the foundation stone of the New Town-Hall.

PERSPECTIVE VIEW OF THE NEW CORN EXCHANGE, LOUTH.

PEARSON BELLAMY, ARCHITECT.

J.R.Jobbins

Corn Exchange

FARMERS, corn merchants, millers and others had met in September 1852, and agreed it was desirable to erect a Corn Exchange in Louth. Within a fortnight a company was formed, with a capital of £3,000, and provisional directors including four Louth merchants and farmers from Well Vale, Great Carlton, Haugham, South Thoresby, Hallington, Acthorpe, Keddington and Burwell. In reporting developments, Brown put in a word for the butter women: 'It is sincerely hoped that, with all the public and private improvements going and contemplated ..., involving an outlay of probably not less than £200,000, the poor butter women will not be forgotten, but the same arrangement will be hit upon to furnish them with suitable accommodation and shelter'.[57]

Matters moved quickly: the Guildhall was bought by Messrs Lucas, by December arrangements had been made to build a Corn Exchange on the site, and Pearson Bellamy (of Bellamy & Hardy) had provided elevations and outline plans. The architect was a busy man, also preparing plans for the Town Hall. A drawing of the Corn Exchange was exhibited in the window of Jackson's, stationers, in the Market Place. Brown repeated his hope that 'accommodation for the females who supply the poultry and butter markets will be provided'.[58] However, his hopes were not met. 'It is much to be regretted', he wrote in January 1853, 'that some provision for ... the wives and daughters of the neighbouring farmers vending poultry and butter in the market has been lost sight of ...'[59]

Tenders for building were received in May: William Kirk, Lincoln £2,280, Thomas Abbott, Alford £2,523, Thomas Lundie, Grimsby £2,424, Robert Young, Lincoln £2,494, Charles Clark, Louth £2,185, John Dales, Louth £2,147, and John Levitt, Louth £2,110. These were much closer than those for the Town Hall, and the contract was awarded to Levitt (he also had the advantage of being a stonemason), who was to have the old materials (from demolishing the Guildhall). Progress was rapid, and Brown noted that 'the pickaxe [was] put into the old building on 12th May'. Actually, the Guildhall had been up less than forty years. It is a plain slate-roofed building on the Panorama sketches, with the name written on. The drawings for the Corn Exchange showed an Italianate front of carved Caen stone, and an unusual roof of four pitches covered with Hartley's colourless rough plate glass.[60] That roof behind the high facade can easily be picked out on the Panorama.

Corn Exchange, Louth.

The laying of the foundation stone on Friday 1st July 1853, following only a fortnight after that for the Town Hall, was accompanied by the usual dinner (in the Mansion House), toasts and speeches. The stone was laid by the Mayor, Samuel Trought, and the statutory parchment in a bottle, placed in the stone with specimens of grain, listed the directors of the Corn Exchange Company: Charles North of South Thoresby (Chairman), Roger Sharpley, Great Carlton; Nathaniel Cartwright, Haugham; Thomas Cartwright, Well Vale; William Scorer, Burwell; Croft Sharpley, Acthorpe; Richard Mason, Keddington; Richard Chatterton, Hallington; Henry Winder, South Thoresby (farmers); Robert Norfolk, Thomas Young and William East (Louth merchants), and William Garfit (banker), with Christopher Ingoldby jun (Secretary). What happened to that bottle and its contents when the building was demolished?

Councillor J. W. Wilson, not only a solicitor but also a fellow artist, had apparently supported Brown's concerns about the butter women. In his speech at the dinner, the Mayor referred to Mr Wilson's concern and said it reminded him of an observation made to him when they were mentioned: 'Surely you are not going to cover up the old lasses! If you do they'll sit like geese and we shall never get them off their roost'. In the evening the 60-70 workmen were regaled with a supper in the Masons Arms. Their 'orderly and respectable appearance was so striking' that the Chairman of directors 'left them a sovereign for their enjoyment, which was protracted till morning'.[61]

The stone facade had reached attic level by December, and exhibited two architectural orders, 'Rusticated' and Doric, with a niche for 'the emblematical figure of agriculture', and a handsome central arch for the main entrance. Wide folding doors led into the stone-flagged Exchange proper, 74 feet by 34½ feet and 25 feet high to the skylights. There were offices at the front with part of the basement re-occupied by Lucas Brothers, wine merchants.

The emblematical figure was Ceres, the Roman goddess of agriculture and the corn-bearing earth, from whom derives our word 'cereal'. The six feet statue held a torch, symbolising the light and warmth of spring, a cornucopia and ears of harvested corn. After more than a century of weathering, the facade was described as 'like a rotting cadaver'.[63] When the Corn Exchange was demolished (it had long outrun its original purpose) and replaced by the Halifax Building Society premises in 1981, the ageing Ceres was pinioned with iron and placed on a concrete shelf overlooking Rosemary Lane. There she decayed further and became unsafe. Poor Ceres. When she was taken down in 1993 she disintegrated. Two years later the Louth Naturalists', Antiquarian & Literary Society, with the aid of funding from the Halifax, commissioned a scaled-down replica. She was carved from a three-quarter-ton block of Ketton limestone by stonecarver Brian Ansell of Riby, and stands in Louth Museum ready to look out on the world again from a niche in the planned extension to the museum.

The Corn Exchange opened for business on 4 January 1854. 'It may be considered a model corn exchange', was Brown's view, but he did not lose sight of its commercial purpose: 'The shareholders, to whom the town and neighbourhood are much indebted for their spirited conduct, are likely to derive a most liberal percentage upon their outlay'.[64] However, the scaffolding was not cleared until April, when the builder doing the interior work, Charles Clark, was still completing the offices.[65]

Thanks to Brown's journalism we have a picture of much building activity in the town – public buildings, houses and shops. This meant full employment for builders (the number of firms more than doubled), bricklayers and stonemasons, carpenters and joiners, plumbers and glaziers, and for painters

The new Ceres statue in Louth Museum, presented by John Simon, Halifax Building Society manager (standing), with David Robinson, President Louth Naturalists', Antiquarian & Literary Society, and Jean Howard, honorary Museum Curator.

(which was Brown's original trade). The left panel of the Panorama shows a remarkable seven brick and brick and tile works at the eastern end of the town, all with Scotch kilns: John Dales off Brackenborough Road; Thomas Simons and Henry Chapman near the Riverhead (between Victoria Road and the railway station); Nicholas Pearson Bellamy between Priory Road and the railway embankment; John Edwards on Monks Dyke (east of the railway); John Dunstan Naull and John Edwards on Charles Street; Thomas Rose on Maiden Row (Church Street); and James Hunter Ryley on Eastgate (Orme Lane).

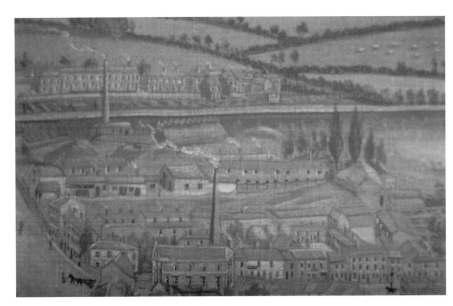

Looking from background to foreground: terrace houses in Trinity Lane, railway, Bellamy's brickworks with chimney and Scotch kiln, Ryall's ropery, Ryley's brickworks, the chimney of Rose's brickworks on Maiden Row (Church Street), and the grey roof of the Free Methodist chapel.

Charles Street brickworks with bricks laid out in the yard and the pit left (now a fishing pond).

Public Cemetery

PERHAPS Brown's most vociferous and prolonged campaign was for a new public cemetery. The problem was not new. St James's churchyard had not been used as a burial ground since 1770, and in 1774 a wall and gates were put up at St Mary's churchyard (now known as the Old Cem).[66] By 1827 the accommodation was insufficient and the burial ground was extended, but in the 1830s there were 1,541 burials (including 380 infants), and the difficulties soon became apparent.[67]

Brown first took up the cudgels in his usual uncompromising style in September 1843. 'St Mary's burial ground ... is ... in such a slovenly condition, that were a man to take a horse and ride, he would not find within a circuit of a hundred miles one so disgracefully neglected. While the town is proverbially improving in the splendour of its dwellings and shops, it is quite seemly that those who in their day materially contributed the means, should have a little more respect paid to their ashes. We hope those whom it immediately concerns will look to this.'[68]

Matters did not improve, and he returned to the attack in January 1845. 'There is ... a grievance ... which, it seems, requires to be repeatedly brought before the public ere its removal can be effected: we refer to the burying-ground of St Mary's: its slovenly condition is a standing reproach to the good taste and feeling of the parish. The rude boys and unconsciously offending sheep should be discharged; the middle path might be blocked up, the broad east path being left open for visitants ...' He also suggested a cottage at the south-east corner for the sexton 'to *efficiently* superintend the whole, and facilitate the solemn rites of sepulture'.[69] The Panorama shows a funeral procession approaching the churchyard, the east path, the offending middle path (still there today), and the crowded gravestones (but no sheep).

The real problems were brought home in June when Brown gave a graphic account of 'the filling in of the grave of Mrs Good.[70] The material dug out of the grave seemed to consist of no fewer than four coffins (four skulls having been cast up): so numerous indeed were the pieces of coffins, leg and thigh-bones, ribs, jaws, and other fragments of mortality, that it was with difficulty the grave-digger found soil enough from the grave to cover them from the sight of surviving friends. One of the spectators ... detected the remains of his father, who had been buried for 17 years ... so grave a violation of respect and decency ... surely cannot possibly exist while any portion of the new burying-ground remains unoccupied'.[71] (That could be where the story came from about the ghost of the sexton – James Smith – with a squeaky wheelbarrow full of bones.)

If there had been a new burying ground in view, nothing had come of it, and three years passed before a special meeting of the Town Council in the Guildhall considered 'the propriety of providing a portion of the borough lands as a public cemetery ... for the present churchyard is inconveniently full'. They also noted the need for ceremonies to be conducted by respective ministers, Establishment and Dissenters. The matter was referred to the Estate Committee. 'The project is entirely in accordance with the ameliorating advances of the age', wrote Brown approvingly.[72] However, many and loud complaints continued from those who found 'the remains of their deceased friends unceremoniously disturbed by the mattock and spade of the sexton'.

In 1849, a year which also saw a cholera epidemic, the Council did select a site of sufficient size, but then found that because it was within 300 yards of human habitation, it was 'disallowed by Act of Parliament'. Brown pressed the point that the subject should 'not be lost sight of by the Council', and ended in typical sepulchral fashion: 'It is hoped that until the desideratum of a public cemetery be prepared, the officials of the dead will in their grave avocations give as little occasion as possible, by the tumbling up of bones and half decomposed corpses, to lacerate the feelings of the mourning spectators of interment'.[73]

Extract from a handbill, published by A RATEPAYER, dated 20 March 1854. It was addressed To the Ratepayers of Louth about the New Burial Ground. Just the sort of short-sighted comment that would have infuriated Brown.

Ten Acres of Land for Burial purposes *cannot surely be needed here!* We find the Town of Stamford satisfied with *Five Acres!* Why should Louth have more? The Old Ground of St. Mary's, being little above *Two Acres,* has afforded accommodation for the burial of the dead for nearly a Century, and on such a calculation the Ten Acres purchased by the Burial Board will suffice for *Five Hundred Years!* Why should the present generation be so unnecessarily burdened? or why should they thus burden posterity? A little reflection will shew the injustice in both cases.

A funeral procession approaches the already overcrowded St Mary's churchyard, where the sexton is preparing another grave among the bones of previous interments.

But the matter was lost sight of by the Council. When the Archdeacon of Lincoln visited Louth in May 1852, the condition of the burial ground was brought to his attention. Brown felt there might be new hope that its disgraceful condition would be remedied 'either by an extension on the adjoining ground or a new cemetery made in another part of town, which would be far better'.[74] Clearly the Archdeacon did make his view known, as a vestry meeting was called for 3rd June to consider 'the best means of providing additional ground for the decent interment of the parishioners'.[75]

What the outcome of that meeting was, Brown did not report, but in September 1852 (nine years after his first complaint), he noted the formation of the 'Louth Cemetery Company'. He then went on in flowery prose, as his pen ran away with him, that it was intended 'to select an eligible spot, easy of access, and to lay it out in a picturesque manner, so as to present a scene of cheerful pensiveness, calculated to excite endearing and solemn feeling in those whose friends may be entombed within its precincts.' Moreover it was to be a 'place of sepulture for all denominations'. The cost was estimated at about £3,000 to be raised in £10 shares'.[76] We suspect that this was Brown's way of giving the process a prod, but in May 1853 the Town Council submitted a petition to the House of Commons for a public cemetery, making explicit the right of dissenters to be buried there.[77] A few dissenting chapels, particularly the General Baptists and Wesleyans, had had limited facilities, and from the 1830s there had been a burial ground at Holy Trinity, but there the incumbent would not read the burial service over one who had not been baptised.[77]

Apparently the petition resulted in action, a Burial Board was formed and they investigated three locations: land owned by Miss Emeris contiguous to St Mary's churchyard, land on the Spilsby (London) road adjoining Julian Bower, and ten acres in two lots belonging to the Ecclesiastical Commissioners on the Horncastle road, considered to be the most eligible. However, there was an objection from the Warden and Six Assistants of the Grammar School that the site on the Horncastle road was too close to the residence (The Lodge) of the headmaster, Dr Charles Badham; and Henry Pye of The Cedars near the existing churchyard had offered more for the Emeris land than the Board felt justified in recommending the Vestry to give. They therefore recommended the purchase of nearly 10½ acres of land at Julian Bower, owned by Mrs Bowling, for £1,260.

Brown approved, and felt sure the parish would also. 'It is situated on a hill, having chalky and dry soil, ... the drainage running away from the town .. it is beyond the precincts of the town, and possesses facilities for two entrances – one on the Spilsby road and the other in Green-lane [now Linden Walk]. It is also a retired and sequestered spot ... and is by far the most eligible place ... which can be procured.'[78] The site is clearly shown on the sketch for the Panorama as a grass field, with a knoll of trees above the London Road cutting. Brown wrote 'Julian Bower' on the knoll of trees, not on the other side of the road where the windmill stood. The building work at the cemetery did not start until after he had put the finishing touches to the Panorama, but he does show that some preparation had been done by felling trees, leaving those on the boundaries.

At the beginning of June 1854, the Burial Board let the contract for building the entrance lodge and two chapels, and laying out of the walks, to John Levitt for £1,082. The other tenders were from Charles Clark £1,697, William Kirk of Lincoln £1,103 and John Dales £1,593. The architects were, yet again, Bellamy & Hardy of Lincoln.[79] James Fowler was then in partnership with James Maugham, and had yet to make his name. Pearson Bellamy on the other hand seems to have been the Council's favoured architect. Reporting the following month, Brown explained that the 'more elevated position of the ground' commanded a 'pleasing view of the German ocean' (North Sea), and that the chapels would be in the Early English style, as would also the lodge which would arch over the entrance through the 18 feet high side of the cutting (made in 1839). And he could not resist a final dig about the former 'notoriously slovenly and neglected graveyard'.[80] Not surprisingly, as he had seen his third wife, Ann, buried there in March that year.

In July the foundation stones of the two chapels were laid by Samuel Trought who was serving another term as Mayor. Each stone contained a sealed bottle with a written memorial 'indicating the two distinct classes of the community (church people and dissenters) for whose use the two portions of the ground were respectively divided'. The mayor said he was gratified that the nonconformists would be able to have their own burial rites and services.[81] The final cost, including land purchase, building the lodge and chapels, enclosing, planting and laying out, was about £2,700. The unconsecrated part was opened for the use of Dissenters in March 1855.[82]

There were however problems for the Established church: the Vicar, Rev E R Mantell, objected to stepping beyond the porch of the Episcopal church to meet a cortege because the roadway to it had not been consecrated. This necessitated a special meeting of the Burial Board and resolution to take counsel's opinion as to whether consecration would prevent passage for users of the unconsecrated part. (The Board had already requested the Bishop to consecrate the chapel and

Brown's preliminary sketch shows a clump of trees on Julian Bower. This was to be the site of the public cemetery.

ground set apart for the church.) Brown was furious: '... why should there by any delay in consecrating the churchmen's portion? ... the boundary stones between the consecrated portion and the portion to be consecrated ... [are] ... sufficient for all possible purposes of distinction ... The demand of a special cemetery for the Church of England within the general cemetery is simply preposterous – neither countenanced by Act of Parliament nor defensible upon any rational principle'.[83] Controversy rumbled on, including decision about the 'dwarf wall' on the west side at the foot of the road cutting, and a stormy vestry meeting in November, until the church portion of the cemetery and its chapel were consecrated by the Bishop on 29 December 1855.[84] It had been twelve years since Brown began his campaign.

Cemetery, Louth.

Self-portrait of William Brown painted from a daguerreotype.

Chapter 5
The man, his family and Methodism

AT THE time of the broken spire and the genesis of his panorama in 1844, William Brown was already 56. He was listed in directories as a painter, which means a housepainter, or what we would call a painter and decorator. (On his death certificate his occupation was given as Master House Painter.) He had additional income as the local reporter for the *Lincoln, Rutland & Stamford Mercury*. He lived above his shop at the Northgate end of Vicker's Lane (formerly Holland Lane) with his second wife Letitia (Lettice) aged 65, and two of his surviving children, Elizabeth (18) and Holland (13). His other family had flown the nest: William, also a housepainter was married with four young children and living in Waite's Yard off Walkergate (Queen Street); Francis was a Wesleyan Methodist Association minister; daughter Mary Ann Holland (24), and stepdaughters Ann (26), and Eliza (25) who was married with children.

Vicker's Lane was a narrow thoroughfare with 18 dwellings and 70-80 inhabitants. Among Brown's neighbours were John Bingley, an agricultural labourer, Abraham Spivey, woollen carpet weaver (probably working in the factory in James Street), Charles Blythe, letter carrier (postman), Ann Gelsthorpe, straw bonnet maker, John Fields, tailor, and William Miller, a woodturner. A short distance away in the Fish Shambles lived his young friend and collaborator, the chemist, druggist, photographer and inventor, William Armitage (30). On the walk to his friend, Brown had to pass three of the town's 26 inns and 19 beerhouses – the White Swan (publican William Cartwright), the Board or the Old Dram Shop (William Spurr; on the site of Mackays), and the Ship & Horns (John Driver: now a charity shop). And pass them he did, for William was a teetotaller and a staunch supporter and advocate of the temperance cause, and his son Holland went on to become one of the honorary secretaries of the City of London Temperance Association.[1]

William was a well-known figure (particularly to Methodists) about the cobbled streets of the town, in his working clothes as a housepainter, or more formal dress with neat black necktie and equally black high-necked, wide lapelled and double-breasted coat on his way to attend or report a meeting or event for the *Stamford Mercury*. Although going bald on top, he wore long sideburns, had a kindly face with well-marked smile lines, and a fairly prominent sharp nose – a feature befitting his enquiring journalistic temperament.

Brown certainly had a quirky sense of humour, as these quotes from his early days of reporting show. 'There is an old Buck now residing in Louth whose ivory-box contains the full number of 32 teeth, and they grind tremendously'.[2] And this conversation he claims to have overheard. ' "A fine day, Sir, a fine day!", said a young knight of the sleeve-board [dandy] to a patriarchal snip [tailor] last week, in Louth market place. "Tolerable, tolerable", responded the old fellow, "but the weather now-a-days is not near so fine as it was when I was a boy. Why Sir," he continued, "I remember at that time a whole year of such fine days, that you might have drawn the coarsest of them thro' the eye of a *twist needle*".'[2]

A drunk being carried along Upgate on a litter on his way to the cells in the Mansion House.

He could also give a humourous twist to a story. Here are two examples. 'On Saturday night last, as the family of Mr Plaskitt, draper, of Louth, were retiring to bed, a hunchback Lothario, named Fox, was discovered sweetly wrapt in the arms of Morpheus, enjoying a share of the maid servant's bed; she too was *dreaming*, but not of the *discovery*. Mr Plaskitt instantly awoke the Don Giovani, and bade him depart *sans* hat, coat, vest, and inexpressibles, which he did, though unwilling, into the open air, and passed his time till morning in a stable, with straw for a covering: his bedfellow likewise suffered an immediate ejectment. He was on Wednesday morning taken to Louth House of Correction as a vagrant.'[3]

The second was headed RECIPROCAL POLITENESS. 'On the fair-day, Mr John Hurst, druggist, had his nervous system suddenly and violently agitated, by the unexpected appearance in his splendid shop of a cow, which, after tranquilly eyeing the toilet bottles, and specimens of rich scents which lay immediately before her olfactory nerves, was happily induced by the exclamatory and gentlemanly remonstrances of the chemist, as politely to back out, *a la mode* the champion, without doing the slightest injury to the elaborated contents of the depot.'[4] It is clear that he had a good vocabulary, and a literary style very much in keeping with the period.

And he wrote this about the town: 'Louth is an odd place; several of its inhabitants are great oddities, and there are oddities peculiar to the place: it has a *Park* without any *deer*, a *Newmarket* without a *race-course*, a *river* without a land *current*, a butchery without a *slaughter-house*, a *churchyard* without a church, a *church* without a *parish*, and a *parish* without a *Vicar*.' But we wonder what his readers thought of it. Were any offended, or did they just regard Brown himself as an oddity?

He crossed swords with the vicar, Rev E R Mantell, a couple of years later about the latter's mode of transport, and wrote it up in the third person. It appears to show a degree of self-importance, but to be fair to Brown, it did contain an apology. It was headed: THE VICAR and the REPORTER.

'A trifling misunderstanding has arisen betwixt these two important personages at Louth, and has become the subject of no small conversation and exaggeration. It appears that the Louth reporter, being wrongly informed as to the manner of the Vicar's arrival in his parish, (stating it to be in a carriage and four instead of a phaeton and pair), instantly recurred to the fact of the Bishop of Lincoln's last visitation, when he came in a carriage and four with outriders bearing staves of office, and with jockeys dressed in scarlet, – inferring that the same spirit of ostentation would be engendered in the inferior clergy, from so conspicuous and powerful an example. This led the reporter to head his article "Fashionable Arrival". The Vicar has commented upon it, and hastily concluded it to be a *malicious fabrication* of the Reporter; and moreover ludicrously charges him with a conspiracy to draw away from the Vicar's ministration, to the pale of the Wesleyan or Warrenite community, his poorer hearers! The Reporter has written the Vicar the following note, and there the matter rests.

"Rev Sir – I am sorry for what has transpired, but I will not now do you the injustice to suppose otherwise than that, after you had made the charge of falsehood and penned the reproof, the charity which 'hopeth all things' suggested 'perhaps, after all, the obnoxious writer of whom I complain may not be solely to blame; he may have been imposed on by others.' And such, Sir, I do assure you, was the case. I acknowledge myself, nevertheless, culpable in some degree in not exercising the rigid scrutiny so continually necessary in a correspondent of the news, when receiving the representations of others. Resolving to be more vigilant in this respect for the future, I beg leave to subscribe myself, Rev, sir, yours etc." '[6]

The vicar and the Warden of the Grammar School in the grounds of the vicarage.

That was in 1842. A dozen years later Brown was referred to as 'querulous' in a newspaper notice from the church: 'We have great pleasure in announcing to our querulous friend, the correspondent to the *Mercury*, that the Thursday evening lectures in the parish church are re-commenced, and we trust that his lawful occupation will not prevent that worthy gentleman's regular attendance'.[7]

However others viewed him, Brown was a good observer of life and change in the town. For example, he would have seen the post van to Gainsborough depart from the King's Head at 9.30 on Monday, Wednesday and Friday mornings, or the London Mail coach leaving the Masons Arms at two in the afternoon, and the daily *Forester* coach service from the White Swan to Grimsby to meet the Hull packet boat. Accidents made good copy for a newspaper reporter: 'On Sunday last, as the Forester coach was entering Louth, on its return from Grimsby, the coachman unfortunately lost all control over the horses which galloped down Tatam's hill [Grimsby Road] at a tremendous rate, until they reached the bridge over Holland's Beck [the headrace of the watermill], where the off wheels caught the kirb-stone, [sic] and both breaking, the coach fell against the west parapet wall, to the great danger of the passengers, who narrowly escaped being either crushed to death or drowned in the Ludd.[8] Brown covered the weekly markets, and noted new rows of working class houses which, along with the coaches and people in the streets, would be translated into paint on the Panorama.

Although an artisan, Brown was very literate, well-read and knew his Bible. He was a keen and active member of the Louth Mechanics' Institute from its formation in 1834, attending and giving lectures, and he had access to its reading room and growing library in the Public Building on Mercer Row (built in 1833 on the corner of Butcher Lane, and until recently Louth Vision Centre).[9] Through the Institute he would have met its Patron, the Rt Hon Charles Tennyson d'Eyncourt of Bayons Manor, Tealby, and known its President, Dr John Bogg, a town alderman who lived at 1 Eastgate, and its Secretary, Alexander Tallents Rogers whose academy was at the Priory, Eastgate. He would also have had access to the Rechabites' (Teetotallers) circulating library and reading room, established in 1839, and he had his own small library of books.

Distinctly radical in his views, Brown had voted for the three North Ward Radical candidates in the 1841 election of councillors for the Borough – Michael Plaskitt (tailor and draper in the Market Place and Wesleyan Methodist local preacher), Joseph Wright Esq, and John Booth Sharpley (coal and corn merchant), another local preacher and a key figure in the Wesleyan Methodist congregation.[10] Brown had been a Wesleyan local preacher, but was expelled from the Society in 1835 for his support of the Wesleyan Reform Association, of which he became secretary (and his son Francis became a minister in the Association, or Warrenites). His recorded speeches at his trial before the local preachers' meeting show him to be well capable of logical argument. He held strong views and was not afraid to voice them in public or record them in print.

During 1844 he was to be seen repeatedly climbing the scaffolded spire of St James's church to make sketches for the panorama he had conceived. To many people in the town he must have been regarded as a rather eccentric character. What, then, was the background of the man now regarded as a key figure in recording the history of mid-19th century Louth?

On one of the preliminary sketches there is a building with a D-shaped roof (right). This was the Public Building, and Brown printed MECHANICS on the upper storey: that was where he went to meetings of the Mechanics' Institute.

John Booth Sharpley.

His family

WILLIAM was the third child of Thomas and Elizabeth Brown, born at New Malton, Yorkshire on 30 May 1788. His father had been born at Hatfield, Yorks in 1768, and his mother (nee Good) at Ingoldmells in 1764. Their two other children were Rebecca and Isaac. The family moved to Kingston upon Hull, probably before the turn of the century, and lived in the parish of St Mary. Nothing is known of William's schooling, but he was a Methodist from the age of 15. Is it possible that he learned to draw with the Hull engravers Goodwill and Lawson (who later engraved at least three of his drawings[11])? His mother died in 1808, aged 44.

On 18 April the following year, 1809, William married Elizabeth, daughter of Francis and Mary Holland, in St James's church, Great Grimsby. He was not quite 21, and she was two months short of 15! He signed with a strong, almost artistic hand, she made her mark. They lived in Grimsby, where William was a (house) painter. However, they did not start their large family until Elizabeth was 19.

Their first child, also William, was born on 20 August 1813 at Royston (Yorkshire), followed by Francis, 22 December 1815, and Thomas, 26 July 1817, both in Grimsby. Thomas died at 11 months, and in 1818 the family moved to Louth, probably living in a rented house in Aswell-lane (Street) next to the Turk's Head (they were certainly there in 1823[12]). Another son, Thomas, arrived on 7 June 1819, but he also lived only 11 months, and was taken to Grimsby for burial.

Within eighteen months Elizabeth gave birth to twins, in Grimsby probably with her parents: Mary Ann Holland was born on 31 December 1820 and her twin brother Edwin Wells Holland half an hour later, but he survived only three months. The next child, Elizabeth, born 26 July 1823, died after six weeks. Another Elizabeth followed on 12 November 1824; she later married.

The family, now with four children – William, Francis, Mary Ann Holland and Elizabeth – had moved to Bridge Street.[13] Isaac was born on 21 June 1826, but died after three months and was buried in Grimsby. The next year Ebenezer Thomas arrived on 8 September, was baptized in Grimsby, but lived only three months and was buried there. The Grimsby connection stopped at that point, as Elizabeth's mother Mary Holland died on 23 November 1827, aged 59, followed soon after by her father Francis on 18 January 1829, aged 72.

William was now 40 and his wife Elizabeth 34, and she continued to conceive. Abigail was born on 2 February 1829 but lived only seven weeks. After the last three children had died in infancy, Holland was born on 5 April 1830. The family were then living in the Fish Shambles.[14] Two years later, on 4 February 1832, Joseph was born but lived only four weeks, and in 1833 Elizabeth was pregnant again and facing her thirteenth confinement in twenty years. However, Satiety was two months premature and died within three hours. It was one birth too many for Elizabeth and she died less than three weeks later, on 19 April. She and William had been married for 24 years and a day, and he was left with five children – William (20), Francis (18), Mary Ann Holland (13), Elizabeth (9) and Holland (3).

William lost not time in marrying again. On Christmas Eve 1833, aged 45, he married Letitia Hales of Louth, a widow of 54 who brought with her two daughters – Ann (15) and Eliza (14). It was now a family household of nine. There would be no more children. They are recorded as living in Eastgate, but it may have been the same house, as the Fish Shambles was not then listed as a separate street.[15] However, we know that by 1837 they were living in Vicker's Lane, where Brown was to remain for the next seventeen years.[16]

The 1830s seemed to mark a turning point or change of direction in Brown's life. It appears that he began to devote

There are five nonconformist chapels on this part of the painting: General Baptist (left), Independent/Congregational (left of Town Hall), Wesleyan Methodist (this side Town Hall), Primitive Methodist (beyond Congregational), and Free Methodist (upper right edge). Brown was a Wesleyan.

more of his energies to matters religious and educational in the town. It was a fortunate coincidence that the Louth Mechanics' Institute was founded in 1834, and that five years later he became the local correspondent for the *Lincoln, Rutland & Stamford Mercury* (although there is evidence that before he had been a correspondent for the *Lincoln Gazette*[17]). In the meanwhile he had been expelled from the Wesleyan Methodists and had joined the Association Methodists. He continued his work as a painter when jobs came his way (there were seven other housepainters in the town) in a decade when the population expanded from 6,927 to 8,848 and the number of houses to 1,985. No record of his business survives, but it is known that in the year before the new Union Workhouse opened (in 1838), Brown had the contract 'to paint all the workhouse bedsteads with two coats of good paint of dark colour, any shade for 9d each.'[18]

Brown's eldest son William married Eliza Donner of Alford on 18 August 1835; they were to have eight children in twelve years, four of whom died in infancy. His stepdaughter Eliza (19) married in 1838; her older sister Ann married later (1848). His son Francis, who had become a Wesleyan Association minister in 1836, married Mary Orme of Scropton, Derbyshire in 1841. The census for that year shows only Elizabeth (15) and Holland (10) living at home, their sister Mary Ann Holland having left (she never married).

With only two children at home (and perhaps his second wife, formerly a widow, had some income of her own?), the need to be fully employed housepainting might have become less important. Certainly he could not have been earning in the daylight hours when he was sketching for the panorama in 1844. And the preparation for the full Panorama and his magic lantern shows, together with reporting and writing must have taken up an increasing amount of his time. His profession was still given as 'Painter' in the 1841 census, but by 1851 it was 'Reporter. Artist (drawing)'. He was then very nearly 63 and had probably given up being a housepainter some time in the late 1840s.

In many ways, 1847 was an *annus horribilis* for Brown: he buried his second wife, two sons, a step son-in-law and two grandsons. But it was also the year of the first exhibition of the Panorama in the Mansion House, and his son Holland won the Mechanics' Institute essay prize.[19] In February his grandson Ebenezer (2) died, followed five days later by grandson Francis (one month) (sons of William and Eliza). At the end of March, Brown's second son Francis died in Maidstone, aged 32; he was buried in the Wesleyan Association chapel in Ipswich. (His widow Mary and daughter Caroline Emily emigrated to America in 1852). Nineteen days later, on 18 April, Brown's eldest son William died, aged 33. He left widow Eliza and four children – Eliza (10), Isaac (7½), William Donner (5½) and Harriet (4).

Brown celebrated his 59th birthday on 30 May, and on 12 July his daughter Elizabeth (22) married Samuel Fairfield Robinson in Hull, but she was to die within two years. His son's widow Eliza remarried on 17 August to W H Gustard of Louth, but he died nineteen days later! (She finally married a third time, on New Year's Day 1851, Thomas Atkinson of Beverley.) And then on 25 September, after fourteen years of marriage, Brown's second wife Letitia died, aged 68.

Ten months later he wed for the third time, this time a younger bride. On 27 July 1848 he married Ann Donner (41), second daughter of John and Elizabeth Donner of Alford. Could it be that she was the elder sister of his son's widow? The wedding took place in the Wesleyan chapel in Louth, the short-lived Warrenite cause in Walkergate (Queen Street) having ceased that year and the chapel sold to the Baptists. We assume that Brown had been accepted back into the Wesleyan fold.[20]

William Brown's painting of his son Francis in preaching mode. He became a Wesleyan Association minister, but died aged only 32.

The youngest of Brown's children, Holland, had left home by the time of the 1851 census, to go to London as a newspaper reporter, taking after his father. He had learned Pitman's shorthand. His father reported in 1845 a lecture given by Holland (then 15) and his teenage friend William Green (who were members of the Phonographic Corresponding Society) at the Temperance Library on Phonography, 'a new art of improved writing [by sound] invented by Isaac Pitman'. In 1852, Holland (22) married Sarah Drayton on 2 September, but she died about five years later. He then married Elizabeth Tooth of Shoreham, Kent, and they had two daughters – Lizzie Holland (2 February 1864 at Crayford, Kent) and Edwenia Edith (15 September 1868 at Ealing). He added an 'e' to his surname, and between the births of his daughters he discarded the Christian name Holland and became Henry Browne; in the 1881 census he was recorded as editor and reporter.

His daughter Edwenia Edith married Arthur Samuel Baxter in 1889, and they had three children – Arthur Henry, Elizabeth Edwinia (1901) and Stanley. The two sons married but Elizabeth Edwinia remained in the family home in Brentwood, and became a romantic novelist and historian. She inherited some of Brown's books and paintings from her grandfather Holland/Henry, and was preparing a biography of her great grandfather.[22] The panorama sketches and other paintings passed to her nephew John Arthur Baxter, and to Anthony Jarvis and Ann Cramphorn (grandchildren of Stanley).

In the 1851 census William Brown was recorded as Reporter and Artist (drawing), and in White's 1856 Directory of Lincolnshire as Artist and Reporter. His third wife, Ann, died on 9 March 1854, after 5½ years of marriage. He was then 65 and did not marry again. She was buried in St Mary's churchyard. There was little wonder that Brown wrote in scathing terms about the state of the churchyard, and depicted on the Panorama a funeral procession approaching and a grave being prepared: he had seen buried there three wives, five children (four in infancy), two grandchildren and a step son-in-law.

The Wesleyan chapel on Eastgate where Brown worshipped when he came to Louth. It was built in 1808 and enlarged in 1820.

Brown the Methodist

BROWN was already a (Wesleyan) Methodist when he arrived in Louth in 1818 and joined the Society with its chapel, built only ten years earlier, in Eastgate. The annual report of the Sunday School for September 1821 listed him as a subscriber.[23] The chapel was already too small for the growing population and was enlarged in 1820, with three strange tunnel entrances from the street and a burial ground between. The Superintendent and second ministers' manses adjoined the chapel; the Superintendent in 1820-21 was Rev Corbet Cooke. The preacher at the opening service on 9 July 1820 was Rev Thomas Galland who had begun his ministry in the Louth Circuit. Among the names on the Preaching Plan that year were local preachers Samuel Horton (47), a grocer in Walkergate (Queen Street) and his son William (20) who had joined the Society through Galland's preaching.

William Horton entered the ministry and later in 1820 went with his young wife to be a pioneer missionary minister in Hobart, Van Dieman's Land (Tasmania), and then to Sydney (1826). He corresponded with his young brother Peter Cross, who had been at Louth Grammar School at the same time as Alfred Tennyson (he left in 1820).[24] It was Rev William Horton who was to return to Louth as Superintendent Minister in 1834-35 and to clash with Brown.

Among the local preachers on the Wesleyan Plan in 1832 were Peter Cross Horton (22), Michael Plaskitt, John Booth Sharpley (32), and William Bond (23), a farmer's son on Monks' Dyke who would enter the ministry in 1834 and return to Louth during the later agitation in 1850-51.[25] Another local preacher Brown knew was George Whelpton, boot and shoe maker in the Butcher Market with his home in Lee Street. Contrary to Conway Walter's account,[26] Bond says that the recipe for the pills that made Whelpton a fortune came from a member of a country chapel where he went to preach.[25] The purifying and stomach pills were effective on Whelpton's wife and were soon in demand locally, and a newspaper published a letter of commendation from a Methodist minister. Whelpton left Louth and made his fortune in Derby and London. Brown would also have met him when using the Mechanics' Institute library where Whelpton became interested in medicine. But did Brown and his family ever take any of those famous pills? Certainly the pills must have remained popular in Louth, as Brown reported in 1841: 'It seems not without reason (judging from the public conduct) that pills are deemed the most elegant mode of administering medicine. Mr [Henry] Hurton [Mercer Row] has just exhibited the contents of another "gigantic pill-box", consisting of 34 pecks: making since 1834 ... 136,608 boxes, averaging 27 pills in each box – total 3,688,416'.(!)[27]

VALUABLE FAMILY MEDICINE.

WHELPTON'S VEGETABLE PURIFYING PILLS.
TRADE MARK.

ESTABLISHED 1835.

By the use of which

FOR UPWARDS OF FORTY YEARS,

Many Thousands of Cures

Have been effected which had been pronounced INCURABLE.

The numerous well-authenticated Testimonials in disorders of the HEAD, CHEST, BOWELS, LIVER, and KIDNEYS; also in RHEUMATISM, ULCERS, SORES, and all SKIN DISEASES, are sufficient to prove the great value of this most useful Family Medicine, it being a DIRECT PURIFIER of the BLOOD and other fluids of the human body.

Many persons have found them of great service both in preventing and relieving SEA-SICKNESS; and in warm climates they are very beneficial in all bilious complaints.

Sold in Boxes, price 7½d., 1s. 1½d., and 2s. 9d., by G. WHELPTON & SON, 3, Crane Court, Fleet Street, London; and by all Chemists and Medicine Vendors at Home and Abroad. Sent free by Post in the United Kingdom for 8, 14, or 33 stamps.

WHELPTON'S VEGETABLE STOMACH PILLS.
TRADE MARK.

A later advertisement for Whelpton's Pills.

Brown does not appear on the Plan as a local preacher until 1834-35. That was a time of change again, with the rebuilding of the chapel to cover the whole site to the street (the frontage to Eastgate as it is today). With tightly packed grey-painted box pews and a large gallery, it was designed to seat a congregation of 1,600. It was probably lit by gas, the gas works having been opened nine years earlier. During the reconstruction work, services were held in the Independent chapel in Cannon Street (now the cinema), the Guildhall (later the site of the Corn Exchange and now the Halifax Building Society), the Sunday School in Lee Street, and elsewhere in the town.

It was also a time of reforming agitation in both town and chapel. 1834 was the last year of the oligarchy of the Warden and Six Assistants; under the application of the Municipal Reform Act 1835, the government of the town was to pass to elected councillors in 1835, and the politically radical element of the town were anticipating change. Their opportunity came in the church rate battle of October 1834.[28] Opposition was led by young solicitor Richard Paddison, supported by Rev Robert Slater Bayley, minister of the Independent chapel since 1830.[29] Bayley criticised the church for failing to promote a library, the

The interior of St James's church showing the galleries. Drawn and lithographed by T W Wallis, 1849.

lack of a 'hall of science', the absence of educational opportunities for young men, and the non-existence of a philosophical or literary society. (In fact the Louth Literary and Philosophical Society had been formed in March 1832 and became the Louth Mechanics' Institute in May 1834.[30]) In response high churchmen derided chapels as conventicles, and belittled their ministers as poorly qualified and motivated by ambition.

All came to a head at the Vestry Meeting in St James's church on Thursday 2 October when up to eight hundred people were present including ladies in the galleries (above the pews in the present north and south aisles)[31]. After a long and exhausting meeting (Brown would have been part of it but is not recorded as having spoken), a poll was set for Friday 3rd, Saturday 4th and Monday 6th. There was much canvassing, cajoling and excitement, and special constables had to be sworn in to keep order. The result was defeat for a church rate on all householders by 589 votes to 573. Brown voted against.[15] Rev William Horton, having arrived in Louth the previous month and living in a tied manse, did not have a vote.

Following the vote, the Wesleyan Methodists, being the most numerous dissenters in the town, were reproached in an anonymous pamphlet 'To those in the Town of LOUTH who once were perhaps conscientious Wesleyan Methodists, but who, by their recent treatment of the Church, have forfeited and lost all claim upon a name so high and venerable'[32]. They were accused of having 'proclaimed an inveterate, perhaps immortal, hatred against the Church of England ... Your vote against the Church-Rate has ... made each of you a Dissenter'. Would John Wesley, it goes on, 'have acted as you have lately acted? Would he, like you, have turned again and fought against his Mother Church?' And so it goes on in similar vein for a dozen pages, claiming the Church of England as providing pure religion, accusing Wesleyan Methodists of treacherous hypocrisy and calling them 'apostate Wesleyans, nondescripts'.

This brought an immediate response from Brown, closely argued and running to twenty-four pages, entitled 'Remarks on sentiments contained in an anonymous pamphlet, addressed to the Wesleyan Methodists in Louth'[33]. He considered there were erroneous statements and reasonings in the pamphlet and 'desired to be useful in conveying more correct information', while not returning 'railing for railing', and hoped 'that it had been written in the heat of the moment'. He questioned what he called a 'sudden change in the behaviour of the Church of England' in 'transforming John Wesley, the fanatic, into a demi-god'. He quoted from Wesley's writings about the principles of Christian liberty (clearly of fundamental importance to Brown, as we shall see), and his references give some idea of the content and extent of his religious library. He concludes that 'a Wesleyan may with the most perfect consistency oppose a Church Rate'. He signed himself 'Not an "Apostate Wesleyan", but a true Methodist. A lover of all good men, and an advocate of Civil and Religious Liberty. And neither ashamed of his name, nor profession. W. Brown. Painter. Fish-Market, Louth. Nov 5th 1834'.

The author of the anonymous pamphlet then revealed himself as Rev George Chaplin, curate of Raithby and Haugham, with a long-winded defence, 'To which are added certain observations submitted to the serious consideration of every protestant dissenter'.[34] This ran to thirty-four pages (!) in high church and high-handed style, saying that some of Brown's remarks 'deserve no better name than mere quibbles, paltry catching at words, and, as such, are worthy of but little, if any, notice'. Perhaps Brown judged that matters had got acrimonious enough, for no more pamphlets on the subject were inflicted on the public.

It would appear that Brown began preaching in September 1834; the Louth Circuit Plan of Wesleyan Preachers' Sabbath Appointments for the first six months of 1835 shows him preaching at Benniworth, Ludborough, Tathwell, Donington, Yarburgh, Grimoldby, Covenham, Legbourne, Elkington and in Louth. For the country appointments he would have walked, or perhaps taken advantage of the local preachers' Horse Hire Fund.

Meanwhile there were events farther afield, the outcome of which were to have a profound effect on Brown. During 1834, a committee recommended to the Wesleyan Conference[35] the establishment of a college to train candidates for the ministry. A member of that committee was Rev Dr Samuel Warren (1781-1862), Superintendent of the Oldham Street Circuit in Manchester. Conference agreed, but when he was not nominated as an officer to bring the college into being, he turned against the proposal. He also wanted lay representation on Conference and self-government for local congregations. After Conference he published a letter violently attacking supporters of the college, and the District Meeting suspended him as Superintendent until the 1835 Conference. Warren then took his case to the Court of Chancery, but the Vice-Chancellor found in favour of the authority and rights of the District, and when he appealed to the Lord High Chancellor the decision was confirmed. Conference had no option but to expel him from the Wesleyan Methodist Church.[25] This was the man who was invited to Louth in May 1835.

Warren delivered an 'impressive lecture' in the Independent chapel to some six hundred people 'comprising Wesleyans and other friends of religious liberty'. The substance of his address which made the front page of the *Stamford Mercury*[36] was in fact written by Brown. Warren spoke of spiritual privileges and scriptural liberty, and the work of the Manchester Wesleyan Reform Association (which he had started). He congratulated the 'peaceful preachers' of Louth, although he thought 'it might not be long so'. One of his key arguments questioned the right of Preachers (Ministers) to make decisions, particularly on expulsions, without the agreement of the majority of lay members.

The Independent chapel (right foreground) is where Dr Warren gave his lecture. In the background is the Primitive Methodist chapel. Between the chapels is a row of terrace houses across the picture: that is Vicker's Lane where Brown lived.

This kind of agitation could not be allowed to pass without some reaction, and indeed retribution on those responsible for inviting Warren. The following Sunday, 24 May, the Superintendent, Rev William Horton, called a prayer meeting at the Lee Street Sunday School at which Warren was caricatured as 'a devil in the shape of a man come to destroy their souls', and 'a violent Conference man vociferated a prayer for "all the apostates that attended Warren's lecture" '. According to Brown's record of the meeting, 'one or two rich high party men scandalized [him] before all the meeting by refusing to shake hands with him, exclaiming "You must repent. You are a wicked man. You abet Warren's wickedness" '. His reply was: 'My good brother hear me. The worst I have said of the Conference party is they are men of a mistaken judgement, but now you unchristianize both me and my friends for mere difference of opinion. Can this be true religion? If you say it is, I pray God save me from such a religion'. But at least his Class Leader, Joseph Larder (grocer on Mercer Row) did shake hands.

A few days later Brown was summoned to appear before the Local Preachers' meeting in the room of William Pearson (baker and flour dealer) in Eastgate on Thursday 18 June to answer charges that 'Brother Brown abetted and sanctioned an illegal meeting [Warren's lecture], slandered the characters of the Preachers and Officers of the Methodist Society in Louth, and conducted himself ... in a manner highly calculated to bring the Methodist Preachers and connexion into disrepute – create discord and strife in a peaceable society – and to check

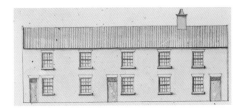

The Sunday School on Lee Street.

the prosperity of the work of God'. He made a detailed report of the meeting and his later trial, which suggests that he used a form of shorthand.[37] This record he felt 'compelled in self-defence (uneducated and poor as he is)' to publish the following November as a pamphlet: 'The Popery of Methodism ('as it is') as exemplified in the Trial etc of W Brown, Painter, Louth. Also an account of an Extraordinary Love Feast.'[38]

In the preface to the pamphlet Brown refers to his 'enemies', and writes that he 'has been accused of want of respect in his defiance ... and the unflinching manner in which he maintained his right to be heard, which circumstances subjected him to ridicule and almost incessant interruption', concluding that 'he may have unwittingly and needlessly offended; if so, he is heartily sorry'.

At the Local Preachers' meeting, which began at 10am, a member proposed the charges be withdrawn, but the Superintendent refused the motion. The proposer then declared himself equally guilty with the accused, and asked 'why did they pounce on the Sprat and pass over the Salmon?' Brown admitted that he had secured the use of the Independent chapel, had distributed tracts about the Reform Association, delivered tickets of admission, had secured contributions to Warren's expenses, and put a note in his shop window that the account of the lecture 'might be read gratis by applying within'.

In response to the second charge, Brown called the conduct of the preachers and leaders in trying to prevent people from hearing Warren 'a rascally piece of work'. Then a letter which had appeared in the *Christian Herald* signed X was read, and Horton asked Brown if he had written it. His second minister, Rev Charles Haydon, added that it was 'an inquisitorial meeting .. and all brethren were bound to confess all they knew on the subject'. Brown declared this to be 'popish', and said it was for his accusers to substantiate the charges.

Matters under the third charge included the fact that Brown had 'got up a social meeting at Hackford's [in the Market Place][39] to hear the statement of two suffering brethren from Hull'. It transpired that the secretary of the meeting, none other than J B Sharpley, had also been at Hackford's, but nothing was said against him. Horton then read letters from the chapels at Covenham, Reston, Carlton, Ludborough and Tathwell requesting that in the new preaching plan Brown's name be omitted for those places.

In his defence, Brown said that 'his sincerity had been repeatedly eulogized during the 32 years he had been a member of the Methodist Society, and never impeached till his friend the secretary [Sharpley] had unhappily seen proper recently to differ from him in opinion'. He pleaded not guilty and averred that 'the meeting in Cannon Street [chapel] was warranted by Scripture as well as necessity', and quoted scriptural sources and Conference minutes and regulations, not least those relating to the duties of Preachers (Ministers). He was interrupted a number of times, but he also provoked laughter: 'Was he in Spain?' he asked, 'in the purlieus of the Inquisition, with the wrack [sic] and the stake before him?'. In all he spoke for 3½ hours! It was to no avail. The verdict was only a short time coming, and he 'was informed they had no longer occasion for his services'.

The following Sunday there was a Wesleyan Love Feast in the Independent chapel. It was a traumatic evening for Brown. After the Superintendent had spoken for some time, a few others were 'so indiscreet as to express themselves strongly against the Wesleyan reformers'. Brown records that 'his son Francis [then 19] spoke his experience in so scriptural a language and with such sobriety of sentiment ... With my eyes rivetted on my boy, and the tears of gratitude to God for his grace, fast falling down my cheeks, I felt impelled to speak of

THE

POPERY

OF

METHODISM

("AS IT IS,")

AS EXEMPLIFIED IN

THE TRIAL,

&c, OF

W. BROWN, PAINTER, LOUTH.

ALSO AN ACCOUNT OF AN

EXTRAORDINARY LOVE FEAST.

"Could the Methodists be invested, by some revolution with the absolute power Rome once possessed, there is reason to fear that, unless checked by the genius of a more humane age, the Conference would equal Rome itself in the spirit of persecution." Lord John Russell.

" They answered and said unto him, thou wast altogether born in sins and dost, thou teach us? And they cast him out." John, IX ch. 34 v.

LOUTH:

PRINTED BY A. G. MARSHALL, MERCER-ROW,

MDCCCXXXV.

[Price Two-Pence.]

his goodness'. As soon as Brown started to speak, the Superintendent rose and pointing at him 'with ... the authority ... of a Roman Dictator ... exclaimed, "Mr Brown, as presiding over this assembly, I insist on your sitting down" '.

However, Brown persisted and said he merely wished to express his gratitude to Heaven and pledged himself not to allude to the disputed topics, claiming a right to speak as a member of the Society, and held up his Class Ticket. One member, Mr Green, called out, 'Mr Horton, let him speak – he has a right to speak', and Brown's son remonstrated with the Superintendent saying, 'Sir, your proceeding I am afraid is unscriptural, my father should be permitted to speak'. Others called out 'That's priest-craft', 'It's time there was a reform in Methodism', and 'Why, this is popery over again'. Some even hissed and several more walked out. Amid the confusion, one 'inspired with a suitable zeal for Methodism' began to sing 'My God the spring of all our joys', and another 'as remarkable for his stentorian voice as for the stern character of his piety' was called on to pray. Brown records that afterwards several members 'condoled' with him, and condemned the conduct of the Superintendent.

But worse was to follow the next day when Brown attended the Leaders' Meeting on the same charges that had been put to the local preachers. And there were also further aggravating circumstances, put by what Brown called 'the dirt collecting and dirt spreading system'. It was a vociferous but shorter meeting, but it was agreed that he could retain the privilege of church membership on certain conditions: 'That W Brown do express his sorrow and regret for his past conduct in this affair. That he give a pledge to the meeting not to interfere in those matters in the future. That he put in his window a document to that effect, to remain there as long as they thought fit. And that he be suspended for a quarter of a year'.

Brown declared that he would even submit to the humiliating conditions if they could disprove the facts of arbitary expulsions of Wesleyan officers and members elsewhere, as stated in the *Christian Advocate* and the *Watchman's Lanthern*, or prove on scriptural principles that the grievances were not of sufficient importance to warrant those actions, but he was required to give an unqualified submission. He declared 'he dared not sacrifice his conscience', and was forthwith expelled from the Wesleyan Methodist Society.

Even despite this final blow, Brown was not one to give up. When the Superintendent called a meeting of the congregation on 26 August, 'in which he culminated Dr Warren most shamefully', Brown sought a note of admission but was refused. Then when he tried to enter the chapel, six men detailed by the minister 'violently cast him out'. This no doubt stimulated him to write on 31 August to the *Stamford Mercury* a long letter about Methodism 'as it was' and Methodism 'as it is'.[40] In this he touched on a meeting in Sheffield of lay reforming delegates (was he one of them?), and slammed the tergiversation [shifting subterfuge or evasive conduct] of the 'high party' in Methodism particularly the Preachers (Ministers), calling for the support of the Friends of Methodism 'as it is'. This probably had little effect, and to ensure that his side of the argument was on record, he published the pamphlet of his trials in June.

Sadly he was debarred from the grand re-opening of the enlarged Wesleyan chapel on Friday 2 October 1835 when Rev Thomas Galland returned again to preach in the morning, with Rev Theophilus Lessey in the afternoon and evening.[41] On Sunday 4th there were no services in the country chapels and people poured into Louth in decorated waggons and carts to hear Rev Dr Jabez Bunting – who had so severely denounced Dr Warren at Conference the previous year.

In the midst of all this hurt for Brown, there was at least one bright spot – when his eldest son William married on 18 August, just two days before his 22nd birthday.

Interior of the enlarged Wesleyan chapel.

LOUTH WESLEYAN CHAPEL.

The first engraving of Brown's drawing of the enlarged Wesleyan chapel. On the far right he shows the Stall-yard which was demolished when the Town Hall was built (see Chapter 4 under Town Hall). Below is the second and later engraving where Brown added the chapels at River Head and New Market (the latter was rebuilt as the Wesleyan Day School in 1858-60, and is now the Playgoers Theatre).

River Head Chapel built 1849

WESLEYAN CHAPEL,
East Gate, Louth.
Built 1808, Enlarged 1820.
Rebuilt 1835.

New Market Chapel built 1849

So, at home in the Fish Shambles with Brown (47) were his wife Letitia (56), Francis (19), Mary Ann Holland (14), Elizabeth (9), Holland (5) and stepdaughters Ann (17) and Eliza (16). William junior appears to have joined the Primitive Methodists, where he became Sunday School secretary,[37] and we must assume that Brown then took his family to the new Wesleyan Methodist Association, who became known as the Warrenites, with Brown as their secretary. In March 1836 they held services in the Guildhall, on three Sundays with Mrs Chester from York preaching, 'the most talented and impressive female speaker we have heard', and a hundred members and friends sat down to tea at a social meeting.[38] Brown's son Francis, who had been working as a cordwainer (almost certainly for George Whelpton), and was also a trustee for the breakaway Methodists, became an Association minister on 17 September 1836, three months short of his twenty-first birthday.

The Warrenites were already planning to build a chapel of their own, and they were able to acquire the pulpit which had been in the Wesleyan chapel before rebuilding. Mounted on an octagonal base and painted, with crimson cushion and drapery, it was auctioned in the market, but there was no buyer. It was purchased afterwards for 22s 6d.[39] Thus by quirk of fate, Brown had the opportunity to ascend the very pulpit from which Horton and others had banned him. The new chapel with a distinctively designed front elevation, was opened in 1837 with seating for 300; the building is still there today as the Masonic Hall in Queen Street, a rare, perhaps unique, survival in Britain. It seems strange that Brown never made a drawing of it. Dr Warren did not lead the Association for long: he took Anglican ordination in 1838 and became rector of All Souls in Manchester.

Throughout these changes in Methodism in Louth, Brown did not neglect the temperance cause, neither in participating nor in reporting for the newspaper. He was one of the speakers along with grocer Frank Whitaker at a public tea party for about a hundred and sixty people in the Mansion House to raise funds for the Louth Temperance Library in June 1841.[45] (Brown also wrote temperance rhymes.)

A couple of months later he turned his attention to the Mormons when, 'in a private house filled with curious hearers', he went to listen to Mr H Herringshaw, an Elder of the Church of the Latter Day Saints in America, as he gave 'utterance to the new-fangled doctrines of Mormonism'. The nature of Brown's report makes clear his scepticism when he spoke for the audience on the suggestion that they should meet again to question Mr Herringshaw, and even added what he would have said if he had not been prevented by the Elder losing his patience and denouncing him as a hypocrite and opposer of the truth! Brown concluded his report, as we might expect, with a round condemnation: 'the company separated, filled with pity for the deluded young man, and an increased conviction that Mormonism is one of the greatest delusions of the day, and based on the avarice and hypocrisy of its chiefs'.[46] A classic piece of Brown reporting.

When the Warrenites or Association Methodists held their annual missionary meeting in 1843, the preachers were from the Primitive and Independent chapels. It was reported that nationally there were over 26,000 members, a hundred ministers, 286 chapels, and missions in Australia and Jamaica.[40] Singing in the Walkergate chapel would be led, as in other chapels, by a choir and orchestra; the Wesleyan chapel was the first to install an organ, at Easter 1844. A former minister there said that 'an organ is a less evil than a quarrelsome choir'.[41] Attendances at the Association continued to increase and required the addition of a 200-seater gallery in 1845.[42] By 1847 they had a minister, Mr Seell, and prided themselves on the 'perfect equality of rights in all the members' and a mutual

The former Warrenite chapel – now the Masonic Hall – in Queen Street.

participation in the management of the affairs of the church'.[50] the very principles for which Brown had campaigned a dozen years before. However, the cause of the Association generally was in decline, and at the end of 1848 the chapel was sold to the General Baptists. Brown wrote a long account of the causes of the secession of the General Baptists, but 'as the misunderstandings among small religious sects can have no interest for the general reader' the *Stamford Mercury* did not use it.[51]

Even during his *annus horribilis*, 1847, Brown found time, with Samuel Ashton (baker), to devote to the Mutual Instruction Society. Membership was about a dozen youths. Brown felt the need to make a report of the proceedings in the *Mercury* (one sentence ran to 24 lines!) as their religious orthodoxy had been 'questioned from the Wesleyan pulpit'. It was said that 'under the pretext of examining science' the youths were 'reasoning themselves into infidelity'. He counters this strongly with a statement about himself and Ashton 'whose stability of religious character and experience in these matters is a sufficient guarantee for the orthodoxy of the youths', and refers to arguments 'in support of the absolute truths of the bible' which will 'fortify them against the ills of life, and prepare them for blissful immortality'(!)[52]

Brown's standing in the teetotal movement was clearly demonstrated in October 1848 at a meeting in the Temperance Hotel (now the site of Kwik Save), Eastgate, run by Reuben Spivey. A new teetotal committee was chosen and Brown was unanimously called to preside and address the meeting. He would have taken some humble pride no doubt in writing that about himself.[53]

A tippler drains a beer bottle, a lady resists attention, and a horse is fed – all going on in the yard of the Greyhound inn.

As we have seen, by 1848 Brown was back in the Wesleyan fold, but only to find the Society embroiled in agitation again from 1849, on similar grounds to those of fifteen years earlier, that is the 'overgrown and tyrannical authority' of the ministers.[54] This time however there was wide popular support: at two simultaneous meetings in the town there were 600 people at each. And Brown was not singled out, although his case was cited at a Leaders' Meeting which he reported in October 1850, under the heading 'People and Peace v Parsons and Power'.[55] A class leader and a local preacher were charged with not paying class and ticket money. When Henry Boothby junior (he would follow Brown as the *Mercury* reporter) started to take notes, the Superintendent, Rev John Stephenson, tried to restrain him, and it was J B Sharpley, now a JP, town alderman and three times mayor, who tried to bring order to the proceedings. A junior minister in the Circuit at the time was Rev William Bond who had grown up in Louth and found it embarrassing that his friends were in opposition.[25]

Matters then went from bad to worse with the arrival in September 1851 of Rev James Loutit as Superintendent, a man known to show little mercy to radicals. At a District Meeting in April 1852, Boothby and others, selected as specially aiding and abetting the reform movement, were declared 'cut off from the church', while Sharpley and Joseph Larder were told that their continuance would depend on their 'future good behaviour'.[56]

Loutit was followed in September 1852 by Rev Richard Ray who was of a similar disposition. At a large gathering of members in the chapel, he read the names of 600 who were known to have reforming sympathies, a list which surely must have included Brown. The ministers said they would be in the Superintendent's manse on the next three mornings to re-admit any who would submit to the rules. No-one came, and all were expelled. Separate preaching services were arranged, and finally in December 1853 the Louth Free Methodist Church was founded. The full story is told in *A History of Methodism in Louth*.[41,57]

During all this unrest, Brown made the acquaintance of a former sailor and drunkard, John Taylor, a man eight years his senior. Born in Louth in 1780, Taylor had served in the Royal Navy on Nelson's flagship at the Battle of Copenhagen, been press-ganged, deserted and flogged many times, been a slave trader and smuggler, and got 'fresh' (drunk) in half the ports of the seven seas. By 1844 he had returned to Louth, tried to be more sober, and sought salvation through the Wesleyan chapel. There Edwin Squire (bookseller on Mercer Row) took him to the Class meeting of George Pearson (boot and shoe maker, Aswell-lane) where he came to 'Praise God for what he's done for me'. Taylor's story was a clear example to Brown of 'the providence and grace of God'. He persuaded Taylor to set down his remarkable narrative, and Brown wrote the introduction; they had it printed in Nottingham in 1852 and sold it in Squire's bookshop.[58]

Brown reported in objective detail the laying of the foundation stone of the Free Methodist chapel in 1854,[59] where he then worshipped and was on the Prayer Leaders' Plan 1857. The new chapel (on the site of the car park on Eastgate) was for some years called 'The House that Jack built' as J B Sharpley, now the natural leader of the reformers, lived opposite in Eastgate House. The secession had been a terrible blow to the Wesleyans, but remarkably all three denominations – Wesleyan, Primitive and Free – flourished: it seemed to be multiplication by division.

Meanwhile Brown's son Holland had gone to London to serve the temperance cause. In 1856 he wrote, and his father published, *A Cycle of Christian Evidences being an outline of arguments proving the Truth of the Bible*. On 29 December that year, when Holland was visiting his father, then living alone in Walkergate (Queen Street), he delivered the opening lecture at the Louth Temperance Society conversazione in the Council Chamber of the new Town Hall, where the Panorama now hangs.[60]

THE

SAILOR'S YARN,

BEING A

TRUE AND INTERESTING NARRATIVE

OF THE EVENTFUL

LIFE OF JOHN TAYLOR,

LOUTH, LINCOLNSHIRE;

LATE A SEAMAN IN THE ROYAL NAVY;

Who went out with the celebrated
Lord Viscount Nelson, when he sailed to the Baltic to frustrate
the designs of the Northern Coalition; and

ACTUALLY FOUGHT IN THE SAME SHIP,—
The "Elephant,"

ALONG WITH THAT RENOWNED ADMIRAL

IN THE

SANGUINARY BATTLE OF COPENHAGEN:

And in whose life is signally displayed both the Providence and
Grace of God.

A piece of biography taken from his own lips, and detailed in
the main, in his own phraseology; tending to minister to the
information, and profiting of both young and old.

"*As I live, saith the Lord God, I have no pleasure in the death
of the wicked : but that the wicked turn from his way and
live.*"—Ezekiel xxxiii. 11.

Louth:
PRINTED FOR JOHN TAYLOR AND WILLIAM BROWN,
OF WHOM IT MAY BE HAD;
ALSO OF E. SQUIRE AND W. SHEPHERD, LOUTH; AND OTHER
BOOKSELLERS.

1852.

ENGLAND'S
Great Curse.

Come all my good friends and country-men dear,
Give ear to my simple relation
And I'll try all I can to convince every man
That strong drink is the curse of the nation.

It is the fore-runner of crimes that are bad,
Leads men to commit depredation,
And the poor distress'd mother, and children ill clad,
Help to prove its the curse of the nation.

It has peopled our jails and the mad-houses too,
Tis a known fact, without disputation,
And the work-houses too would sometimes have but few,
Were it not for the curse of the nation.

The publicans say this Tee-total wont do,
It will bring on us sad desolation
But we'll try all we can to convince every man
That strong drink's not the curse of the nation.

But Tee-totalers cry oh ! all ye that pass by,
What e're be your rank or your station,
Dash from you the bowl that would ruin your soul,
And rob you of Eternal Salvation.

It has ruin'd its thousands both body and soul,
And sent them to eternal damnation ;
And those who are under its baneful controul,
Must confess its the curse of the nation.

WILLIAM CRISP,

Donington, March 10th, 1841.

Marshall, Printer, Mercer-Row, Louth.

Wonders of Nature

Chapter 6
The Polyopticorama and Brown the artist

THERE can be little doubt that Brown's religious beliefs and experiences as a dissenting Methodist influenced his art. Moreover, his response to new ideas in science was strong, and he was particularly enthusiastic about photography and about the use of the magic lantern for education and entertainment. He saw no real conflict between religion and science, and the traits of his beliefs and interests developed together in 1845 into a production or exhibition he designed: the Polyopticorama. This was a new term coined by Brown from 'polyorama', as using an optical apparatus for presenting many views. Before we look at this in detail, we need to trace Brown's artistic development from earlier years in Louth, and in particular his friendship with William Armitage (1814-1849).

It is speculation of course, but is it possible that Brown went to the Louth Theatre (on the site of the Halifax in the Cornmarket) in September 1823, or would it have been beyond the pale for a Methodist? Maybe 9-year old William Armitage was taken by his father (children under ten half-price). It would certainly have appealed to his enquiring and inventive mind. The event was an exhibition by the Royal Mechanical and Optical Museum. The programme on the bill-poster showed that it included a representation of the recent explosion of Mount Vesuvius, a moonlight piece with changes in the horizon, a panoramic view of London taken from Primrose Hill, automatons, a mechanical peacock, and optical and chemical pyrotechnics.[1] The show was probably a mix of phantasmagoria and dissolving views using more than one magic lantern. Certainly elements of the show presaged what Brown and Armitage would themselves exhibit some twenty years later.

There is little hard evidence, only deduction, about any artistic painting Brown may have done before we have documentary evidence after the formation in 1834 of the Louth Mechanics' Institution, of which he was a member, and his own reporting in the *Stamford Mercury*. The purpose of the Mechanics' Institution, as expressed by Brown's predecessor as newspaper correspondent, fitted Brown's own aspirations and aims: 'to improve the moral and intellectual condition of the rising generation of middle and working classes'.[2] The Institute flourished: 70 members in the first year and 260 in the second (annual subscription was 15s – about £30 in today's money), a growing library, and a museum collection of fossils, shells and stuffed birds. There were regular classes in chemistry, drawing, stenography and botany.[3] It is not difficult to imagine Brown brushing up on his shorthand (stenography) and improving his drawing skills.

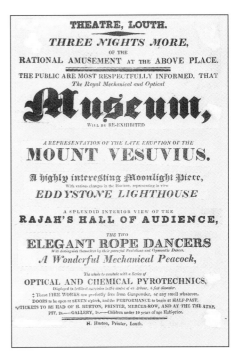

Extracts from the Louth Theatre handbill for September 1823.

Bennett Hubbard.

Among items at the Institute exhibition in February 1835 was work by the artist Bennett Hubbard (29), who would within a few years go on to exhibit at the Royal Academy, and a 'Peripatetic Diorama' by William Brown.[4] Did they walk round it, or did the diorama move? And what was the subject of the diorama? All we can be sure of, perhaps, is that it was an early example of Brown as an artist painter. The next exhibition included tube retorts, dropping, syringe, deflagrating and test tubes, all 'of glass blown by the ingenious experimenter of the chemical class' William Armitage (21), who also demonstrated a 'high pressure railway steam-carriage which moved round an adjoining room'.[5] Armitage's standing among members was such that the following year (1836) he was re-elected to the committee with the third highest number of votes.[6]

William was the son of Thomas Darley Armitage, brazier and tinner, and had the benefit of a partial grammar school education.[7] Brown and Armitage had been neighbours or near neighbours in the Fish Shambles for five or six years from the time the latter was a teenager. Although Brown was twenty-six years the senior, their complementary interests forged a collaborative friendship. No doubt when Lorenco Louis Bellatti of Grantham brought his 'Shop of Novelty' to Louth, they would have been interested in the optical, mathematical and philosophical instruments, barometers and thermometers (aside from his watches, jewellery and spectacles).[8] And a few months later Mr Barth visited the town to exhibit his hydro-oxygen microscope which could magnify a flea to twelve feet in length.[9] Similarly perhaps they were together eight years later when H Lefevre lectured to the Mechanics Institute on astronomy, illustrating it with 'a transparent orrery illuminated by the newly invented solar lamp'.[10]

We know of Armitage's inventions through Brown's reports in the *Mercury*: for example a hydraulic pump capable of moving 500 to 1,000 gallons of water a minute,[11] and his work on electrography (the process of copying an engraving on an electro-copper plate).[12] His father Thomas also took out a patent for an 'improved life-preserver', designated the Yarborough Life Buoy after his patron the Earl of Yarborough.[13] The previous year (1844) Brown reported that Richard Hoyle (tanner, currier and leather cutter) on Bridge Street had invented a machine called Neptune's Chariot, not unlike an ammonite in structure, 'for the preservation of life from shipwreck'.[14]

A Vice-President of the Mechanics' Institute and Clerk to the Louth Union Board of Guardians was solicitor James William Wilson (1811-1894). 'He had a facile pencil and brush' and took lessons in drawing and painting from William Espin (The Priory, Eastgate).[15] His volume of *Sketches of Louth* was published by J & J Jackson of Louth in 1840 (when he was 29) and much admired, not least one suspects by Brown. It may even have been part of the stimulus for what he did in sketching the panorama in 1844.

However, the *Stamford Mercury* in 1843 gives the first hard evidence that Brown had already had some experience as an artist. He lectured on 'Painting' at the Louth Poor Men's Library and News-room, but it didn't take him long to get on his puritan platform. He described 'the kinds of materials and methods of that art', without, unfortunately, leaving us any detail, and then 'aminadverted on those disorders of art which had given a licence to some of the more skilful painters to minister to the increasing debauchery of the day, by the indecent representation of figures when painted either in a state of nudity, or so thinly clad as more effectually to poison the mind of the spectator and admirer of the *chef d'oeuvre* [masterpiece]. The lecturer argued that this was more criminal (as the instrument of evil was more durable) than if the painter,

Part of a sketch (coloured later) by J W Wilson, looking along the canal towards the Riverhead.

or his archetypes, had violated public decency by running naked in the streets.'[16]

Unfortunately Brown does not say in the report (he wrote it of course) what subjects he painted, but one wonders if there was some connection with his trade as an interior house decorator. One might reasonably speculate that when employed to do interior work in some of the larger houses in the town, he may have painted decorative friezes and surrounds in a semi-Regency style.

In February 1845, Brown reported that the committee of the Mechanics' Institute had 'at great cost' arranged a Chinese Exhibition by an eminent London artist 'for the gratification as well as instruction of the members and of the public' in their rooms on Mercer Row. The exhibition consisted of a 'beautiful and unique series of revolving views, representing with fidelity the peculiar scenery, manners and customs of China'. It was 'accompanied by a band of music led by that eminent violinist Mr [Richard] Hubbard'[17]. The paintings, each measuring 10 feet by 7 feet, included Hong Kong, the Great Wall and an Imperial Travelling Palace, the whole being mechanically operated. Such was the demand that the exhibition was open for two months.[18]

Perhaps Brown gained a few more ideas for his 'polyopticorama, or many optical views' which he exhibited for the first time in June 1845. The event was a public tea-meeting of the members and friends of the Temperance Library and News-room, held in the Mansion House. The many views he 'distributed into classes representing among other objects of interest portraits of distinguished persons, sovereigns, statesmen, philanthropists, and divines: he dexterously introduced to the great amusement of the company, a full-sized and striking likeness of himself, which he made to answer by a graceful bow, the acclamations of the audience: then followed zoological rarities, natural phenomena, pagan superstitions, impressive morals, celestial scenery, and the *way to be happy* – a highly instructive series of figures with appropriate mottoes, and a clear painting of a ship riding at anchor, with its corresponding motion'.[19]

This was a magic lantern show, the effect of movement being achieved by a strip of glass which could be moved over the fixed glass of the slide. The opening in London of the Royal Polytechnic Institution with its own lantern theatre in 1838 had encouraged a growing trade in lanterns and lantern slides, so Brown probably used some commercial slides. But it is also clear that most of them were painted by himself, and Armitage may well have helped by making the glass slides and moving parts, and provided the chemical, lime, for the illuminant (as for theatre footlights, hence 'in the limelight'). It means that Brown as an artist was also a miniaturist, which skill he put to good use in the figures on the Panorama which are only an inch or two high. Moreover, Brown would have had his own lantern. Two years earlier his son William showed transparencies, which he also could have painted, to an anniversary meeting of the Primitive Methodist Sunday School.[20]

Brown's next show, in April 1846, to 260 children of all denominations (be it noted) packed into the vestry of the Wesleyan chapel, confirms the friendly collaborations with Armitage and gives further insight into what Brown was painting. They 'exhibited a large number of phantasmagorical views (painted by Mr Brown) on the dissolving principle, as exhibited in the Polytechnic Institute in London. The artist seems to have carefully avoided the offensively comic subjects of the magic lantern, the scenes being fraught with scientific, moral, and religious instruction throughout, and affording great gratification ... Such was the interest taken in the

Was this the likeness of himself that Brown made to bow gracefully on the screen?

exhibition ... that we believe the series of figures representing "the seven steps to happiness" will be long remembered'.[21]

'Phantasmagorical views' were imaginary figures, optical illusions and changing scenes of different elements. The 'dissolving principle' was the use of two synchronised lanterns (the second could have been Armitage's) to execute a slow transformation from a summer to a winter scene or a volcano suddenly erupting. And it was all carefully designed and arranged to be instructional. It also shows that Brown got on well with the Wesleyan Methodist minister then stationed in Louth, even though Brown was still a Warrenite. The third show of which Brown has given us an account introduced three new elements. It took place in January 1847 and is worth quoting in full.[22]

> JUVENILE TEA MEETING ... Rev W Hales, Wesleyan minister ... conducted an excellent tea-meeting liberally provided by the friends of the scriptural instruction for the children ... in the large vestry adjoining the chapel in Eastgate. Three hundred of these ... were afterwards highly delighted by again witnessing Mr Wm Brown's exhibition of his "Polyopticorama" – a series of phantasmagorical paintings executed by himself, arranged under the heads of distinguished sovereigns, eminent statesmen, divines &c, extraordinary animals, surprising inventions, celestial scenery, natural phenomena, impressive morals and sacred topography. Amongst the more remarkable of these ... was the "railway to Louth", consisting of a distant view of the town, and a series of first, second and third-class railway carriages, with luggage trains &c, swiftly gliding past and as swiftly returning: – views of the Holy Land, calculated to infuse into the mind devotional feelings; – the striking portrait of the exhibitor, painted from a clever daguerreotype taken last summer; and the final revolving pyrotechnicorama or artificial Chinese *coup de feu* in honour of Her Majesty Queen Victoria, which elicited from the juvenile audience loud and repeated bursts of joy and irrepressible applause. The portraits of eminent men were not at all inferior to these in quality, nor the "way to be happy" less likely than formerly to stimulate the youthful mind to habits of virtue and piety. The whole passed off with great hilarity, and the children separated about nine o'clock, highly delighted with the rational amusements of the evening'.

The trains Brown painted on the Panorama, and made to steam back and forth on the screen with the aid of the magic lantern.

Brown had cleverly anticipated the opening of the East Lincolnshire railway: the first VIP train to Grimsby would not be until September that year, with a full service the following September.[23] The effect of movement was achieved by moving an additional painted strip of glass to and fro in front of the main image slide. The 'revolving pyrotechnicorama' was a double circular movement of geometric patterns, by simple gearing and a little winding handle on the slide carrier, which the children called 'artificial fireworks' (technically a chromotrope).

We can be reasonably sure that Brown's lantern slides were being used a few years later from a report about a 'Mechanics' Lecture' in 1851. Held in the Mansion House and organised by the Mechanics' Institute committee, the lecture by Rev John Theodore Barker, pastor of the Congregational chapel in Cannon Street and Vice-President of the Institute, was on Astronomy. It was illustrated by 'diagrams thrown on a medium by the phantasmagoria lantern ably managed by Mr Portas, master of the Lee-street [Wesleyan] school seminary', and afterwards 'several beautiful dissolving views were exhibited, closing with a brilliant specimen of revolving chromotrope paintings'.[24]

The mention of daguerreotype in the 1847 report takes us back to the William Armitage connection. Nine years earlier the Frenchman Louis Daguerre (1789-1851) invented a photographic process – the daguerreotype as it became known. This reversed mirror image was produced on a silver-plated surface made sensitive with iodine vapour. The exposed image was developed by fuming with mercury vapour and fixed by immersion in a solution of common salt. This 'mirror with memory' was patented and licences issued in this country on a county basis. The Lincolnshire licencee, a Mr Cooke, was in Louth in July and August 1845 and faithfully reported by Brown.[25]

New Graphic Wonders – the Daguerreotype. In this age of discovery and invention, it is wonderful with what railroad speed art and science advance, and how with their bright rays they illuminate even the densest portions of the empire. Louth, which a few years ago was nearly as ignorant of the achievements of science as the aborigines of Lapland, has already become familiar with, and has its own adepts in, the arena of nature: and is not infrequently visited by savans [sic] of science and art from distant spots. We are at present favoured with the temporary visit of Mr Cooke, the Lincolnshire licencee for Daguerreotype or Photographic Portraits. These the artist takes in a few seconds, in his elegant moveable portrait-rooms, situate in James-street. Every line, every touch in the picture produced, is from the pencil of nature: the chance of a mistake precluded, a fac-simile of the sitter is of necessity produced. Several clever specimens are exhibited in the windows of Messrs Jacksons, stationers, [now Oxfam in the Market Place] and shown at the rooms; among which we may name as likenesses peculiarly striking those of Mr Campbell, of the firm of Campbell, Bowmar and Ranshaw [now Eve & Ranshaw]: Thos Jackson Esq, the Rev Mr Hodgson, Rev Mr Simpkis, Mr W Armitage, chemist, several ladies, and our correspondent; all which are truthful pictures, free from the usual defects of painted portraits, whether of intentional flattery or of imperfect observation. To all who desire (and who is there that does not) to preserve or transmit to their friends the faithful memorials of connubial or parental bliss, the most precious gift that can be given to those who love us while living, and who will cherish our memory when dead; we earnestly urge not to let slip so favourable an opportunity of acquiring these gems, on such remarkable terms as are offered'.

'The Flight into Egypt'. A typical lantern slide, from later in the century, used in Sunday School teaching.

We do not know what happened to the daguerreotypes of Brown and Armitage, but the latter, described as an 'eminent practical chemist', apparently obtained a licence himself. In the yard behind his shop in the Fish Shambles was a kitchen with a 'tincture room' above it and a two storey warehouse for drugs. At the end of the yard he built 'a rather elegant apartment, raised to a second storey on posts, and mostly covered with glass (called the "glasshouse") ... used for the purpose of taking daguerreotype likenesses'.[26]

In 1848, Armitage had been experimenting with detonating railway fog signals. These were fixed to the rails by narrow trips of lead which, when run over by the locomotive 'suddenly transformed the thick foggy darkness of the night into a most transparent and splendid red light'. The signals were successfully demonstrated on the newly opened East Lincolnshire line and the Great Northern Railway company operating the line placed orders with Armitage. In August 1849, the Mechanics' Institute made arrangements for their 'ingenious chemist ... to exemplify the practical applications of the detonating alarm fog signals' (presumably out of doors!).[27]

The explosion waiting to happen.
(Lincolnshire Life).

Portrait of Henry Hurton by Bennett
Hubbard. (Louth Town Council).

In the manufacturing process the explosive part had to be dried and this usually took a couple of days. However, in November 1849 Armitage had received a large order, and to save time placed fifty of them in the kitchen oven to dry. He then went to take 'likenesses by daguerreotype' in the glasshouse before lunch and afterwards to develop some. When he returned to the kitchen, his housekeeper Eliza Wilson told him the oven was getting too warm. He opened the oven doors and there was a violent explosion.

At his home in Vicker's Lane, Brown heard the explosion and 'was speedily at the place, and observed a lurid gunpowder cloud arising from the back of the premises and towering far above', and found the studio, kitchen, tincture room and part of the warehouse 'a commingled mass of ruins'. Also quickly on the scene was Wesleyan minister Rev John H Beech who, like Eliza Wilson, had 'remonstrated with Mr Armitage on the impropriety of ... drying ... signals in the oven'. The explosion killed Armitage, his father Thomas, his two young assistants Stephen and Mary Evans, and his housekeeper who died very shortly afterwards. His apprentice George Wright Walker (26) survived and, with his brother William, carried on the chemists' business until 1853.[28]

The dageurreotype however was soon overtaken by photography on the collodion principle (first demonstrated at the 1851 Great Exhibition). Brown himself did not report it, but by September 1854 Thomas Ward, Aswell-lane (Street) was using the new wet-plate process; he had also taken over and improved the production of detonating fog signals.[29] Later that month a professional photographer, a Mr Pickering, visited Louth, taking portraits of people and groups.[30] By 1856 there were two more 'photographic artists' in the town – William Parker, Eastgate, and Joseph Willey (1829-1893) of 7 Aswell-lane. Competition had reduced the charge for a portrait to 1s 6d, including a frame (probably of papier mâché).[31] Willey had taken daguerreotypes, and ambrotypes (developed in England in 1851 and popular in the 1850s because of their cheapness).[32] Is it just possible that, because of his interest in photography, Brown was one who had his portrait taken then?

What can we make of Brown's relationship with two eminent but much younger artists in the town – Bennett Hubbard (1806-1870), painter, and Thomas Wilkinson Wallis (1821-1903), sculptor in wood. All three were members of the Louth Mechanics' Institute and Wallis became curator in 1851. Hubbard painted portraits of many local people, and animals and scenery. His first painting to be exhibited at the Royal Academy, in 1839, was of Bob, a favourite pony of John Naull, ironmonger, nailmaker and cutler in the Market Place.[33] Brown was generous in his assessment of Hubbard's masterly portrait of Henry (Harry) Hurton (printer, binder and bookseller, Mercer Row) in 1842: 'the likeness is allowed to be a successful specimen of the talent of the artist'.[34] Brown also noted Hubbard's painting exhibited at the Royal Academy in 1852 – a portrait of 8-year old Lucy Jane, daughter of Robert Beatneffe.[35]

The nature of Brown's relationship with Wallis is more problematical. They were from much the same social background, but with different aspirations and of opposing religious persuasions. Brown, as far as we know, had served no apprenticeship, and represented the low church, dissenting, artisan tradition of the *Stamford Mercury*; Wallis on the other hand, had 'made good' and joined the aspiring middle class. It seems surprising that Wallis never mentioned Brown sketching when writing about the fashionable activity of ascending the scaffolding surrounding the spire in 1844.[36] Perhaps they did not both ascend at the same time, and what was unusual about a newspaper reporter in late middle-age making sketches?

Almost certainly neither of them realised how significant the work would become.

Nor did Wallis mention the exhibition of the finished Panorama in 1847, even though he had joined the Mechanics' Institute in March that year. At the time of Brown exhibiting the Gallery of Illustration at the festivities for the stonelaying of the Town Hall in May 1853, Wallis noted in his diary 'I was stoical enough to work all day'.[37] On the occasion of the celebrations for peace in the Crimea, when Brown exhibited the Panorama in the new Corn Exchange, Wallis was in London.[38] And when Wallis was writing his autobiography forty years later, the Panorama had disappeared from both view and memory.

However, Brown devoted many column inches to the work of Wallis in relation to the Great Exhibition of 1851 where he won a gold medal for the woodcarving Trophy of Spring (one of seven works he exhibited). In October 1850, under a heading *The Fine Arts*, Brown linked himself with Wallis and Hubbard and reported: 'Mr Wallis is producing by his skilful and careful hand specimens of the richest and most delicate carvings; Mr Hubbard is painting portraits on canvas which literally seem to breathe the life of the sitters; Mr Brown is supplying the public with copies of his neat and pleasing engravings – memorials of places of religious worship in the town'.[39] Brown was aged 62, Hubbard 44 and Wallis 29.

The following February, Brown described Trophy of Spring in detail. 'It consists of an immense nosegay representing Spring, composed of 1,000 representations of 47 kinds of spring flowers and buds, elegantly entwined round stalks of the apple-tree in blossom, and accompanied by their usual attendants, the caterpillar and other insects. The whole, which is carved in lime tree wood, is suspended by carved drapery in the form of ribbons &c, from the head of a lamb, supported by a shepherd's crook, encentred by a nest of the blue-capped tit-mouse, with the old birds conveying food to the young brood in the nest; and ornamented with a beautiful grape cluster and vine leaves as a pendant'.[40]

Such was the 'rush of people who had been invited to view Mr Wallis's masterpiece in the art of woodcarving', Brown reported a fortnight later, 'that his window and some other property in his shop were broken, and he was compelled to lay on a fee of 3d admission ... 1,466 persons visited the studio'.[41] In June he quoted the description of the carving in the *Builder*, in July that 'orders from those who had visited the Great Exhibition would keep [Wallis] in work for two years',[42] and in August noted that the *Morning Chronicle* recognised Wallis as 'a worthy successor and rival to Grinling Gibbons'.[43] The next month there were two reports in glowing terms of his carving of a golden plover, from a single block of wood,[44] which was exhibited in his shop window in Upgate in December.[45]

Wallis featured again the next year when Brown extracted from the juries' report on the Great Exhibition what was said about the medal-winning carving,[46] and also reported that Wallis had carved the reading-desk designed for St James's church, Louth by (James) Maughan and (James) Fowler, architects.[47] In 1853, Brown wrote, 'we have been much gratified in seeing in the atelier [sculptor's studio/workshop] ... Mr Wallis's several studies of dead game in a progressive state of woodcarving ... one of rather collosal proportions ... of the winged heron, bulrush, and the ever-twisting ivy branch ... nearly six feet high'.[48] And then, in 1856, of a 'statuette group of birds ... snipe, water wagtail and robin ... composed with an old thorn stump ... the whole design is equal to the details, and these are rendered with a truthfulness to nature seldom if ever surpassed'.[49]

It would appear, therefore, that Brown was quite fulsome in his appreciation of the sculptor about half his age. Wallis on the

T W Wallis
– self portrait.
(Louth Town Council).

Partridges and Ivy
T W Wallis, 1871.

other hand seems to have shown little or no interest in Brown's painting, neither the Panorama, the Gallery of Illustration nor his Polyopticorama. Was it just that – lack of interest – or may there have been some personal animus? We cannot help surmising that when Wallis organised the grand three-day bazaar in the Mansion House in summer 1853 to raise funds to purchase that building from the Corporation, Brown would have been disappointed not to be asked to exhibit the Panorama.

Of Brown's architectural drawings, we have seen four – St James's church (1844-45) and three chapels: Wesleyan (1849), General Baptist (1850) and Primitive (1850). The chapels were engraved by Goodwill & Lawson in Hull. There are two versions of the Wesleyan: one oval which also shows on the right the Stall-yard where the Town Hall now stands, and the other with two vignettes of the River Head and New Market chapels. An original Brown drawing, in pen and ink with ink wash appeared in a Louth auction sale in the early 1980s. It shows **Eastgate, Louth** looking towards St James's, with the shops of dyer Lambert Harrison and grocer James Standaland, 'Drawn from Nature' in 1852. Also in 1852 he sketched the **Destruction of Jerusalem by Titus AD70**, which is noted in one of the obituaries. This is 10 inches by 6 inches and shows sacking by fire (but what is the ice-berg like feature in the foreground?).

Destruction of JERUSALEM, by Titus, A.D. 70. Sketched by Wm Brown, Painter & Reporter, Louth. 1852.

It would appear that one of Brown's most popular and best remembered works was the set of studies from Pilgrim's Progress; this is mentioned in all three of his obituaries. The 40 scenes were drawn and painted, the latter for his Gallery of Illustration exhibitions in 1853 and 1856. The drawings, or rather a series combined into one continuous story, were titled **The Pictorial Pilgrim's Progress – From the City of Destruction to the Celestial City and the chief incidents of his Journey**, and engraved by Goodwill & Co of Hull in 1850. The work is oval and measures $13\frac{1}{4}$ inches by $10\frac{1}{4}$ inches. The story starts lower left and ascends in alternating directions in seven lines of drawings. The drawn figures of the characters are $\frac{1}{4}$ inch to $\frac{1}{2}$ inch high. Examples are Xn (Christian) and Pliable in the Slough of Despond, Xn's conflict with Apollyan (Ye Devil), Madam Wanton resisted, Xn escapes from Doubting Castle, Hopeful describes his conversion at the Mercy Seat, concluding with crossing the river of Death. The work was regarded as a masterpiece which 'evinced a large amount of imaginative and manual skill'.[50] It demonstrates Brown as a clever miniaturist. The original (?) was bequeathed to the Louth Free Evening School which had opened in what had been the Wesleyan and then Free Methodist Sunday School in Lee Street in 1856. It was for those 'who may have been so unfortunate as to be taken too early from school', a purpose with which Brown would have fully concurred.[51]

One of Brown's obituaries[52] mentions a number of other religious engravings and paintings, only one of which is known to have survived – the **Protestant Christian's Memento**. This depicts (left to right) Calvin, Cranmer, Luther and Knox standing on the Rock of Truth, with explanatory text. Copies engraved by Goodwill & Lawson, about 1850, cost 3d each. Others noted, and now lost, were 'Crucifixion' and his last and unfinished painting titled 'Last Day' showing 'about 200 portraits of the good and wise of all generations as about to ascend to glory'. On the back of one or two of the panorama sketch panels drawn in pencil are groups of crude circles, ovals and face outlines, each with a shortened form of the names of those who would have made up the painting. Most are now illegible, but it is possible to identify Old Testament names – Abraham, Job, Moses, Samuel, Isaiah, David and Jeremiah, and from the New Testament, Matthew, Mark, Luke, John, Peter and Paul, along with St Polycarp and St Francis. We must suppose that all those and other 'distinguished persons', suitably classified, were ones he first painted individually onto lantern slides for his polyopticorama. These and his other slides are now lost.

THE PROTESTANT CHRISTIAN'S MEMENTO.

THE four principal figures, standing upon the Rock are intended to represent the chief PROTESTANT REFORMERS: Luther in the centre, Cranmer on his right hand, Knox on his left, and Calvin on his extreme right; each holding in his hand a manuscript or printed copy of the word of God. The Rock is intended to denote the TRUTH of the doctrine of the Divine Oracles on which as on an immutable Rock the Reformers rested all their claims in labouring to restore pure Christianity. Around the Rock of Truth the waves of Error and Superstition are seen dashing, and in that sea appear struggling for existence the four chief supporters of the Papal Antichrist. The principal figure represents HIS HOLINESS THE POPE, grasping in one hand his once dreadful *Bull*, and in the other his formerly terrible sceptre. On his right hand appears a bloated MENDICANT FRIAR; on the left a wily JESUIT; and on his extreme right a ROMISH DIGNITARY, each with his peculiar symbols of *hypocrisy, imposture,* and *terror,* but all become useless to their possessors in the presence of the published HOLY SCRIPTURES.

LUTHER, CALVIN, CRANMER, and KNOX, have laid Europe and the whole world under the greatest obligations to them by their courageous, indefatigable, and successful labours; overthrowing the Priestcraft of Popery, that blasphemous 'MAN OF SIN' and 'MYSTERY OF INIQUITY,' 2 Thess. ii; and restoring to the people the Holy Scriptures as their only infallible directory in matters of Religion.

Goodwill & Lawson Engravers. Hull.

PRICE, 3ᵈ. To be had of W. Brown, Vicker's Lane, Louth.

According to the *Advertiser* obituary, [52] Brown was also preparing to paint pictorial illustrations of the 'Fulfilment of the Prophecies of Daniel'. The obituary further refers to views of Holbein's *Imagen Mortis* or Dance of Death. The 25 scenes from this and 16 sketches from Harriet Beecher Stowe's *Uncle Tom's Cabin*, together with the 40 scenes from *Pilgrim's Progress* made up the 150 feet of canvas in the Gallery of Illustration. It seems most likely that, as with Pilgrim's Progress, the Dance of Death and Uncle Tom's Cabin scenes started in miniature before being painted very large on canvas (both are now lost). It would have been a cheap hemp canvas, as used in theatre scenery, and painted with tempera. [53] It was easily rolled and would have a short life.

What have survived are four examples of Brown's painting, each with miniaturist detail of the kind he applied to the Panorama. **Wonders of Art No 1** is, according to the obituary, one of six views he did of the wonders of nature and art. It measures 31 inches by 13 inches, and has a London background – the Embankment with monuments, fountain and obelisk, the Thames and the Tower of London, St Paul's Cathedral, and Westminster Abbey, but not in prospect order. In the middle ground is the ascent of a decorated Montgolfier hot air balloon with suspended basket, and above right is Blanchard's 'flying ship' balloon with revolving paddle blades. Hot air ballooning began in France in the 1780s, but in this country aeronaut Charles Green was using coal gas to fill his balloon, and had made an ascent from Louth in August 1826 to mark the opening of the gas works at the Riverhead. The event was advertised in the *Stamford Mercury* with a small illustration, and reported in detail. [54] Brown surely must have seen the brightly coloured balloon as it soared over the town.

In the foreground of Wonders of Art, we see what Brown called 'surprising inventions' when he illustrated them for the polyopticorama in 1845-47. These include steam carriages and an engine towing coal wagons, an orrery, (a working model of the solar system), a miniature post-mill on a three-legged base, printing presses, a microscope, a wind-propelled horseless carriage, a wheelbarrow with a sail, hobby horses, a pedal operated conical screw in a box (for what purpose?) and, of course, a magic lantern. Where did Brown see these objects to copy?

Green's balloon
over Louth in 1826.

From the mid-1830s the Mechanics' Institute reading room had a number of weekly, monthly and quarterly journals and magazines, including the *Mechanics' Magazine* which was illustrated. There were over eight hundred books in the Institute library including *Ree's Cyclopaedia* (45 volumes), *Buffon's Natural History* (15 volumes) and *Mavor's Voyages and Travels* (31 volumes), and members made borrowings of around four thousand books a year. And from 1842 members had access to the *Illustrated London News*.[55]

Two paintings have no title and there is no reference to content in the obituaries, but they could be called **Wonders of Nature No 2 and No 3**. We have Brown's description of subjects in the polyopticorama – zoological rarities and extraordinary animals, natural phenomena, and pagan superstitions. The paintings, damaged on the right margin, and measuring 31 inches by 16 inches and 29 inches by 16 inches respectively, both incorporate all those subjects. The foreground landscape of **No 2** has a river with waterfalls, curious cone-capped porous columns (very thick bamboo?), native huts, a geyser spouting rocks with a man on his hands and knees cooking something in the boiling water, palm trees and a native climbing for coconuts. There is a coastline of basalt columns and Fingal's Cave, an arid landscape with sharp pinnacles, the Bay of Naples with Vesuvius erupting, another quiet volcano which may well be Mt. Hekla, and a strange red and steaming mass which may represent lava flowing into the sea, upon which there are various sailing vessels. There are also three men in a boat, one of them attacking an octopus with an axe. And swimming in the sea is a creature not without resemblance to the popular image of the Loch Ness monster.

Brown's painting of Fingal's Cave is a reverse of the drawing by John Frederick Miller, made when Sir Joseph Banks of Revesby (1743-1820) visited the Island of Staffa in August 1772. The drawing was engraved in *A Tour of Scotland and Voyage to the Hebrides* by Thomas Pennant, published in 1774. Moreover, Brown's depiction of the geyser is remarkably similar to the watercolour with ink by John Clevely (he and Miller were employed by Banks as draughtsmen) made when Banks visited the Great Geyser at Haukadal in Iceland in September 1772; the party also climbed Mt Hekla on that occasion. Of the visit to Fingal's Cave, Banks wrote, 'Compared to this what are

Cameleopard
Thomas Bewick engraving

Wonders of Nature No 2

Cathedrals or the palaces built by man? Mere models or playthings, imitations as diminutive as his works will always be when compared to those of Nature .... How amply does Nature repay those who study her wonderful works'. Brown would surely have agreed with those sentiments. On the visit to Iceland, Banks had a ptarmigan which he had shot cooked in the boiling waters of the geyser. Could we even conjecture that Brown meant the man in the red jacket to be Banks and the seated man to be the artist?

Scattered in the foreground and middle ground are sea creatures including octopus, whale, flying fish, corals, starfish, crab, and gryphaea (devil's toenail) fossils. Animals include a large crocodile, with young breaking from an egg, a zebra caught by a python, a coiled and a two-headed snake, beaver, birds, monkeys, a flying squirrel and a cameleopard or giraffe. And on a flat rock on the bottom right of the painting is a part-cowled bearded face: who was he meant to represent? .

The composition of **No 3** is similar, with landscapes in the background and animals in the foreground. There is also a mix of continent and climate, in this case Africa and Asia, with a touch of Australia. The mix, one might even say muddle, could have been Brown's way of creating a children's 'see what you can find' visual aid. Or perhaps they were just a reflection of his quirky nature. Here we have in the background a mountain pass, rising spray from the Victoria Falls, part of the red rock city of Petra, the Roman Appian Way, and what was thought to be the water feature of the Hanging Gardens of Babylon.

A major river with a cataract (and therefore probably the Nile) has a canopied barge on calmer water. On the far bank is a date palm and a large banyan tree with aerial roots, and even a man lying on a bed of nails. In the foreground an Indian elephant with palatial howdah takes centre stage. To the left is an opossum, a beehive, an orang-outang sitting on a stool, duck-billed platypus, porcupine, kangaroo, and cobra. To the right are antelopes, a hippopotamus, a rhinoceros and an ostrich, together with a goat, a locust, a Chinaman with tea plants, humming birds and a large raven pecking the eye of a sheep. Most intriguing is a row of bending and rhythmically working black slaves under a canopy, with songster and slave-drivers; it appears that the slaves are treading something in flowing water, possibly sisal.

Kanguroo
Thomas Bewick engraving.

Wonders of Nature No 3

The sources of Brown's inspiration were undoubtedly the illustrated books and publications in the Mechanics' library. We can, in fact, demonstrate that Brown used one book in particular for the animals he painted – *A General History of Quadrapeds* with wood engravings by Thomas Bewick (1753-1828), published in 1790. Of about a dozen of Bewick's engravings we have identified that Brown used, in almost every instance he created a clever mirror image (perhaps to obscure the fact that he had made a copy) – cameleopard (giraffe), rhinoceros, Indian elephant and flying squirrel for example. Two others are particularly clear: the kanguroo (the original spelling) which Bewick engraved from a painting in 1772 by George Stubbs (1724-1806) from a skin brought back from New South Wales by Joseph Banks, to which Brown added a joey in the pouch; and the orang-outang or wild man of the woods.

Orang-outang.
Thomas Bewick engraving.

The other painting which survives with Brown's descendants – **Battle of the Nile** (22 inches by 10½ inches), is more of a mystery. The battle took place in August 1798, and the following year the official painting was executed by Philipe Jacques de Loutherberg. The painting illustrated here was done in strips and pasted on a backing sheet *en echelon* to show the line of English ships in relation to the French fleet (the main protagonists are identified) and the destruction of *L'Orient*. Below the painting Brown had written in pencil 'Sent from cousin Joseph Brown on board the Hibernia 120 guns'. The *Hibernia* was not in the battle, and there is no trace of cousin Joseph in the family tree (as we know it). It is further complicated by writing in ink at the top mentioning Malta and dated 11 December 1845. It is a dramatic picture, but on this evidence is a copy rather than an original composition.

The Battle of the Nile.

Finally, there is a painting Brown did of his son Francis in preaching mode; Brown must have been proud of him as a Wesleyan Association (Warrenite) minister. He died in 1847, aged 31. And the painting Brown did of himself from a daguerreotype taken in 1845: did he use this also to make himself bow when projected by magic lantern? Certainly the projection of surprising inventions, zoological rarities and exploding volcanoes enthralled the young audiences Brown sought to educate as well as entertain.

Taking the full range of Brown's known drawings and paintings, it seems that they all date from the early to mid-1840s onwards. It is reasonable to suppose that his drawing skills had improved through classes at the Mechanics' Institute in the mid to late-1830s, and that the application of paint came from knowledge of the materials of his trade. That period of the 1830s was also the time when he had access to illustrated publications. These postulations fit with other evidence for a change of direction in his life in the 1830s, a time when his fertile and omnivorous imagination was finding new means of expression.

THE

MORAL MISCELLANY;

or, Lines descriptive of the moving Figures exhibiting (large as life) in Brown's

MAGIC TUTOR.

WISDOM.

O wifdom, fource of true fubftantial blifs
Whofe worth exceeds all human happinefs,
If now thou deign'ft inftruction to convey
O teach us truth till error flee away.

BRITANNIA.

2. Ye Britons fair, 'tis true you rule the main,
But rul'd by vice, your boaft of freedom's vain;
O fly the follies of the age; be wife;
So fhall your fame be lafting as the fkies.

THE REGENT.

3. Illuftrious Prince of Britain's favor'd Ifle;
Long may he reign beneath the Almighty's fmile,
Encourage every virtuous act, and prove
By virtuous practice he that virtue loves.

ALEXANDER.

4 When Europe groan'd beneath th' afflicting rod
Of war and tyranny, an angry God
Awak'd revenge in Alexander's breaft,
Who quell'd the fiend and gave to Europe reft.

BONAPARTE.

5 See the late Emp'ror, Bonaparte fee,
How fall'n that pride, how bafh'd that vanity:
May heaven forgive the man; from Europe chace
Such monfters cruel and fuch tyrants bafe.

WELLINGTON.

6 He comes; the conq'ring Wellington; O Spain,
O Portugal, he fav'd your finking fame;
O might you but efpoufe a better caufe
And banifh all your anti chriftian laws.

BLUCHER.

7 When France in all the boafting pride of war
Refolv'd on conquefts, fee a Pruffian dare
Their rage defy: the vet'ran Blucher hurl'd
Th' afpirants down, and all their power control'd.

THE OURANG OUTANG.

14 How grand's the fcale of being: man's confeft
The nobleft creature heav'n with life hath bleft;
Yet fee how fine's the feparating line,
How man refembles the Ourang Outang.

GUILDHALL.

15 The gothic pile you view is nam'd Guildhall,
Where my lord mayor attends the city's call,
And rights of citizens adjufts; here feafts
Are fometimes held which many ills create.

PEACE.

16 All hail, fweet peace! ye thankful nations praife
The gracious hand who fent thofe golden days:
To concord rear this beauteous temple then;
Your thanks exprefs by your good will to men.

THE PAGODA.

17 The chinefe bridge or grand pagoda fee
In jubiliftic pride and vanity:
Sad fate befel it, furious flames burnt down
This chriftian heathen temple of renown.

THE INDIAMAN.

18 Fair blows the breeze, the veffel glides along
With India's riches fraught; ye worldly throng,
Lade you with grace tow'rds heav'n your veffel fteer
So fhall you fwim when all have perifh'd here.

THE BALLOON.

19 Sadler's balloon's an emblem of the heart:
Fill'd with pure air 'twill rife and heav'nward ftart;
The gas let out, the common air let in,
'Twill foon defcend, an emblem then of fin.

CURIOSITY.

20 This antique fair, all eye all ear you fee;
Her name you afk, 'tis curiofity;
The prying dame with quick difcerning eye
Seeks all your fecrets, marks your vanity.

VENUS.

21 When a pure flame invades the guiltlefs breaft
'Tis Venus rules, the goddefs is confeft:
The youthful figh, the maiden blufh, declare
'Tis love alone their wedded bofoms fhare.

DIANA.

22 The Ephefians fond of making filver fhrines
To enrich their goddefs with, Diana fhines
The idol of their foul.—Love you no thing
In preference to heaven's glorious King.

THE MOON.

23 The fage well fkill'd in fair aftronomy
With curious mind and telefcopic eye
Infpects the moon, at length with wonder fpies
Volcanos huge, and numerous hillocks rife.

JOSEPH.

24 Reft Jofeph reft till heav'n to thee make known
Thy brethren's bafenefs and thy own renown;
Fair fun, fair moon, ye twinkling ftars obey,
And to this youth your foft obeifance pay.

SAMUEL.

25 The firft crownd head that Judah's fceptre fwayd
Sought help of witches, in difguife array'd;
The forcerefs ftamp'd, old Samuel's ghoft arofe,
And doomed the king to fuffer dreadful woes.

ELIJAH.

26 Elijah faw nor death nor putrid earth:
A fiery chariot as the fcripture faith,
Convey'd the prophet far above the fky,
O bleft reward of genuine piety.

BELSHAZZAR.

27 The proud Belfhazzar Chaldea's king fuggefts
A feaft, and names a thoufand lords his guefts,
A hand tranfcribes the haughty monarch's ftate,
His crimes are weighed he trembles at his fate.

THE BATTLE OF ARMAGEDDON.

34 Arrayed in power the king of kings makes war,
And conquers all the infernal hofts that dare
His followers vex: the beaft and all his foes
Sink in the lake that burns with dreadful woes.

THE LAST ENEMY.

35 Death's the laft foe, fad foe indeed to thofe
Who for the world care not their fouls to lofe;
But friendly guides unto the realms of blifs
Thofe wifer fouls who love the prince of peace.

THE END OF TIME.

36 On earth and fea an angel ftands and rears
His head: he lifts his mighty arm and fwears,
By him that lives and reigns for evermore,
Ye mortals lift; time, time fhall be no more.

THE YEAR'S REVOLUTION.

37 On the earth's orbit fee the various figns,
Mark where the fun, our year completing, fhines;
Firft the bright ram his languid ray improves,
Next glaring watry through the bull he moves.

38 The amorous twins admit his genial ray;
Now burning through the crab he takes his way;
The lion flaming bears the folar power;
The virgin faints beneath the fultry fhower.

39 Now the juft balance weighs his equal force;
The flimy ferpent fwelters in his courfe;
The fable archer clouds his languid face;
The goat with tempefts urges on his race.

40 Now in the water his faint beams appear
And the cold fifhes end the circling year;
Thus years roll on—it is for men to gain
That wifdom here, which ever fhall remain.

Chapter 7
A Window in Time – what the Panorama shows

THE AMOUNT of detail Brown drew and painted on his Panorama is astonishing, almost obsessive. One of the remarkable but perhaps little appreciated aspects of the painting was his skill in scaling up about ten times from the small sketch panels to the two canvasses each about nine feet wide and six feet high, while retaining the proportions and perspective. He transferred the shape and pattern of flower beds in gardens, the patchwork of fields and hedgerow trees, the network of town streets and country roads, and the fenestration, roofs and chimneys of buildings. Even the direction of smoke from chimney pots (kitchen fires for cooking were still needed in the summer) is true to the anticyclonic weather of summer 1844: a sea breeze with fluffy cumulus clouds over the Wolds. And then, based on daily observation as he moved about the town, he peopled the streets, workyards, school playgrounds and gardens of the town with almost Lowry-like figures. Among this plethora of detail spreading out into the countryside and to the coast, let us examine some of those themes.

Garden fashions

There are interesting examples of contrast in styles of garden design then fashionable. On the right panel and left foreground are the grey pitched roofs of the Vicarage (now the Rectory), a relatively new building designed by Louth architect C J Carter in 1832. Walking along the gravel path is the vicar, Rev E R Mantell, with perhaps the Warden of the Grammar School, while in the shade of a tree two ladies sit, one with a white parasol. There are a few small flower beds, but the rest is lawn with trees and arboreal arches leading towards an arbour with statues, wall hangings, a bamboo table and chairs. Between the arbour and the seated ladies is a column of the top stones taken from the church spire during the restoration, and therefore added in the later stages of completing the painting. Moreover, the sketches show two flower beds and no arches, so the garden plan was being changed by Mantell, or more likely by his wife Sarah. Perhaps she had read Jane Loudon's *Ladies' Companion to the Flower Garden*, first published in 1841: 'the object of shrubbery is to produce as ... interesting [a] walk as the nature, extent and ... circumstances of the place will permit'.[1]

Mantell's predecessor, Rev Wolley Jolland (1745-1831), had built a hermitage folly in the garden, but all that remained was an urn, the base of which still bears the inscription 'Sacred to the memory of George and Justina, Revered Parents of the Hermit ...'[2] and perhaps the rustic chair on which Mrs Mantell (?) is seated. There is one other small object in the garden worth noting; to the left of the ladies is what appears to be a lawnmower, or roller. The lawnmower was invented by Edwin Budding in 1830 and manufactured by Ransome of Norwich from 1833. However, by the 1840s the lawn was losing its popularity, being seen more as the setting for decorations.[3]

Ladies in the vicarage garden with stones from the spire and arbour.

Wolley Jolland's hermitage folly, by Thomas Espin.

Inscribed base of the urn.

To the right of the vicarage are the rear gardens of Church Precincts, Arnold House, The Limes and the front garden of Lindsey House. The formal 18th century parterre design of the small Church Precincts garden contrasts with the new and more fashionable scrollwork pattern of the main part of the Arnold House garden, in the 'gardenesque' style then being advocated by J C Loudon (1783-1843), editor of *Gardener's Magazine*.[4] He is regarded as the father of the English garden, and wrote that gardens were 'intended to show that they are works of art and to display the taste and wealth of the owner'. Loudon was also an advocate of gravel paths, and here Brown depicts the master of the house with his wife, daughter and the family dog. The sketch, but not the painting, shows a roller on the gravel path.

In the garden of Arnold House.

The garden of The Limes, the home of Mrs Elizabeth Emeris, has a rectangular lawn and a balanced pattern of disconnected geometrically curved flower beds, with a surrounding gravel walk, very much the new fashion. A similar design is in the adjacent front garden of Miss F Emeris's newly built villa, Lindsey House. The same is found again in part of the garden of Westgate House, beyond Schoolhouse Lane, where two areas of new design have been carved out of the earlier formal parterre beds. This must have been done at the behest of Miss Mary Sophia Ansell, whose name Brown wrote on the garden path in the sketch.

'Nothing harmonises and adorns the female mind more surely than a taste for ornamental gardening', wrote Mrs Louisa Johnson in *Every Lady in her Flower Garden* (1845). Clearly Miss Ansell and the Emeris ladies had such a taste. Perhaps they also followed Mrs Loudon's advice, as offered in *The Lady's Country Companion* (1845), of 'regular geometric figures planted in masses, each bed containing flowers of one kind'. Miss Ansell also had a greenhouse on a south-facing wall, and there was a free-standing one between the kitchen garden and the stables at The Sycamores on the other side of Breakneck Lane. Of the grounds of The Sycamores (a large house which had been done up in the artisan mannerist style by C J Carter for the Hobart family only a few years before, about 1837), only a small part had been given over to the new style of flower beds.

A conversation in the garden of Masson House. Note the bird table.

Next to the grounds of The Sycamores to the west is The Mansion. When it was offered for sale in 1843, the garden was described as having 'a spacious lawn ornamented with flowering shrubs, evergreens, forest trees and gravel walks'. There was also a back lawn, flower garden and gardener's toolhouse.[5] On the north side of Westgate we see ladies strolling in the garden of Masson House. The gardens of other houses here all stretch down to the river: the garden of the white house, at the junction of Westgate and Breakneck Lane, has a delicately scalloped lawn with a small ornamental pond. Some also have a private bridge to property, and sometimes a garden extension, on the north side of the river.

Gardens on the north side of Westgate stretch down to the river.

Opposite:
Gardens on Westgate (L-R): Church Precincts, Arnold House, The Limes, Lindsey House and Westgate House.

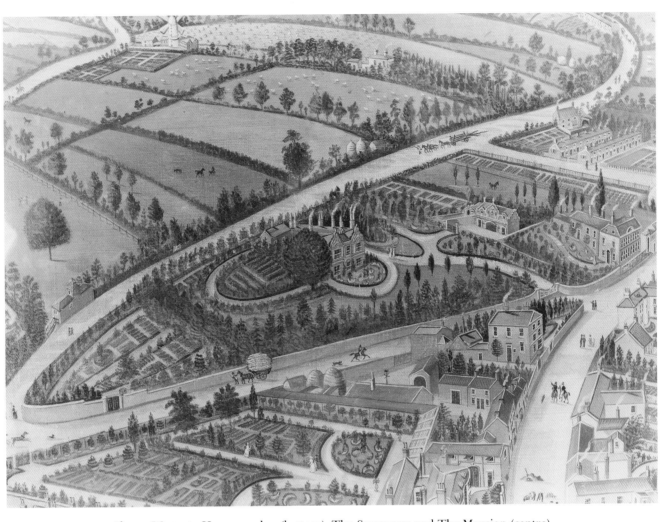

Above: Westgate House garden (bottom), The Sycamores and The Mansion (centre),
and The Hill (white; built between sketch and painting, and now Golf Club) on Crowtree Lane.

The Cedars ...... and the nursery across St Mary's Lane.

Thorpe Hall.

At the west end of St Mary's Lane stand The Cedars, built in 1830 by solicitor Henry Pye,[6] with a garden and ha-ha looking across parkland, formerly part of Wilderness Close, newly planted with trees, to a lake which had been made in the river. Was it his wife Charlotte Mary and daughter Charlotte portrayed in the grounds? On the other side of St Mary's Lane were nursery gardens with a small windmill, a pagoda-like feature (a dovecote?) and other buildings (shown on the left edge of the other painting panel); a greenhouse once part of the complex is still in use. The gardens of Thorpe Hall, beyond The Cedars and in South Elkington parish, are hidden from view, but is that John Fytche and his wife walking the path in the park?

On the lower left of the same panel are other formal gardens, including one of about a fifth of an acre attached to Bridge Street House by a bridge over the river. Bridge Street House was built about 1822, and the garden extension leased by Dr Thomas Philbrick who, in 1838, built the 'ornamental, lofty, latticed bridge of singular beauty and design' that appears on the Panorama. However, in the years between the sketch and the painting the decking of the bridge appears to have gone, and soon after the bridge had to be replaced with a more sturdy and practical structure.[7]

Bridge Street House garden on the sketch.

The gardens behind Bridge Street Terrace (left) and the houses of Field Flowers Goe and Henry Orme (right).

On the opposite side of Bridge Street is Bridge Street Terrace, built in 1825, just about the time Brown moved into a cottage in the street from Aswell-lane (Street). The gardens behind the Terrace are formal, but the scroll-like paths in the adjacent large garden, the property of solicitor Field Flowers Goe,[8] suggests someone wishing to show off gardening design skills (albeit taken from Loudon's *Gardener's Magazine*). And his neighbour, Henry Orme, also a solicitor (and commissioner for taking acknowledgements of married women), had made three adaptations of the formal: one square bed with concave cut-out corners, one rounded and another subdivided, each with a central shrub or pedestal and urn. The small formal garden next along, near the hay ricks, boasts an obelisk which must be about twenty feet high and makes a striking focal point. Then look across the river to the garden leading up to the tall white brick and grey-slated house on Cisterngate: formal beds near the river, a zig-zag green fence and then a square pedestal carrying the statue of a man with arms outstretched. Who was he? – we don't know.

There is a charming scene in the garden of St Mary's Close or Mount on Bridge Street: one lady sits half seen in an arbour and another welcomes two visitors. The two ladies were the maiden sisters and landed proprietors, Ann and Elizabeth Pettener. Across the Grimsby Road are the neat gardens of the White House where Mrs Ann Elizabeth Paddison lived. Brown showed that formal, probably parterre, gardens still remained within the town, particularly those on Cannon Street. Moving back to the right panel of the painting, on the left edge we see orchards round the British (Kidgate) School. When the school was built in 1840-41, it was necessary to clear 24 apple and 19 pear trees, currant and gooseberry bushes, and plots of rhubarb and mercury. The nurseryman, Morgan Jones, was paid £67 15s in compensation.[9]

At the time the Panorama was created, there were ten or more gardeners, nursery and seedsmen in the town, including Richard and his son Thomas Cocking who had a shop in Mercer Row, John Mitchell who took over from Morgan Jones, Newton North on Monks Dyke, William Howell with a nursery at Riverhead, William Robinson on Newmarket, George Tuxworth whose nursery was on Westgate (the town side of Irish Hill), and George Moody on Holmes Lane (now High Holme Road). The Panorama shows Moody's nursery, and the firm was still advertising in the county directory more than a century after it was founded in 1830.[10] By 1856 the number had increased to at least fifteen. These were the men who supplied the seeds and plants for town gardens, and some would also sell fruit and vegetables on market stalls.

The Cisterngate gardens and the impressive statue.

The Misses Pettener in the gardens of St Mary's Mount.

George Moody's nursery, and advertisement of 1937.

The import from foreign lands of exotic seeds, cuttings and plants had started for the rich in the 18th century. After Sir Joseph Banks of Revesby had co-founded the (later Royal) Horticultural Society in 1804, quantities increased and prices fell. The dahlia from Mexico became fashionable from the 1820s, and roses, the aspidistra, chrysanthemums and hydrangea from China in the 1830s, and there was improvement of fruit and vegetable gardens and the introduction of Bramley Seedling and Cox's Orange Pippin apples.

It is no surprise therefore to find that Louth had a flourishing Floral and Horticultural Society, which evinced the usual fierce competition. At the first show of 1841, in June, Brown reported that 'the display of flowers and costly plants was considerably better than last year, and the quality of the vegetables superior to any previous year'.[11] The second show at the end of July was also held in the Infant Schoolroom, that is the ground floor of the National Girls' and Infants' School (on the site of the car park on Broadbank). On that occasion 'a heavy charge of partiality [was] brought against the Society by a poor man [a journeyman cabinetmaker] who is such a connoisseur in flowers as to excel to a high degree his rich competitors, not infrequently eclipsing their glory [with] his own superior specimens ... and the jealously of his rivals ... led to the refusal of his claim to exhibit on the alleged ground that he was not a "cottager" as described but a tradesman!' Brown concluded his report with a typical caustic comment. 'We hope that in future the better informed in such technicalities will not suffer so manifest a quibble on a word, which our best lexicographers decide includes both the mechanic and the artisan, to stifle in the breast of the humblest of Flora's admirers a taste for the beauties of creation.'[12] A fashionable garden may impress fellow gentry but did not guarantee first prize at the show.

One other thing to notice is the type and distribution of trees in gardens and in grass closes on the edge of town. Most appear to be deciduous – beech, lime, horsechestnut, ash and oak, but there are conifers in Westgate and Bridge Street gardens for example. Lines of poplars also appear in places – along the south side of St Mary's cemetery, and quite prominently in Gospelgate in front of the house called The Poplars. The latter Brown showed to be well grown; the year after he died one of those poplars was blown down in a severe gale and damaged the house of T W Wallis on the other side of the street, and there was other storm damage to other trees and buildings in the town.[13]

Fields and farming

Out in the country the patchwork of hedged fields was relatively new. The enclosure of Louth's two large medieval open fields, North and South (the smaller East Field worked with the South), formerly ploughed in strips, had only been completed forty years earlier under the Award of 1805. Before that the boundary of the old town closes and paddocks was St Mary's Lane (formerly Paradise Lane) and High Holme Road (Holmes Lane) on the left painting, and Horncastle Road and Newmarket on the right painting. More than a third of the common land went in extinguishing the hated tithes, in fact a total of 608 acres out of 1,700; the lords of the manor received another 178 acres. Of the private landowners, only four were allotted between 50 and 100 acres (William Stephenson and William Wright jointly, Wharfe Preston, tanner, John Simpson, and Richard Codd), 42 received one to ten acres each, and 67 less than an acre.[14] It had been for owners of the new allotments in the former open fields to set their own hedges. Brown therefore accurately shows the hedges beyond the old closes as lower (younger) with fewer, smaller hedgerow trees.

Looking west to farming on the Wolds.

Out on the Marsh (mainly the left painting) the majority of the fields are shown green – the 'fatting' pastures for longwool sheep and horned cattle. The Wolds on the other hand (right painting) show many corn fields, including one near the five-sail windmill on the Horncastle Road as part harvested with lines of stooks. Not all the landowners with new farms had yet built their farmsteads and barns (for example there is no Northfield Farm on Fanthorpe Lane), so it is no surprise to find hay ricks and corn stacks in the town – on Cisterngate, off Chequergate and even in Bridge Street (left painting), appropriately in the yard of the Wheatsheaf inn on Westgate and by the Lion inn at the corner of Upgate and Newmarket (right painting). It was quite usual for innkeepers also to be farmers, and fodder was needed for horses stabled at the inns.

Pigs and haystacks in the yard of the Wheatsheaf inn.

The farmers of whom there is a record at the time the Panorama was created were Benjamin and John Ashton on the Grimsby Road, William Bond on Monks Dyke, Susanna Bowling (widow of Samuel) at Louth Grange on the London Road, Richard Cox, Eastgate, William Fytche and John Maltby at Louth Park, William Heath, Westgate Place, and Joseph Maltby, Louth Field (Grimsby Road). They were not necessarily landowners, but more likely to be renting land from the vicar or from the Grammar School. On the other hand, the land awarded to William Robinson in 1805 became the family nursery business which continued until the new housing development off Mount Pleasant in the late 20th century.

Some closes near the town not taken up for building were still horse paddocks, as Brown shows; others were grazed by sheep. And there is one mystery field – on the north side of the river, part on the left edge of the left painting and part on the right edge of the right one. The latter shows a rectangular water tank (note the reflections) and the other has what appears to be washing hanging out to dry. How was the water tank filled? Was it simply town laundresses[15] using the field as a drying ground? Or was it about retting and drying flax? Brown left no clues.

The drying ground for the town laundresses?

A horse-drawn society

Snaking over the Wolds into Louth are the turnpikes – the Dexthorpe from Bawtry, joined by the Lincoln turnpike at the double gate tollbar at South Elkington (just in view on the painting); the Louth turnpike from Horncastle (with Stanmore tollbar at the corner of Halfpenny Lane), and the Dexthorpe again coming down from Kenwick Bar. If that is the daily London Royal Mail coach Brown painted trotting across the Plough crossroads on Upgate, we can allow him a little artistic licence: the shadows are afternoon but the coach was due to arrive at the Masons Arms at 11.56am, according to the timetable of R. Fagg & Co who had the contract to run the service.[16] What a contrast Brown paints to the blizzard conditions of late December 1835 and early January 1836 when the Louth Mail was 'stopt by snow' on the Wolds south of Kenwick, the 'letter bags sent forward with the guard on a post-chaise and four'.

The London Royal Mail coach.

The Louth Mail stopt by snow, December 1835. Drawn by J Pollard.

Open landau in Mercer Row.

On Upgate (Dog and Duck pub on right).

In the yard of the Greyhound inn.

Leaving Louth along Bridge Street, Brown shows an open coach on the back of which he painted 'Grimsby – HULL – Louth'. This could have been the *Forester* operating daily from the White Swan or the *Pelham* from the Masons Arms. There is actually another coach on the Grimsby road near the junction with Fanthorpe Lane. Those coaches used the Scartho and Louth Turnpike from Hollowgate Head (the top of the cutting on the Grimsby Road) with the first toll at Brackenborough (later Cordeaux's) Corner.

There is a stage coach in the Market Place, but the other carriages Brown painted were private conveyances: the open landau with a gentleman and three ladies driving along Mercer Row, and on Bridge Street (near the church on the left painting) the landau with two liveried postillions, clearly of someone with means if not also title. Whoever was driving the carriage and pair along Westgate was heading for trouble: workmen have dug a hole in the road ahead and are standing discussing it!

The most charming depiction of fashionable transport in Louth is at the junction of Edward Street and Breakneck Lane: it is the latest cab-phaeton, which came to be known as the Victoria. When Brown painted the beginning of the railway age, the iron horse with carriages merely coach bodies on rail bogies, did he quite realise that the days of the stage coach were numbered?

There are no carriers' carts on the streets, but Brown chose not to paint a market day. However, there are two in the yard of the Royal Oak inn on Upgate (conveniently named on the roof of the building on the sketch). The landlord was William Wallis Gowthorpe and his yard was used on Wednesdays by carriers William Smith from Binbrook, John Thistlewood from Market Rasen, John Reed from Alford, and Martin Harnies and James Ingleby from North Thoresby. In the 1840s there were 31 carriers converging on Louth on market days from all parts of the hinterland painted on the Panorama. Teetotaller Brown might have been, but on the sketches he wrote the names of some of the many pubs – Boar's Head, Rising Sun, Fleece, (Crown &) Woolpack (Cornmarket), Greyhound, King's Head, Black Bull (Upgate), and even the humble Dog and Duck (facing the chancel of St James's and next to Dr Bogg's house on the corner of Upgate and Eastgate). Some names he also painted on the Panorama. Brown was a stickler for detail.

He illustrates the evils of drink with a drunk swigging from a beer bottle at the back of the Greyhound, and another being carried on a stretcher along Upgate. There are pigstyes and pigs in the yards of the Wheatsheaf and the Greyhound. And people on the church green and a man with a telescope on Church Walk look up at him sketching atop the spire.

Commercial activity is also apparent on the roads and streets: a timber waggon approaches on Crowtree Lane, laden hay or corn waggons along St Mary's Lane and High Holme Road, covered waggons can be seen in Eastgate and George Street, and there are other loaded carts in the town streets, with sacks being unloaded from one in the Cornmarket. Not omitting the sheep being driven along South Street, on their way to market or perhaps to pasture on the Marsh.

As much as anything therefore the Panorama is a record of a horse-drawn society, with the clatter of iron-shod hooves and wheels, and the dust, dirt and horse droppings, And Brown did not fail to record the water-carrier filling his cart in the mill dam on Bridge Street, preparatory to watering the dusty streets, the lack of which he had complained about in such caustic terms in 1839.

Landau and liveried postillions on Bridge Street.

A horse-drawn society

Waggon and delivery dray on Northgate.

The latest cab-phaeton, the Victoria.

A smart gig on Gospelgate.

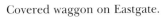

Covered waggon on Eastgate.

A laden cart approaches town along Breakneck Lane.

Elkington toll-gate.

Elkington toll-house and gates for two turnpikes, Dexthorpe (left) and Lincoln.
(Artist unknown).

Carriers' carts in the Royal Oak yard.

Johnson, Carrier, and side entrance
to New King's Head inn.

Having difficulty with a horse in the yard of the Bluestone inn.

Public buildings

We have already noted, in the decade before Brown prepared his panorama sketches, that there had been considerable building activity. Holy Trinity church, a chapel of ease, was built in 1834 at the far end of Eastgate to serve the growing population at the Riverhead,[17] and the Catholic chapel (as named by Brown and now St Mary's), at the corner of Upgate and Newmarket, was rebuilt and faced with stone in 1833 and the priest's house built in 1839. The nonconformist chapels, the Town Hall and the Corn Exchange have been considered in detail in earlier chapters. On the west face of the Town Hall, where the District Council office is now, are painted the words POLICE STATION. The British (Kidgate) School opened in 1841, has been referred to: it is on the left edge of the right painting. There were already two National Schools,[18] for boys (1811) in Westgate, and for Girls and Infants (1833-34) on Enginegate (Broadbank). The latter two-storey building is easily picked out on the Panorama as Brown depicts the children in the playground with two maypoles and a central circle of grass.

National Girls' and Infants' school.

Boys are in the playground of the Grammar School, clearly seen on Schoolhouse Lane (on the right painting). The bedehouses (occupying the ground floor with a separate yard) and schoolroom above were built in 1766. This is where Alfred Tennyson was an unhappy pupil from 1816 to 1820, unlike the carefree boys with a hoop in the lane. They needed to watch out though, for the man driving his gig towards them is waving them out of the way – an example of how Brown imbued his Panorama with life and a little drama. Within a decade of Brown's death, a new school was designed by James Fowler[19] and built in the playground before the old building was demolished so as not to interrupt the flow of education.

Grammar School.

On the right edge of the left panel is the grey D-shaped roof, with conical glass lantern, of the Public Building (1833), at the corner of Mercer Row and Butcher Lane. This building played a significant part in Brown's life. Many would be the time between 1834 and 1853 he climbed the circular stairs, lit by the roof lantern, to the meeting rooms of the Louth Mechanics' Institute on the top floor. It is not without significance that on the sketch at that level he wrote simply 'Mechanics'.

Impending drama on Schoolhouse Lane.

The building of a sessions house adjacent to the House of Correction, the Prison, was recorded by Brown in 1852. The tall prison, first built in 1680, rises above the trees down Eastgate. The complex comprised the governor's house, cells, a treadmill, the Petty Sessions Court and the new Sessions House, the prisoners kept in by a 23 feet high wall. The buildings were taken down in 1872 and the Orme Almshouses, designed by James Fowler, built on the site in 1885.[20] The Poor House or House of Industry was built in Padehole (Northgate) in 1734; on the Panorama it is part hidden behind the Primitive Methodist chapel. Perhaps the most prominent building on the Panorama is the three-storey Union Workhouse (left centre of the left painting). Designed by George Gilbert Scott, building started in 1837, and the first paupers were admitted in July the next year. The gatehouse entrance with Guardians' boardroom and a chapel is in white brick, and the main building in local red brick. The 'Union' served 86 parishes, most of them within the circle of the Panorama, and its prominent position served as a reminder of the shame of having to end up there. There was a school in the Workhouse and boys are shown in the high-walled recreation yard. The Workhouse closed in 1935, and re-opened as the County Infirmary in 1938.[21] At the time Brown was engaged on the Panorama, John Joseph Brian was the governor of the Prison with his wife Diana Earle as matron. At the Workhouse Thomas Sargent was Master and his wife Ann the matron, and they had charge of around two hundred paupers, of whom just over half were under 15 years of age.

Union Workhouse.

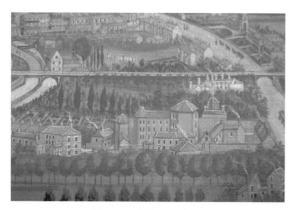

House of Correction.
(White building beyond is The Priory.)

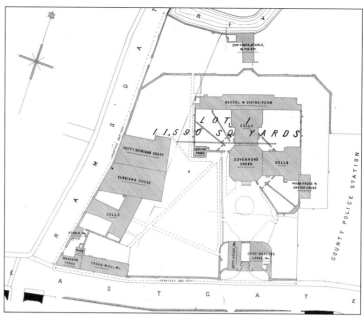

Plan of Prison, Courts and Treadmill, 1872.

Streets and shops

If you ascend the tower of St James's church to the gallery, you are at just over half the height from which Brown made his sketches. Looking out over the town and country you need reference points before you can appreciate the detail of the panoramic view before you. It was the same for Brown, and his starting point would be the pattern of streets and roads. He also had the advantage of another 130 feet in height, where less of the street pattern was hidden behind buildings. The ancient trackway of Louth (or Barton) Street – London Road – Upgate – Bridge Street – Grimsby Road – Fanthorpe Lane – is on both panels of the painting, with curved approaches (to reduce gradient) to the original ford across the Lud. On the right panel Westgate follows the natural curve of the river, in contrast to the straight George Street which was laid out towards the end of George III's reign (after the Enclosure Award). What shows clearly on the left painting are the planned parallel medieval streets of Chequergate-Northgate, Eastgate, and Mercer Row-Queen Street, and the open Cornmarket (formerly Butcher-market).

This is where the commercial core of town shops is found, and Brown obligingly identified a number of businesses by painting their names on the buildings in minute capitals. One of the easiest to read is that of his Methodist friend Abraham Gouldsborough MARSHALL (bookseller, stationer, bookbinder, printer and pawnbroker), with bow windows facing Mercer Row at the corner with Upgate. Looking along Mercer Row we find BANK (Garfit, Claypon & Co, now Lloyds TSB), SNOWDEN (Samuel and David, linen drapers and hatters), PRINTING OFFICE – H Hurton (Henry, bookseller, printer, bookbinder, stationer, paperhanging warehouse and patent medicine vendor), SUTTON & PETTINGER (linen and woollen drapers and hatters), and ASHTON (Thomas Showler) FLEECE Commercial INN. Brown's description of the shops on Mercer Row can be found in Chapter 4.

Continuing into the Market Place, from right to left are the shops of LEES (John Bailey, ironmonger), VICTORIA (HOUSE) BRADY (Robert Henry, linen draper),[22] JACKSON & Co (John and Thomas, booksellers, printers, bookbinders and stationers; publishers of *Poems by Two Brothers*, Alfred and

Marshall, bookseller & stationer on the corner of Mercer Row and Upgate.

Market Place.

Pulley and tackle for hoisting paper in Jackson's print works.
(ATS survey, August-September 1943).

The commercial core of the town.

Mercer Row.

Charles Tennyson, in 1827; now Oxfam), PEARSON (Henry Jackson, tailor, draper and hatter), GRAHAM & Co (baker and confectioner), MITCHELL (Richard) GROCER, and SIMPSON (John Henry, chemist and druggist).

Business names to be found in Bridge Street are HUBBARD (John, joiner and builder), DAN KEELING Hawker 1847,[23] HILL-GROCER and ALLISON (John, miller and baker); and in Westgate is PADDISON (William, boot and shoe maker) next to the Wheatsheaf inn. On Upgate are SUDBURY (John) Three Tuns and JOHNSON (Thomas) CARRIER (to Lincoln), both on the site of the present petrol filling station, and next to the Plough inn on London Road are the premises of George EMERSON, carpenter and builder. In Gospelgate is the stonemasons' yard of Thomas ABLEWHITE who was the master mason for the repairs to the church spire. Further along is the GEORGE INN, now demolished and replaced by a modern building; the publican in the 1840s was George James Marshall, but the name over the door is GRESSWELL (Dan), a veterinary surgeon who moved there from Lee Street.

George Inn.

Hubbard's timber yard.

Horn's tanyard.

Hallam's malthouse and beerhouse.

Esberger's coach building business, and their 1907 advert.

From his vantage point of three hundred feet, Brown could look down into the workyards of properties. The most obvious is in the foreground of the left painting, where men are unloading sawn timber in the yard of joiner and builder John Hubbard. Now turn from Bridge Street into Chequergate, and facing on the left are two signs on a building: HUNT'S • CHINA GLASS. This was James Hunt, a wheelwright employing three apprentices, who was also a grocer and glass and china dealer! He no doubt made wheels for ESBERGER Coach Maker, the other sign on the wall. The works of Frederick Esberger & Co can be seen along Ludgate to the left (the street no longer exists), with part-built coaches in the yard, the forge and bellows, and even a dog on a chain. There were 14 labourers, master coachbuilder Richard Mason lived in Ludgate and coachsmith David Esberger lived in nearby Healey's Court. Between the Court and the river is the tanyard, with its stack of hides, of William Horn, tanner and fellmonger: not the most pleasant aroma to have next to the National School.

Back to Chequergate and follow into Northgate. At the corner with Enginegate (Broadbank) is a single storey building: this is the Mapletoft and Hardie charity school for poor children, headmaster Samuel Cresswell who came to Louth from Dale Abbey, Derbyshire.[24] Brown even painted three boys outside the school. The next yard along on the left, with two hay or corn stacks and a three-storey malthouse, is that of John Hallam, maltster, ironmonger and farmer of 56 acres employing three men. He came to Louth from Stannington, Yorkshire, and his beerhouse became the Malt Shovel, later run by his widow Sarah; it is now inappropriately renamed the Miller's Daughter.

Details of all shops and trades are given in the Louth extract from White's *Lincolnshire Directory* for 1842. The numbers reveal the burgeoning nature of the town Brown painted, with the numbers in brackets those of ten years later: 18 (30) bakers, 30 (42) boot and shoe makers, 28 (38) butchers, 4 (12) confectioners, 12 (36) milliners and dressmakers, 20 (31) grocers and tea dealers, 6 (12) hatters, 23 (35) tailors – just to quote the most numerous of a wide range of shops and services. In most cases families lived above the shop.

At the other end of the scale from the grand houses of Westgate are the rows of working class terrace houses – on Newmarket, Church Street, Irish Hill (demolished), Spital Hill, Priory Road (was Union Court), Grays Road and Cannon Street Court (now a car park) for example. Brown's pictorial record shows what a close-knit town it was in the 1840s. It is also worth noting the number of grey roofs, a direct result of the import of slate along the navigation canal after 1770.

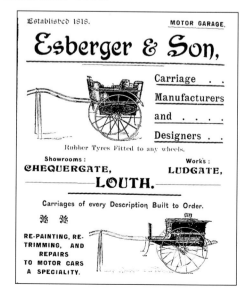

Workers' terrace housing on Irish Hill for Grounsell's agricultural implements works.

Industries

When Brown created his Panorama, Louth was the third largest town in Lincolnshire after Lincoln and Boston. It was 'the emporium of a rich grazing and agricultural district'.[25] Situated between Wolds and Marsh it was, and still is a market town, and developed industries to serve its hinterland, which Brown carefully recorded. The construction of the navigation canal, which opened to the Riverhead in 1770, bringing in timber, coal and 'groceries', and exporting corn and wool, generated industries such as malting and brewing, a ropery and a soapery, a tannery and a leather factory, making cattle cake and a bonemill.[26] Although the Riverhead is a mile from Brown's sketch point, he shows the complex of warehouses and factories, chimneys, windmill, terrace houses and the masts of boats in the basin. And out in the country are the sails of other sloops and keels navigating the canal to the sea lock at Tetney.

The import of coal was key to the establishment of iron founding and the making of agricultural implements. The three big firms in the town were William Grounsell, who made a patent drill, on Westgate (Brown painted his name over the entrance, at the foot of Irish Hill), John Sanderson – the factory with the tall chimney on the site of what is now Hawthorne Avenue, and William Watkinson, who was also a brassfounder, on Upgate.

In addition to two ropemakers at the Riverhead (John North and William Wray), and Luke Harrison Youle also making sails and waggon covers, there was (Elisha) RYALL'S ROPERY – the name painted on the building – along Eastgate on Priory Road. Brown and the teetotal movement had little effect on the growing number of breweries in the town: there were at least nine in the 1840s. Three were on Walkergate (Queen Street): William East (the name is on the panorama sketches), Robert Andrews, and Richard Luck and his son Peter.[27]

There was also water and wind power. Following the Lud from Hubbard's Hills, we find Chaplin's mill for grinding corn (then tenanted by Jonathan Swift); at Westgate bridge is the Thorpe Hall mill, where James Henry Carr had made paper until 1842 when it reverted to corn milling (and was later a trout farm);[28] on Bridge Street is Holland's mill, reconstructed in 1755 and run by Robert Foster; it had a breastshot wheel under the extension to the mill, just to the left of where the three boys are fishing in the tailrace; and at the bottom of Grays Road Brown painted a small waterwheel over the river, but we don't know what it powered. The next mill is the large carpet, rug and blanket manufactory (built in 1787) straddling the river and with a tall chimney. It had two waterwheels driving twenty machines. Adam Eve, who lived in James Street, had the lease from 1791 until he died in 1831. At the time of the

The Riverhead and navigation canal. The buildings in the distance are Saltfleet.

Thorpe Hall paper, later corn mill.

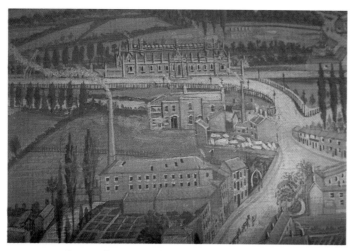

Carpet factory, with railway station beyond.

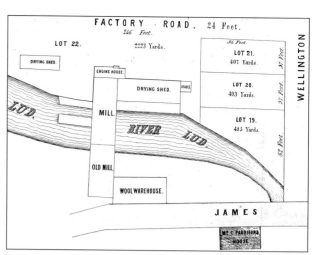

Plan of factory and grounds 1852.

The small waterwheel at the foot of Grays Road.

Panorama it was managed by Charles Paddison with a workforce of about sixty for carding, spinning, reeling, dyeing and weaving.[29] The grass paddock on the other side of the river was a drying ground for the wool. Carpets made in this factory are on display in Louth Museum. Finally to be seen on the Panorama is the watermill in Ramsgate Road (later Bryan Hall's and now flats).

Wind was the other power source, chiefly for grinding corn. The Panorama shows four brick tower mills, painted white with ogee caps and all except one with four sails, on higher ground on the edge of town. On the right painting are the slender five-storey mill on Little Lane, the distinctive five-sailed mill on Horncastle Road (run by James Scarborough), and the Julian Bower mill of John Bush Cox. On the other painting the five-storey black-tarred mill at the Riverhead ground bark for the tannery and was run by John Taylor Griffin, and there is a wooden post mill beyond the limekilns on St Mary's Lane. There are also two smaller tower mills at the brickyards of John Edwards on Monks Dyke and John Dales off Brackenborough Road, probably used for pumping water out of the clay pits, plus the small mill in nursery gardens on St. Mary's Lane which could have been a water pump.

However, Brown's sketches show two other windmills which are not on the Panorama. One was a tower mill at High Holme, to the right of the Union Workhouse; by the time Brown completed the painting the windmill had gone and there was an impressive three-storey house, High Holme, with an elaborate walled greenhouse at the end of a long garden. It became the residence of Henry Hynman Allenby, (son of

Julian Bower windmill.

Five-sail windmill on Horncastle Road.

114

Hynman Raddish Allenby of Kenwick House), and was later a ladies' boarding school run by the Misses Ann and Charlotte Chappell. The other was a wooden post mill on the other side of the Workhouse at the top of Grimsby Road hill, and was actually painted on the Panorama. It must have been taken down in the late 1840s, when Brown painted it out but left a 'ghost' of it in the paint texture. Not a vestige of any of the windmills remain today.

Lime burning was a major industry in Louth from the time coal became available by canal, and the white chalk quarry faces show up on both panels of the Panorama. There were nine limeburners producing mainly agricultural lime. On London Road was the Julian Bower Lime Works of Samuel Appleby and Charles Mumby, and a smaller pit on the other side of the road (now Quarryside). William Hurst had a small pit at the top of Aswell Street (hence the steep rise to Newmarket). Richard Hurley and his son Joseph Cradock branched out from being grocers in the 1840s to whiting manufacture in the Saturday Pits on Kenwick Road, with cottages for manager and workers. Chalk was ground in water and dried into ball whiting. The works and cottages are on the Panorama, beyond the grey-slated Southfield House, home of grocer Benjamin Hyde, conveniently identified by name for us on Brown's sketch. On the left panel, on St Mary's Lane, are the limekilns of George and Thomas Tatam; their directory address was Limekiln-hill. Brown painted a workman top-loading the kilns with alternate layers of chalk and coal. Bungalows now occupy the site.[30]

The 'ghost' of the wooden post mill Brown painted out of the Panorama.

Tatam's limeworks on St Mary's Lane, with close-up of the kilns being top-loaded

The lime quarries on London Road – the oldest in the town. Chalk was taken from here in the 12th and 13th centuries for the building of Louth Park Abbey.

Sheep being droved along South Street to the market pens near the Boar's Head inn on Newmarket.

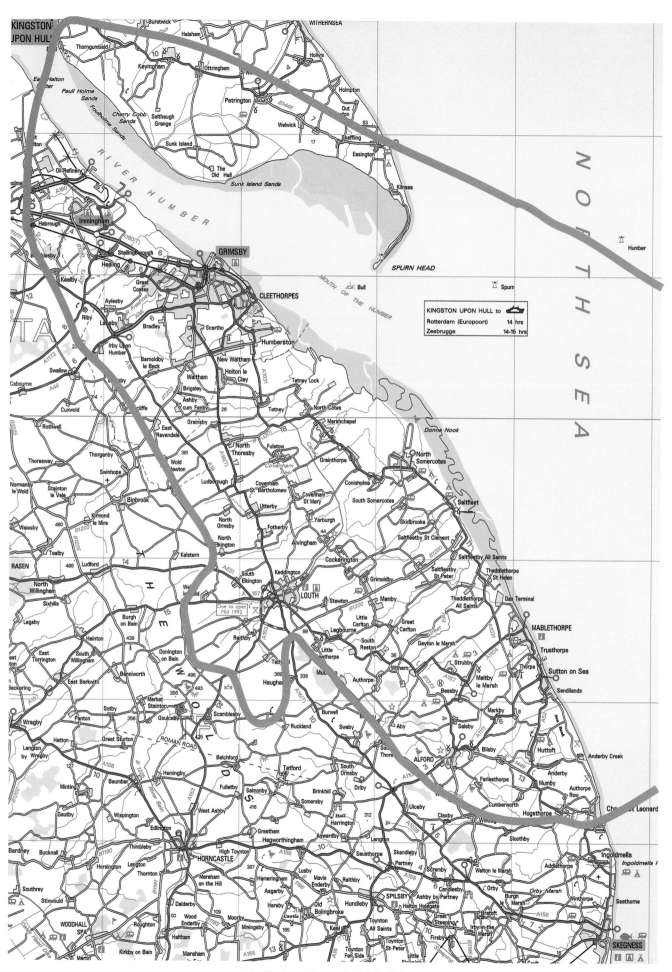

The limits of Brown's field of view.
Reproduced by permission of Ordnance Survey on behalf of The Controller of Her Majesty's Stationery Office
© Crown Copyright. MC 100033809.

In the distance

We have already commented on Brown's clever anticipation of the opening of the East Lincolnshire railway, and his skill of incorporating it on the painting between 1847 (see below) and the showings of the Panorama in 1848 and 1856. What we have therefore is a train of first and second class carriages, goods and third class wagons and more goods wagons, a load of some twenty vehicles, steaming south; the Keddington Road crossing, a large goods shed, the railway station, bridges over Ramsgate, the River Lud and Eastgate, and the Monks Dyke crossing with crossing keeper's house; with another train steaming north, which trails back onto the right panel.

From an early East Lincolnshire Railway timetable.

Beyond are the Marsh villages, with churches, windmills, prominent buildings and scattered farms, a sweep from Utterby to Well near Alford, and all carefully named on the sketches – vital evidence in confirming one's line of sight. However, it is not too difficult to identify, for example, the old Fotherby church (St Mary's; demolished in 1863 and replaced by a James Fowler design),[31] the whitewashed St Edith's church and the Hall at Little Grimsby, two churches in the same churchyard at Alvingham,[32] and the exaggerated spire of St Peter's at South Somercotes. Less easy to detect are All Saints church and the Abbey (house) at Legbourne, and the two white marks to the north-east which are all that remained of the chalk core of the chancel walls of Louth Park Abbey. On the sketch Brown wrote 'Abbey Ruins'; only one wall, the south, is upstanding today.

Little Grimsby Hall with St Edith's church (left).

Looking over the Wolds, on the left panel a broad light brown strip extends across Elkington Cowpasture towards the new Italianate Elkington Hall in grey brick, designed by W A Nicholson[33] and built in 1841, the seat of Rev William Smyth. Beyond is a windmill on the horizon towards Kelstern. To the left of that Brown marked Girsby Wood on the sketch, but on the painting the land rises strangely and therefore the horizon does not fit the right edge of the right painting (although the sketches show a perfect match). Continuing on the right painting, roads snake over the Wolds to Donington on Bain and Market Stainton, and to Horncastle past Slates (Raithby) Farm. Showing next on the horizon is the tall Government Observatory (see Chapter 3), then the elegant spire of All Saints, Haugham, clearly a copy in miniature of the Louth spire by G R Willoughby,[34] and finally the Kenwick Toll Bar on the London Road.

All that remains today of Louth Park Abbey.

The coastline extends from the Humber above Grimsby to Chapel (St Leonards; 17 miles from Louth), which is named on the sketch. Also on the sketch beyond Huttoft is the outline of two towers on the horizon, but these are barely discernible on the painting. Moving north on the left painting, on the edge are Trusthorpe church and windmill, and a red flag, probably the coastguard station. A few buildings mark Mablethorpe, and then undulating grass covered sand-dunes now a National Nature Reserve.[35] Next is a group of red brick buildings, including the three-storey New Inn, on the dunes: this is the port and sea bathing resort of Saltfleet,[36] together with a beacon pole on Toby's Hill.

The sweep back to the Humber, past the beacon at Donna Nook, brings us to view the canal warehouses at Tetney Lock (nearly in line with Spurn lighthouse). The rather exaggerated hump in the ground (compared with the sketch) is the higher land at Cleethorpes, and then the new red brick Grimsby Dock Tower (1852; which Brown also put on the sketch). He must have had some days of really good visibility to record the detail on the Yorkshire side of the Humber: the spire of Patrington church and the square tower of Hedon church (22 miles from Louth), and half a dozen windmills. On Spurn Point we can see the 90 feet red brick lighthouse built by John Smeaton in 1776, and the auxiliary navigation beacons.[37]

Elkington Hall, with All Saints church beyond.

Donna Nook beacon is right centre. Sails in the foreground are boats on the navigation canal.

The spire of South Somercotes church is on the left. To the right are the houses of Saltfleet on the dunes, including the tall New Inn.

Donna Nook Beacon.

Out to sea the ships of the Royal Squadron, seen off Spurn by Brown on 2 October 1844, are but specks on the horizon on both sketch and Panorama. An opera glass, as he put in his advertisement, would certainly be needed to see them when the paintings were exhibited in the Mansion House. What Brown did add to the paintings were a number of sailing barques and smaller coastwise craft, including one with auxiliary steam as it progressed out of the Humber. His paintings of the ships and the billowing attitude of the sails, though minute, are accurate and consistent with the prevailing breeze he applied to other aspects of the Panorama.

Both panels of the Panorama are signed, on a brown (!) roof, the clearest in the lower left corner of the left painting:

**W^M BROWN. LOUTH. Drew &
Painted, 1847.**

LOUTH DIRECTORY 1849

GENTRY.

Adlard Mr. Thomas, Broad bank
Alington Mrs. West gate
Allen Mr. George, Victoria terrace
Allen Mr. John B. South street
Allenby Mr. John, Lee street
Allison William Grant, esq. West gate
Ansell Mrs. Mary Sophia, West gate
Ashton Mr. Edward, New market ter
Baker Mr. Henry Fitzwilliam, James st
Banks John Tatam, esq. Stewton house
Barker Rev. John Theodore [Independent], Lee street
Beach Rev. John H. [Wesleyan], Lee st
Bellwood Mr. Charles, West gate
Blathwayt William, esq. Up gate
Bogg John, esq. East gate
Bond Mr. Christopher, Up gate
Bourne Mr. John, North gate
Bourne Septimus, esq. Mercer row
Brady Mrs. Matilda, Union hill
Brickhill Mrs. Bridge street
Buckeridge Rev. R. [curate], South st
Bumstead Rev. J. [Wesleyan], Nichol hl
Burgess Mrs. Jane, Up gate
Byron Christopher, esq. New street
Byron Mrs. Broad bank
Cartwright Thos. Turnill, esq. Up gate
Chapman Mr. John, West gate
Coulam Mrs. Rebecca, East gate
Cross Mr. Thomas Leech, Up gate

Dale Rev. Thos. Aquila, B.A. Bridge st
Dalton Mr. Robert, South street
Denniston John, esq. Trinity terrace
Ditchett William Day, esq. Up gate
Dymock Archibald, esq. West gate
Egremont Mrs. West gate
Egremont Mrs. Godfrey, West gate
Emeris Mrs. West gate
Emeris Miss, Crowtree lane
Falkner Henry, esq. Trinity terrace
Farrow Mrs. North gate
Fowler Mrs. Mary, Up gate
Fredlington Mr. David, East gate
Furlong Misses, West gate
Gace Miss, West gate
Goe Field Flowers, esq. Bridge street
Goy Henry Cox, esq. Up gate
Grant Mrs. John, Lee street
Grant Thomas, sen. esq. Nichol hill
Grant Thomas, jun. esq. West gate
Griffin Mr. William, South street
Hall Rev. Henry [Catholic], Up gate
Hannath John, esq. South street
Harneis Mrs. Mary, West gate
Hildyard Isle Grant, esq. West gate
Hodgson Grantham, esq. Market place
Hubbert Mr. William, George street
Hudson Mrs. Hannah, Up gate
Hudson Thomas, esq. Chequer gate
Hunt Mr. Baxter, New market terrace
Hyde William, sen. esq. Park place

Hyde William, jun. esq. West gate
Ingham Rev. Richard [Baptist], New market terrace
Ingoldby Christopher, sen. esq. South st
Ingoldby Christophr. jun.esq.Trinity ter
Jackson Mr. John, sen. Up gate
James Thomas, esq. Up gate
Johnson Henry Allen, esq. Lee street
Kiddall Rev. James [Baptist], Up gate
Kime Miss Sarah, Walker gate
Larder Mr. Joseph, sen. West gate
Lister Mrs. South street
Loft Mrs. Ramsgate
Longbottom Mr. Michael, Up gate
Lucas Mrs. Elizabeth, James street
Lucas St. John Wells, esq. Gospel gate
Ludlam Mrs. Mary, Bridge street
Mantell Rev. Edward Reginald, M.A. [vicar], West gate
Marsden Rev. Wm. Delabene, James st
Morley Miss Ann, East gate
Nevitt William, esq. West gate
Newbald Henry, esq. West gate
Norris Mrs. Susannah, West gate
Norton Rev. John Hutchinson [Wesleyan], Up gate
Odling Mrs. Susannah, South street
Orme Mrs. esq. Chequer gate
Overton Miss, South street
Overton Mrs. Helen Martha, West gate
Paddison Mrs. Ann, White house

Parker Cornelius, esq. West gate
Peters Miss Charlotte, East gate
Pettener Misses Elzbth.&Ann,Bridge st
Philbrick Thomas, esq. Bridge street
Prescott Rev. John, M.A. Trinity ter
Preston Mrs. Harriet, West gate
Pye Henry, esq. West gate
Richardson Rev. Edmund, Trinity ter
Robinson Mrs. Sarah, West gate
Rule Rev. William Harris [Wesleyan], Lee street
Samuel Mr. Samuel, London road

Searle Maurice, esq. West gate
Sharpley John Booth, esq. East gate
Sooby Mrs. Elizabeth, George street
Strachan Rev. Alexander [Wesleyan], Nichol hill
Tate Frederick Septimus, esq. Up gate
Taylor Mrs. Ann, South street
Thimbleby Mr. William, East gate
Thorold Mrs. River head
Topham Mrs. Jane, Up gate
Toynbee Samuel, esq. East gate
Trought Samuel, esq. Mercer row

Waite Rev. John, M.A. Edward street
Waite Rev. John Deane,M.A.Edward st
Waite Thos. Phillips, esq.§West gate
Ward Mrs. James street
Wemyss Mrs. George street
Wilson James William,esq. West gate
Wilson Miss, West gate
Wimberley Rev. Conrad Makings, B.A. Trinity terrace
Yolland Mrs. Up gate
Young John, esq. Home cottage
Young Mrs. Ann, Up gate

TRADERS.

Ablewhite Thomas, stone & marble mason, Gospel gate
Ablewhite Thomas Ranson, grocer, Walker gate
Adamson Thomas, auctioneer, Aswell lane
Adlard Charles, grocer, Walker gate
Adlard James, watch maker, East gate
Allenby & Bourne, solicitors, Mercer row
Allison & Co. wine & brandy merchants, Corn market
Allison John, miller & baker, James street
Allison William Grant, solicitor, & clerk to the Louth gas light company, & agent to the County fire & to the Crown life assurances, Mercer row
Anderson David, tailor, East gate
Andrews Frow, chemist & druggist, Market place
Andrews Holland, baker, Gospel gate
Andrews Robert, brewer & maltster, Walker gate
Arliss John, butcher, Walker gate
Armitage & Son, coal & corn merchants, & wharfingers, River head
Armitage William, operative chemist,& railway signal manufacturer, East gate
Ashley Thomas, blacksmith, Cannon street
Ashton Mrs. Elizabeth, farmer, Grimsby road
Ashton John, farmer, Grimsby road
Ashton Richard, hairdresser, Corn market
Ashton Richard, turner, &c. Kid gate
Ashton Thomas Showler, farmer, Up gate
Ashton William, ironmonger, & agent to the Clerical, Medical & General life assurance, Market place
Ashton William, boot & shoe maker, East gate
Askey Thomas, tailor & draper, East gate
Atkin John, carpenter, Engine gate
Atkinson Newby, miller & baker, Maiden row
Atkinson Plant, baker, Up gate
Baines George, grocer, Mercer row
Baines Joseph, baker, Mercer row
Bains William, agricultural implement manufacturer & wire worker, Up gate
Baldock William, ' Crown & Woolpack,' New street
Banks John Tatam, physician, Stewton house
Barker Joseph, boot & shoe maker, Nichol hill
Barnes Shadrach, butcher, James street
Barnes Thomas, butcher, Nichol hill
Barret & Co. tobacconists, &c. East gate
Batterham Nathaniel Hammond, linen & woollen draper, East gate
Beaumont William, wheelwright, Paradise road
Bee Thomas, beer retailer, New market
Beech William, tailor, Walker gate
Beedall James, grocer, East gate
Beeten&Annison (Misses),ladies' boarding school,North gate
Bellamy Nicholas Pearson,plumber & brickmaker, Up gate
Bellatti James, tinman & brazier, East gate
Bingham John, tailor, Corn market
Birkett Jonathan, agent to the Alliance fire & life assurance, Corn market
Birkett Joseph, grocer, East gate
Blair James, grocer, East gate
Blakelock & Son, saddle & harness makers, Market place
Blakelock Thomas, boot & shoe maker, East gate
Blanchard John Taylor, grocer, New street
Blanchard Edward, grocer, East gate
Blathwayt William, surgeon, Up gate
Blow Charles, butcher, Broad bank
Bogg John, surgeon, East gate
Bond Charles, surveyor of taxes, Up gate
Bond John, jun. butcher, Market place
Bond William, farmer, Walker gate
Booth John, coal dealer, Walker gate
Boothby & Son, boot & shoe warehouse, & patten & clog makers, Market place
Borrows Frederick, wheelwright, New market
Boswell Edward, basket maker, East gate

Bourne & Co. tailors & woollendrapers, Mercer row
Bourne Septimus, solicitor, & agent to the Nottinghamshire & Derbyshire fire & life assurance, Mercer row
Bourne William, land surveyor, Public buildings
Brady Robert Henry, linendraper, Market place
Bratley Smith, beer retailer, West gate
Brett Mrs. Elizabeth, grocer, Aswell lane
Brett William, tailor, linendraper & hatmaker, Mercer row
Brewster George, boot & shoe maker, East gate
Briggs Benjamin, wholesale druggist, Mercer row
Broadley John, boot & shoe maker, Mercer row
Broadley John, hairdresser & glover, New street
Broddell Thomas, baker, Cistern gate
Brotherton & Co. linen & woollen drapers, & hatters, Market place
Brown Charles, boot & shoe maker, Aswell lane
Brown Mrs. Ann, porter & spirit merchant, East gate
Brown Mrs. Francis, lodging house keeper, Up gate
Brown Samuel, carpenter & wheelwright, River head
Brown William, painter, Vicker's lane
Brumpton Misses Sarah & Mary, milliners & dressmakers, North gate
Bryan John, currier & leather cutter, East gate
Burke John, tailor, Aswell lane
Burnett John & Henry, boot & shoe makers, Kid gate
Burton George, tailor, East gate
Burton John, saddle & harness maker, Up gate
Burton Mrs. John, lodging house keeper, Up gate
Burton Thomas, tailor, Up gate
Bush & Co. painters & house decorators, Bridge street
Butterfield Francis, surgeon, Walker gate
Byron Christopher, solicitor, & agent to the North of England fire & life assurance, New street
Campbell, Bowmar & Ranshaw, linen & woollen drapers, man's mercers,&c. Market place
Campion Henry, fishmonger, Up gate
Carratt John, blacksmith, Kid gate
Carritt William, chemist & druggist, & grocer, Corn market
Carter Charles John, architect & surveyor, Up gate
Cartwright Edward, farmer, Keddington road
Cartwright Salah, ironmonger, Corn market
Cash & Meanwell, general carriers, Walker gate
Catling Mrs. Grace, milliner, Market place
Chapman William, beer retailer, River head
Clapham Thomas, ' Wheatsheaf,' West gate
Clark George, ' White Swan,' East gate
Clark William, beer retailer, River head
Clarkson Richard, ' Ship & Horns,' East gate
Clipsham Michael, blacksmith, River head
Cocking Thomas, nurseryman & seedsman, Mercer row
Colam William, carpenter, London road
Colbeck Joseph, blacksmith, Lud gate
Cole Mark, butcher, River head
Cole Thomas, eating house, Mercer row
Cole Thomas, farmer
Collis Chas. Smith, saddle & harness maker, East gate
Cotten George, boot & shoe maker, James street
Coulam Henry, builder & cabinet maker, East gate
Coulam William, builder & cabinet maker, East gate
Coulbeck John, wheelwright, Engine gate
Coultan Thomas, shopkeeper, Aswell lane
Coviller Mrs. Ann, ironmonger, Corn market
Cowley Mrs. Ellen, china, glass, & earthenware dealer, Market place
Cox John Bush, miller, Julian bower
Crampton James, cabinet maker, Aswell lane
Crashley Mrs. Mary, beer retailer, Walker gate
Cresswell Samuel, classical & commercial academy, North gt
Croft James & Co. tailors & drapers, Walker gate
Croft David, tailor, East gate
Croft Thomas, painter, East gate
Crofts Francis, boot & shoe maker, Mercer row
Crofts Richard, tailor, East gate

Cropper Robert, surveyor of roads, South cottage, South st
Crow Vincent Cross, '*Black Bull*,' Up gate
Dales Benjamin, sen. builder, Broad bank
Dales Benjamin, jun. cabinet maker, upholsterer, & builder, East gate
Dales John, builder & brick & tile maker, West gate
Dales John, grocer, River head
Dales William, bricklayer, Bridge street
Darby Thomas & Son, veterinary surgeons, Walker gate
Davey Jonathan, bed & mattress maker, North gate
Davis William, carver & gilder, looking glass & picture frame maker, & printseller, East gate
Dawson John, boot & shoe maker, Lee street
Dawson John Wood, butcher, East gate
Dawson Simpson Clark, grocer & butcher, River head
Dawson William, broker, East gate
Dawson Wm. Bennet, butcher, East gate
Day John, shopkeeper, Up gate
Day William, '*Woolpack*,' River head
Dean Henry, butcher, Gospel gate
Ditchett William Day, surgeon, Up gate
Dixon Joseph, wheelwright, Bridge street
Dobbs William, baker, Lee street
Dodson Edmund, boot & shoe maker, Corn market
Dodson Edwin, gun maker & bellhanger, Up gate
Dowse Edward, basket maker, East gate
Dowse Francis, plumber & glazier, East gate
Dowse William, basket maker, Bridge street
Drew William, brewer, Cistern gate
Dunham Thomas, beer retailer, James street
Dunn Wm. Allison, sub-distributor of stamps, Corn market
Dyas George, blacksmith, East gate
Dyas Richard, builder, James street
Dymock Archibald, physician, West gate
Earl William, tailor & grocer, Aswell lane
East William, brewer & maltster, Maiden row & Walker gate
Edwards William, printer, bookbinder, bookseller & stationer, & agent to the Church of England fire & life assurance, Corn market
Elliott William, stone mason, Engine gate
Emerson George, carpenter & builder, London road
Emerson George, jun. coal & coke merchant, River head
England William, miller & baker, East gate
Esberger Frederick & Co. coach builders, Lud gate
Evison John, butcher, Walker gate
Fairweather John, tailor, East gate
Falkner Henry, solicitor, vestry clerk, master extraordinary in Chancery, & commissioner for taking affidavits in law courts, & agent to the Norwich fire & life assurance, East gate
Fanthorpe John, glass & china dealer, East gate
Farrow Wm. road & land surveyor, Walker gate
Flinders Miss Henrietta, milliner & dressmaker, Up gate
Forman Henry, confectioner, Market place
Forman Mrs. Kezia, dressmaker, Market place
Forman Thos. baker, confectioner, & dining rooms, East gate
Foster Frederick, tailor, Corn market
Foster Mrs. Frances, eating house, Aswell lane
Foster Preston, tailor, Walker gate
Foster William, builder, West gate
Freeman Thomas, patten, clog & last maker, East gate
Freeman William, last & patten maker, James street
French Mrs. Elizabeth, '*Pack Horse*,' East gate
Furnish William, boot & shoe maker, North gate
Garfit, Claypons & Garfits, bankers, Mercer row
Garnet William, shopkeeper, Walker gate
Gelsthorp Mrs. Jane, straw bonnet maker, East gate
Gelsthorpe John, fellmonger & tanner, Walker gate
Gibson Abraham, miller & baker, East gate
Gillot John, beer retailer, New market
Girdham William, boot & shoe maker, East gate
Glazier Mrs. Jemima, baker, Aswell lane
Goddard William, carpenter, New market
Goe & Wilson, solicitors, West gate
Good Edward, cooper, Aswell lane
Gowthorpe Wm. Wallis, butcher, East gate
Goy Henry Cox, solicitor, & agent to the General fire & life assurance, Up gate
Graham & Ashton, bakers & confectioners, Market place
Grant Thomas, jun. solicitor, & treasurer to the Louth Gas company, & to the Louth Turnpike trust; commissioner for taking acknowledgments of married women, & agent to the Imperial fire & life assurance, & to the Globe fire & life assurance, West gate
Graves Henry, baker, Walker gate
Graves Robert, corn, coal & timber merchant, River head

Gray Charles, bookseller, Up gate
Gray Miss Rebecca, ladies' boarding school, West gate
Gray William Henry, boot & shoe maker, Market place
Green John, grocer, Aswell lane
Green Mrs. Sarah, beer retailer, Pade hole
Green Robert, ironmonger & bar iron merchant, Market pl
Greenwood Mrs. Sarah, grocer, East gate
Gresham John & Co. woollen drapers, hatters, & tailors, & ready made clothes warehouse, Corn market
Gresswell Dan, veterinary surgeon, George street
Griffin John Taylor, miller & baker, East gate
Grounsell William, ironfounder & agricultural implement manufacturer, West gate
Grundy William, blacksmith, East gate
Gunnil James, blacksmith, River head
Gustard John Robert, cabinet maker, East gate
Hackford Edward, miller & baker, East gate
Hall & Robinson, brewers, North gate
Hall Charles, beer retailer, North gate
Hall John, butcher, Aswell lane
Hall William, baker, Up gate
Hall William, currier & leather cutter, North gate
Hallam John, ironmonger, tinplate wrkr. & maltster, Mercer rw
Hampson Kenric, baker & corn chandler, Bridge street
Harness Benjamin, tailor & hatter, East gate
Harrison James, beer retailer, Walker gate
Harrison James, butcher, East gate
Harrison Lambert, dyer, East gate
Harrison Thomas, brewer, Rams gate
Harper Alfred, watch & clock maker, Kid gate
Harvey John, eating house, East gate
Hawson John, hatter & furrier, East gate
Headland William, tailor, Aswell lane
Heath William, inspector of weights & measures, Mercer rw
Heaton Joseph, tailor, Brackenborough gate
Hempstock Benjamin, saddle & harness maker, Mercer row
Herringshaw William, grocer, East gate
Hewson Robert, '*Royal Oak*,' Up gate
Hewson Thomas, builder, Broad bank
Hewison John, Temperance coffee house
Hildyard Isle Grant, surgeon, West gate
Hill Michael, grocer, East gate
Hill William, blacksmith, West gate
Hobson Isaac, bookbinder, North gate
Hodgson John, blacksmith, New market
Hogg Joseph, fishmonger & cheese & bacon dealer, East gate
Holden John, grocer, East gate
Holroyd Wm. Henry, dyer, Walker gate
Hopper Henry, shopkeeper, Cistern gate
Househam John, miller & baker, James street
Howard Samuel, farmer, Up gate
Hoyland William, professor of music, Nichol hill
Hoyle Richard, tanner, currier & leather cutter, Bridge st
Hubbard John, cabinet maker & grocer, Bridge street
Hubbard Richard, engraver & lithographic printer, New st
Hunt James, grocer, wheelwright, & china & glass dealer, Chequer gate
Hunter William, grocer, East gate
Hurley Richard, grocer & confectioner, East gate
Hurst John, chemist & druggist, & sharebroker, Mercer row
Hurton Henry, bookseller, printer, bookbinder, stationer, paperhanging warehouse, pat. medicine vendor, Mercr. rw
Hutchinson Thomas, '*Black Horse*,' Aswell lane
Hyde, Smith & Tate, grocers, soap makers & tallow chandlers, Up gate
Ingoldby Christopher & Son, solicitors & agents to the London fire & life assurance, South street
Ingoldby Christopher, jun. solicitor, town clerk & clerk to the Borough magistrates, South street
Jacklin William, confectioner, Walker gate
Jackson John & Thomas, booksellers, printers, bookbinders & stationers, Market place
Jackson John, agent to the Atlas fire & life ass. Market place
Jackson Thomas, auctioneer & appraiser, & land agt. Market pl
Jackson William, coal & corn merchant, East gate
James Thomas, surgeon, Up gate
Johnson Charles, beer retailer, Maiden row
Johnson Henry Allen, surgeon, Lee street
Johnson Thomas, carrier to Lincoln, Up gate
Kemp & Gilson, tanners & fellmongers, North gate
Kew Jonathan, gun maker, Mercer row
Kew William, hairdresser, Up gate
Kew William, hairdresser & perfumer, East gate
Kidd Thos. Dowse, cabinet maker & builder, Walker gate
Kime Joshua, butcher, East gate
King John, carter, East gate

Kirk Benjamin, tinman & brazier, Aswell lane
Kirk John, blacksmith, Pade hole
Kirk William, blacksmith, New market
Kitching William, grocer & provision dealer, Mercer row
Lambert Robert, shopkeeper, Cistern gate
Langworth Edmund, hairdresser, East gate
Larder Joseph, jun. grocer & provision dealer, Mercer row
Larder West, limeburner, Broad bank
Lawrence Teft, watch & clock maker, Walker gate
Leak Edward, builder, East gate
Leak Mrs. Mary, builder, East gate
Leake & Darnill, plumbers & glaziers, James street
Lees John Bailey, ironmonger, Market place
Levitt John, stone & marble mason, Up gate
Lill William, baker, North gate
Lincoln & Lindsey Banking Company (Mr. John Nesbitt, manager),Corn market; draw on Prescott,Grote&Co.Lndn
Longbottom Barnard, linendraper, Up gate
Lucas Chas. Edward & Brothers, wine & spirit, & ale & porter merchants, Corn market
Lucas Charles Edward, agent to the Pelican life, the Phœnix fire, & the Scottish Equitable life ass. Corn market
Lucas Lionel Richard, agent to the British Guarantee association, Corn market
Lucas St. John Wells, surgeon, Gospel gate
Luck Peter, brewer, Walker gate
Lundie William, plumber & glazier, Walker gate
Mackinder Charles, blacksmith, Walker gate
Maddison Charles, builder & cabinet maker, Up gate
Malam William, beer retailer, Up gate
Maltby Joseph, farmer, Grimsby road
Marfleet William, farmer, Vicarage farm
Markham John, auctioneer & beer retailer, Rams gate
Markham Thomas, coach builder & house & ornamental painter, Corn market
Marris John, ivory & wood turner, East gate
Marshall Abraham Goulsborough, bookseller & stationer, bookbinder, printer, & pawnbroker, Mercer row
Marshall George James, *George inn*, Gospel gate
Mason Wright, chemist & druggist, Up gate
Mawer James, grocer, Kid gate
Mawer Thomas, grocer & cheese & bacon factor, East gate
Mawer William, hairdresser & glover, East gate
Meanwell John, ' *Ship*,' River head
Middleton George, cabinet maker, East gate
Miller William, turner, Vicker's lane
Milson James, carter, West gate
Mitchell Richard, grocer & provision dealer, Market place
Mitchell Richard, *Masons' Arms commercial inn & posting house*, Corn market
Moncaster Robert, brewer, Kid gate
Morton Charles Wilson, grocer, East gate
Morton Joseph, ironmonger, ironfounder, bar iron merchant & tin plate worker, East gate
Morton Mrs. Jane, ' *Turk's Head*,' Aswell lane
Mountain Charles, furniture broker, Corn market
Musgrave Philip, maltster, Louth
Musson Balthasar, watch & clock maker, East gate
Myers Louis, london, birmingham &sheffield war.Mercr.row
Naylor John, shopkeeper, River head
Naylor William, grocer, Gospel gate
Nell William,corn&coal mer.wharfinger&shipbldr.Rivr.head
Nelthorpe John, surgeon, Trinity terrace
Nesbitt John, agent to the Yorkshire fire & life assurance & mangr. to the Lincoln & Lindsey banking comp.Corn mkt
Newman William, miller,corn merchant,&bone crshr.East gt
Norfolk Robert, miller, corn & coal merchant, & linseed & bone crusher, River head
North John, ropemaker, Ramsgate
Northend Mrs. Mary, worsted manufacturer, West gate
Norton & Gray, coach builders, Walker gate
Norton Hugh, grocer & cabinet maker, James street
Norton Mrs. Brancby, brazier & confectioner, East gate
Nundy Thomas, ' *New Rein Deer*,' Market place
Oates Thomas, cutler, Aswell lane
Odling Edward, baker, Walker gate
Odling Edward, saddle & harness maker, Corn market
Oliver George, brazier & tinplate worker, East gate
Orme Henry, solicitor, clerk to the paving & lighting commissioners, commissioner for taking acknowledgments of married women, & agent to the West of England fire & life assurance, Chequer gate
Overton & East, corn & coal merchants, & spirit merchants, East gate
Overton Thomas, wine merchant, East gate
Paddison Charles, carpet, rug & blanket manuftr. James st

Paddison William, boot & shoe maker, West gate
Parker James William, clerk to commissioners of assessed taxes, New market
Parkin William, accountant, seed merchant, agent to the Royal Exchange fire & life assurance, & registrar of births & deaths for the Louth district, Edward street
Pearce George, brazier & tinplate worker, East gate
Pearson William & Son, millers, bakers & cornfctrs. East gt
Pearson George, boot & shoe maker, Aswell lane
Pearson Henry Jackson, tailor, draper & hatter, Market pl
Pearson John, watchmaker & jeweller, Corn market
Pearson William, chemist & druggist, & grocer, Market pl
Pettinger Thos. Blanchard, auctioneer & appraiser, & furniture broker, Up gate
Philbrick & Tate, surgeons, Bridge street
Phillipson John, butcher, Corn market
Phillipson William, butcher, Corn market
Pickering Thomas, builder, James street
Pickford & Co. railway carriers (Patrick McKeevor, agent), Walker gate
Pipe Allen, supervisor of excise, South street
Plaskitt Michael, linen & woollen draper, tailor, straw bonnet manuf. & agent to the Star fire & life as.Market pl
Portas Mrs. Rebecca, ' *Rising Sun*,' Walker gate
Porter John, accountant & reg.of marriages forLth.Wst.gte
Porteus Henry, butcher, Walker gate
Potter William, grocer & tallow chandler, Mercer row
Proctor William, boot & shoe maker & beer ret. Aswell lane
Pullon William, cork cutter, West gate
Pye, Waite & Newbald, solicitors, & agents to the Sun fire & life assurance, Gospel gate
Rains William, harness maker, New market
Reed Henry, patten & clog maker, Up gate
Reed Matthias, cabinet maker &builder, Walker gate
Renison Charles, baker, Maiden row
Renison Thomas, cabinet maker, Aswell lane
Richardson Bankey, bricklayer, North gate
Richardson Joseph, ' *Old Rein Deer*,' Mercer row
Richardson Thomas, tailor, Kid gate
Rickit Stephen, *Blue Stone tavern*, Up gate
Rickit Mrs. Caroline, milliner, New street
Rickit William, posting, hearse, & funeral carriage depôt, *Blue Stone tavern*, Up gate, & at New street
Robinson John, butcher, Mercer row
Robson John, chemist & druggist, Market place
Rogers Alexander Tallent, classical & commercial boarding school, the Priory
Rogerson John, rope maker, River head
Roper William, boot & shoe maker, North gate
Ryall Elisha & William, saddle & harness mak. Market pl
Ryall Elisha, rope & twine maker, Market place
Ryall Richard, builder, Up gate
Ryley Benjamin, grocer, Up gate
Ryley Charles, watch & clock maker, Up gate
Ryley Charles Hunter, maltster, Walker gate
Ryley James Hunter, stone & marble mason, & brick maker, Chequer gate
Rysdale William, boot & shoe maker, Chequer gate
Samuel Abraham, watch & clock maker, silversmith & jeweller, Mercer row
Sanderson John, sen. millwright, Ramsgate
Sanderson John, ironfounder, millwright, & agricultural implement manufacturer, Broad bank
Satchwell John, cooper, Kid gate
Saunby John, ' *Woodman*,' East gate
Scarborough James, carter, New market
Scott Charles, beer retailer, London road
Scott Henry, carver & gilder, & optician, East gate
Scott Thomas, shopkeeper, West gate
Scupham Charles, grocer, Walker gate
Sellers George, cooper, East gate
Sharp Henry, grocer, River head
Sharp William, tailor, East gate
Sharpley & Laurence, coal merchants, River head
Sharpley John Booth, corn merchant, River head
Shepherd William, bookseller,printer, stationer, bookbinder & paper hanger, Market place
Simons Mrs. Lucy, milliner, Burnt hill lane
Simons Thomas, postmaster, chemist & druggist, grocer, seedsman & cheese & bacon factor, East gate
Simpson, Morris & Co. general outfitters, Up gate
Simpson John Henry, chemist & druggist, Market place
Simpson Joseph, nail maker, Walker gate
Slight John, tailor, East gate
Slocombe Miss Mary, ladies' boarding school, West gate
Smith Cornelius Stovin, milliner, &c. Up gate

Smith Edward, watch maker, Mercer row
Smith Isaac, grocer, Mercer row
Smith James, hairdresser, Walker gate
Smith John hairdresser, East gate
Smith Misses, Susannah, Harriet, & Fanny, milliners, &c. East gate
Smith Mrs. Eliza, straw bonnet maker, East gate
Smith Richard, butcher, Market place
Snowden Saml. & David, linendrapers & hatters, Mercer row
Snowden Richard, butcher, East gate
Sowden William John, chemist & druggist, Mercer row
Spivey Reuben, tailor, & boarding & lodging house keeper, East gate
Spurr William, ' Old Dram Shop,' East gate
Squire Edwin, bookseller, stationer, bookbinder & dealer in musical instruments, Mercer row
Standaland James, grocer, East gate
Stephenson John, house & ornamental painter, East gate
Storr William & Co. tanners & fellmongers, North gate
Stovin Mrs. Jane, grocer, Up gate
Strawson Charles, painter, East gate
Strawson Paul, wheelwright, East gate
Sudbury John, butcher, Up gate
Sudbury Mrs. Ann, ' Three Tuns,' Up gate
Surfleet William, saddle & harness maker, Up gate
Sutton & Pettinger, linen & woollendrapers & hatters, Mercer row
Sutton George, corn & coal merchant & linseed cake merchant, River head   [Lee street
Sutton George William, proprietor of patent medicines,
Sutton Robert Carter, grocer & druggist, James street
Swaby George, tailor, James street
Swaby William, general carrier, James street
Tacey John William, agent to the Victoria life assurance, & superintendent of police, Up gate
Tate David, whitesmith & bellhanger, East gate
Taylor Henry, hat manufacturer, Market place
Taylor James, carpenter, East gate
Thompson Geo. beer retailer & boot & shoe mak. London rd
Thompson Henry, furniture dealer, Market place
Thompson John, cabinet maker, Aswell lane
Thompson John, tobacco pipe maker, New market
Thompson Joe, butcher, London road
Thompson Samuel, blacksmith, Aswell lane
Thomson James, grocer & baker, New market
Thorpe John, butcher, East gate
Titley John, ' Marquis of Granby,' East gate
Topham Thomas, miller & baker, River head
Topham Timothy Wold, miller & baker, East gate
Toynbee Samuel, solicitor, East gate
Trafford George, carrier, Spring gardens
Trought Samuel, surgeon, Mercer row
Tupholme John, tailor, New street
Turner James, brushmaker & beer retailer, Burnt hill lane
Towl John, beer retailer, wheelwright & carpenter, River hd
Tuxworth Joseph, grocer, Walker gate
Tuxworth William, beer retailer, Maiden row
Vickers James, currier & leather cutter, Aswell lane

Waite Robert Keighley & Son, tailors & drapers, Corn mkt
Wakelin James, carter, Up gate
Wakelin Thomas, hairdresser, Mercer row
Walker Thomas, Fleece commercial inn & posting house, Market place
Walker William, assistant overseer, Lee street
Wallis Thomas Wilkinson, carver & gilder & lithographic artist, Up gate
Walmsley John, grocer, Market place
Warburton Abraham, worsted manufacturer
Watkinson William, iron & brass founder & agricultural implement manufacturer, Up gate
Webster John, butcher, Walker gate
Webster Samuel, cooper, Vicker's lane
Weldale Miss Christiana, dyer, Vicker's lane
Wells Joseph, basket maker, East gate
West George, gunmaker & bellhanger, East gate
West John, butcher, Corn market
West Joseph, blacksmith, Gospel gate
Whitaker Frank, grocer, East gate
White Henry, grocer & beer retailer, West gate
White John, haircutter, Up gate
Whiting John, butcher, Mercer row
Wileman William, boot & shoe maker, East gate
Wilkinson Charles, steam cooking apparatus manufacturer, East gate
Wilkinson Daniel, corn chandler, Kid gate
Wilkinson Thomas, boot & shoe maker, Nichol hill
Willey Charles Robert, tailor, Aswell lane
Williams John, broker, Up gate
Willoughby George Rivis, King's Head family hotel & posting house, & wine & spirit merchant, Mercer row
Wilman Joseph, toy dealer, East gate
Wilson Joseph & Son, tailors, East gate
Wilson George, baker, Mercer row
Wilson James William, solicitor, & clerk to board of guardians of Louth Union, & agent to the Royal Naval, Military, East India & general life assurance, & superintendent registrar of births, deaths, & marriages, West gate
Wilson John, maltster & corn merchant, Aswell lane
Wilson Mrs. Diana, ' Greyhound,' Up gate
Wilson William, beer retailer, Broad bank
Wilson William, boot & shoe maker, Up gate
Winn Henry, cabinet & blind maker, James street
Winter William, sailmaker, River head
Woodhouse Edward, job master & livery stable keeper
Woolley Stephen, hairdresser, Corn market
Wrangham Miss Lucy Dunn, ladies' boarding school, South Trinity parade
Wray Jonathan, saddle & harness maker, Up gate
Wray Thomas, ship builder, River head
Wright Miss Eliz. ladies' boarding & day school, East gate
Yarnell George, ' Red Lion,' Aswell lane
Youle Luke Harrison & Son, rope & twine makers, & manufacturers of waterproof covers for stacks, waggons, &c. Market place
Young George, ' Jolly Sailor,' East gate
Young Thomas, corn, coal & timber merchant, River head

POST OFFICE.—Mr. Thos. Simons, postmaster, East gate

Letters from	Arrive at	Despatched.	Box closes.
Alford	4 40 a.m	8 15 p.m	7 30 p.m
Boston	4 40 a.m	8 15 p.m	7 30 p.m
Gt. Grimsby	{ 10 30 a.m } { 8 30 p.m }	{ 3 0 p.m } { 4 30 a.m }	{ 2 30 p.m } { 9 0 p.m }
Hull	{ 10 30 a.m } { 8 30 p.m }	{ 3 0 p.m } { 4 30 a.m }	{ 2 30 p.m } { 9 0 p.m }
London	4 40 a.m	8 15 p.m	7 30 p.m
Peterborough	4 40 a.m	8 15 p.m	7 30 p.m
Spalding	4 40 a.m	8 15 p.m	7 30 p.m
Spilsby	4 40 a.m	8 15 p.m	7 30 p.m

Letters for any of the above places may be posted till within 10 minutes of despatching on payment of a fee of 1d. Money orders are granted and paid from 9 till 6 daily, Sundays excepted

CORPORATION :—
High Steward, the Right Hon. C. T. D'Eyncourt, M.P
Aldermen,

John Booth Sharpley, esq.	Mr. John Campbell
mayor	Samuel Trought, esq
Field Flowers Goe, esq	John Bogg, esq
James William Wilson, esq	

Councillors,

Mr. William Shepherd	Mr. John Allenby
Mr. Robert Green	Mr. William East
Mr. Michael Plaskitt	Mr. William Armitage
Christphr. Ingoldby, sen. esq	Mr. A. Goulsboro' Marshall
Mr. William Potter	William Day Ditchett, esq
Mr. William Ashton	Mr. Edward Sutton
Mr. Charles Bowmar	Mr. John Hurst
Mr. Luke Harrison Youle	Thomas Philbrick, esq
Mr. John Henry Simpson	Mr. William Nell

Borough Magistrates,

John Booth Sharpley, esq	Samuel Trought, esq
John Fytche, esq. Thorpe hll	Cornelius Parker, esq

John Tatam Banks, esq. Stewton house

BANKERS :—
Lincoln & Lindsey Banking Company, Corn market, open from 10 to 1 & 3 to 5 daily (Mr. John Nesbitt, manager); draw on Prescott, Grote & Co. London
Garfit, Claypons & Garfits, Mercer row, open from 10 to 1 & 3 to 5 daily; draw on Masterman & Co. London
Savings' Bank, Public buildings, open every wednesday from 1 till 2, & on saturday evenings from 7 till 8 in winter, & from 8 till 9 in summer, Mr. John Nesbitt, actuary

INSURANCE AGENTS :—
Alliance Fire & Life, Mr. Jonathan Birkett, Corn market
Atlas Fire & Life. Mr. John Jackson, Market place

Church of England Fire & Life, Mr. Wm. Edwards, Corn market

Clerical, Medical & General Life, Mr. Wm. Ashton, Market place

County Fire, William Grant Allison, esq. Mercer row

Crown Life, William Grant Allison, esq. Mercer row

Etonian Life, Thomas, Philbrick, esq. Bridge street

General Fire & Life, Henry Cox Goy, esq. Up gate

Globe Fire & Life, Thomas Grant, jun. esq. West gate

Imperial Fire & Life, Thomas Grant, jun. esq. West gate

London Fire & Life, Christphr. Ingoldby & Son, South st

North of England Fire & Life, Christopher Byron, esq. New street

Norwich Fire & Life, Henry Falkner, esq. East gate

Nottinghamshire & Derbyshire Fire & Life, Septimus Bourne, esq. Mercer row

Pelican Life, Mr. Charles Edward Lucas, Corn market

Phœnix Fire, Mr. Charles Edward Lucas, Corn market

Royal Exchange Fire & Life, Mr. Wm. Parkin, Edward st

Royal Naval, Military, East India & General Life, Jas. Wm. Wilson, esq. West gate

Scottish Equitable Life, Mr. Chas. Edwd. Lucas, Corn mkt

Star Fire & Life, Mr. Michael Plaskitt, Market place

Sun Fire & Life, Pye, Waite & Newbald, Gospel gate

Victoria Life, Mr. John William Tacey, Up gate

West of England Fire & Life, Hy. Orme, esq. Chequer gte

Yorkshire Fire & Life, Mr. John Nesbitt, Corn market

PUBLIC ESTABLISHMENTS, &c.:—

Engine House, Engine gate

Excise Office, at the King's Head hotel, Mercer row

Gas House, River head, Alexander Milne, superintendent

Mansion House, Up gate

Police Station, Up gate, John Wm. Tacey, superintendent

Prison, East gate, Mr. John Joseph Brian, governor; Mrs. Diana Earle Brian, matron; Rev. Thos. Aquila Dale, B.A., chaplain; Mr. John Bogg, surgeon

Sessions House, Ramsgate

Stamp Office, Corn market, Wm. Allison Dunn, sub-distributor

Town Hall, Corn market

Workhouse, Broad bank, Mr. Thomas Sargent, governor; Mrs. Ann Sargent, matron; Rev. Edward Reginald Mantell, M.A. chaplain; Charles Watmough, Edward Brown & Joseph Jepson, relieving officers

PUBLIC SOCIETIES, &c.:—

Depôt of Society for Promoting Christian Knowledge, National school-room, West gate

Louth Association for Prosecuting Felons, Goe & Wilson, secretaries

Louth Book Club, East gate (open from 10 to 1 & 2 to 5, daily); Wm. Whitton, librarian

Louth Eske Association for Prosecuting Felons, Henry Falkner, esq. treasurer

Louth General Friendly Society, Public buildings, Mercer row, Christopher Ingoldby, jun. esq. steward; Henry Cotten, actuary

Mechanics' Institution, Public buildings, Mercer row (open daily from 10 a.m. till 10 p.m.); Wm. Walker & Jas. Seller Forster, secs.; Miss Mary Foster, librarian

Subscription Library, News & Billiard Rooms, Corn mkt

PUBLIC OFFICERS:—

Assistant Overseer, Mr. William Walker, Lee street

Boroughreeve, William Heath, Mercer row

Clerk to Board of Guardians of Louth Union, Jas. Wm. Wilson, esq. West gate

Clerk to Borough Magistrates, Christopher Ingoldby, jun. esq

Clerks to Commissioners of Louth Navigation, Goe & Wilson, West gate

Clerk to County Court, Thos. Phillips Waite, esq. West gate

Clerk to Justices for the parts of Lindsey acting for the division of Louth Eske & Ludborough, James William Wilson, esq. West gate

Clerk to Louth Gas Light Company, William Grant Allison, esq. Mercer row

Clerks to Louth & Dexthorpe Turnpike Trusts, Pye & Waite, Gospel gate

Clerk to Trustees of Scartho Turnpike Trust, Wm. Grant Allison, esq. Mercer row

Clerk to Paving & Lighting Commissioners, Henry Orme, esq. Chequer gate

Commissioners for taking Acknowledgments of Married Women, Henry Pye, esq. West gate; Henry Orme, esq. Chequer gate; Thomas Grant, jun. esq. West gate

Coroner, Field Flowers Goe, esq. Bridge street

Deputy Coroner, James William Wilson, esq. West gate

Deputy Registrar of Births & Deaths for Louth District, Charles Watmough, Up gate

High Constable of the Wold Division of Louth Eske, Mr. Charles Edward Lucas, Corn market

Inspector of Weights & Measures, Wm. Heath, Mercer row

Parish Clerk, Mr. William Parkin, Edward street

Registrar of Births & Deaths for Louth District, Mr. Wm. Parkin, Edward street

Registrar of Marriages for Louth District, Mr. John Porter, West gate

Relieving Officer for Louth District, Mr. Charles Watmough, Up gate

Sub Distributor of Stamps, Mr. William Allison Dunn, Corn market

Superintendent of Police, Mr. John Wm. Tacey, Up gate

Superintendent Registrar of Births, Deaths, & Marriages for Louth Union, Jas. Wm. Wilson, esq. West gate

Supervisor of Excise, Mr. Allen Pipe, South street

Surveyor of Roads, Mr. Robert Cropper, South street

Surveyor of Taxes, Mr. Charles Bond, Up gate

Town Clerk, Christopher Ingoldby, jun. esq

Town Crier, James Turner, Burnt hill lane

Treasurer to the Louth Eske & Ludborough Court of Sewers, Henry Orme, esq. Chequer gate

Treasurer to Louth Turnpike Trust, Thomas Grant, jun. esq. West gate

Treasurer to the Warden & Six Assistants, Henry Falkner, esq. East gate

Vestry Clerk, Henry Falkner, esq. East gate

PUBLIC SCHOOLS:—

Free Grammar, Schoolhouse lane, Rev. John Waite, M.A. head master; Rev. Thomas Aquila Dale, B.A. second master; Mr. Isaac Drape, English master; Mr. William Atherstone Hales, assistant master

Mapletoft's & Hardie's Free Commercial, North gate, Mr. Samuel Cresswell, master

British, Paradise road, Jas. Seller Forster, master; Miss Eliza Frances Davis, mistress

National (Boys), West gate, George Tidman, master

National (Girls), Engine gate, Miss Elizh. Tidman, mistress

Infant, Engine gate, Mrs. Mary Ann Perry, mistress

PLACES OF WORSHIP:—

St. James's Church, Rev. Edward Reginald Mantell, M.A. vicar; Rev. Richard Buckeridge, curate

Trinity Chapel of Ease, East gate, Rev. Edward Richardson, minister

Catholic Chapel, Up gate, Rev. Henry Hall, priest

Baptist Chapel, Cannon gate, Rev. Richard Ingham, minister

Independent Chapel, Cannon gate, Rev. John Theodore Barker, minister

Wesleyan Chapel, East gate
Wesleyan Chapel, River head
Wesleyan Chapel, New market
— Rev. Alex. Strachan, Rev. Wm. Harris Rule, Rev. John H. Beech, Rev. John H. Norton, ministers

Primitive Methodist Chapel, Walker gate, ministers various

Primitive Methodist Chapel, Pade hole, ministers various

General Baptist Chapel, Walker gate, Rev. James Kiddall, minister

POSTING HOUSES:—

King's Head hotel, Mercer row, George Rivis Willoughby

Mason's Arms hotel, Corn market, Richard Mitchell

Fleece inn, Market place, Thomas Walker

Blue Stone tavern, Up gate, Stephen Rickit

AN OMNIBUS leaves the King's Head & Mason's Arms hotels, in time for every train

TRADING VESSELS for London, Hull, Wakefield, & Leeds, sail from Nell's wharf, Riverhead, weekly, & for Newcastle monthly

CARRIERS TO:—

ALFORD—William Swaby, every tues. from his own house, James street; John Reed, wed. from the 'Royal Oak;' & Jesse Tickelpenny, wed. from 'Rising Sun'

ASHBY-CUM-FENBY—Michael West, wed. from 'Rising Sun'

ASTERBY—James Heaton, wed. from the 'Greyhound;' Thomas Hatcliff, wed. from the 'Greyhound;' & Moses Crow, wed. from the 'Three Tuns'

BAGENDERBY—Thomas Bark, wed. from the 'New Rein Deer'

BELCHFORD—Stephen Hudson, wed. from the 'Three Tuns'

BENNIWORTH—Edward Tacey, wed. from the 'Three Tuns;' & Edward Kent, wed. from the 'Greyhound'

BILSBY—William Stevenson, wed. from the 'Red Lion'
BINBROOK—John Carpenter, wed. from the 'Greyhound;'
Matthew Hackfaith, wed. from the 'New Rein Deer;' &
William Smith, wed. from 'Royal Oak'
CAISTOR—Robert Eyre, wed. from the 'New Rein Deer;'
& Benjamin Dawson, wed. from the 'Greyhound'
CONISHOLME—John Lowis, wed. from the 'Pack Horse'
COVENHAM—George Leeman, wed. & sat. from the
'Marquis of Granby'
DONINGTON—John Prescott, wed. from the 'Greyhound'
FULSTOW—Thos. Storr, wed. & sat. from the 'Jolly Sailor'
GAYTON-LE-MARSH—Thos. Evison, wed. from the 'Rising
Sun;' & John Mason, wed. from the 'Rising Sun'
GRAINTHORPE—John Wilson, wed. from the 'Jolly
Sailor;' & John Green, wed. & sat. from the 'Pack Horse'
GRANTHAM—David Johnson, mon. wed. & fri
GREAT CARLTON—Isaac Smith, wed. & sat. from the
'Fleece'
GRIMSBY—James Curtis, wed. from the 'Marquis of
Granby'
GRIMOLDBY—Samuel Vamplew, wed. from the 'White
Swan;' & Wm. Leake, wed. & sat. from the 'Rising Sun'
HAINTON—Robert Brumpton, wed. & sat. from the
'Wheatsheaf'
HOGSTHORP—Richard Sturr, wed. from the 'Three Tuns'
HORNCASTLE—Thomas Vinter, mon. wed. & fri. from
'Marquis of Granby;' George Hatcliff, mon. wed. & fri.
from the 'White Swan;' & Cash & Meanwell, sat. from
their office, Walker gate; & Wm. Swaby, from his own
house, James street
HOVINGHAM—Doe, wed. & sat. from the 'Woodman'
HULL—George Trafford, mon. & thurs. from his own house,
Spring gardens
LACEBY—James Markham, wed. from the 'Wheatsheaf;'
& John Markham; wed. from the 'Wheatsheaf'
LINCOLN—Thomas Johnson, mon. & thurs. from his own
house, Up gate
LUDFORD—Richard Marshall, wed. & sat. from the
'Wheatsheaf;' & James Wright, wed. & sat. from the
'Wheatsheaf'
MABLETHORPE—Thos. Triffit, wed. & sat. from the 'Jolly
Sailor'
MANBY—William Ascough, wed. from the 'Rising Sun'
MARKET RASEN—John Thistlewood, wed. from the
'Royal Oak'
MARSH CHAPEL—William Wright, wed. & sat. from the
'Rising Sun;' & James Neale, wed. & sat. from the 'Jolly
Sailor'

MUCKTON—Wm. Neal, wed. & sat. from the 'Rising Sun'
NORTH SOMERCOTES—Richard Huffton, wed. & sat. from
'Marquis of Granby;' Mark Riggall, wed. & sat. from
'Marquis of Granby;' Townend, wed. from the 'White
Swan;' George Sutton, wed. & sat. from the 'Jolly
Sailor;' Robert Short, wed. from 'Jolly Sailor;' & John
Jacklin, wed. from the 'Jolly Sailor'
NORTH THORESBY—James Andrews, wed. from the
'Greyhound;' Martin Harnies, wed. & sat. from the
'Royal Oak;' & James Ingleby, wed. & sat. from the
'Royal Oak'
SALTFLEET—Wm. Sampson, wed. & sat. from the 'New
Rein Deer;' Mrs. Elizabeth Parrish, wed. from 'Jolly
Sailor;' & Slater Borman, wed. & sat. from 'Jolly Sailor'
SALTFLEETBY ALL SAINTS—Wm. Leake, wed. & sat.
from 'Rising Sun'
SALTFLEETBY ST. CLEMENTS—John Stubbs, jun. wed.
from 'Red Lion'
SAUSTHORPE—Chas. North, wed. from the 'Greyhound'
SCAMBLESBY—Joseph Hayes, wed. from the 'Marquis of
Granby;' & John Crowson, wed. from the 'Greyhound'
SOUTH COCKERINGTON—Slater Borman, wed. & sat.
from the 'Jolly Sailor'
SOUTH SOMERCOTES—Wm. Lancaster, wed. from the
'Pack Horse'
SOUTH WILLINGHAM—John Howssam, wed. & sat. from
'Wheatsheaf'
SPILSBY—Cash & Meanwell, mon. & thurs. from their
office, at Walker gate; & Wm. Swaby, mon. from his
house, James street
STAINTON—Jsph. Babington, wed. from the 'Black Bull'
SWABY—John Townend, wed. from the 'Three Tuns;' &
Wm. Walter, wed. from the 'Greyhound'
TEALBY—T. P. Simons, wed. from 'Marquis of Granby'
TETFORD—Thos. Carter, wed. from the 'Greyhound;' &
John Bell, wed. from the 'Three Tuns'
TETNEY—Joseph Drury, wed. from the 'Woolpack;'
Henry Grimolby, wed. from the 'Marquis of Granby;'
Wm. Hackfaith, wed. from the 'Marquis of Granby;'
Thos. Nicholson, wed. from 'Marquis of Granby;' & John
Smith, wed. from 'Marquis of Granby'
THEDDLETHORPE—James Phillips, wed. from the 'Turk's
Head;' William Atkinson, wed. & sat. from the 'Jolly
Sailor;' & Edward Keal, wed. from the 'Rising Sun'
WAINFLEET—William Baxter, wed. from the 'Red Lion'
WALTHAM—George Gray, wed. from 'Marquis of Granby'
WITHERN—William Bagley, wed. & sat. from 'Marquis
of Granby'

LOUTH PARK is an extra-parochial liberty, ½ a mile east from the town and station of Louth, containing 87 people, and about 770 acres of land. An extensive abbey was founded here by Alexander, Bishop of Lincoln, in 1139, for monks of the Cistercian order, dedicated to the Virgin Mary; the foundation and portions of some of the walls remain; its revenue, in 1296, amounted to £246 9s. 3d., and at the dissolution to £169 5s. 6½d. Louth Park house is the residence of Thomas Charles Oldham, Esq.

Naull Mrs. Susannah, Louth park bldgs
Oldham Thomas Charles, esq. Louth park house

Atkin Moses, wheelwright & carpenter
Fytche William, beer retailer
Goodwin John, blacksmith
Mackinder Mrs. Elizabeth, shopkeeper

Humphries William Ferguson, principal coast officer, Louth park buildings
Maltby John, farmer
Letters received through Louth

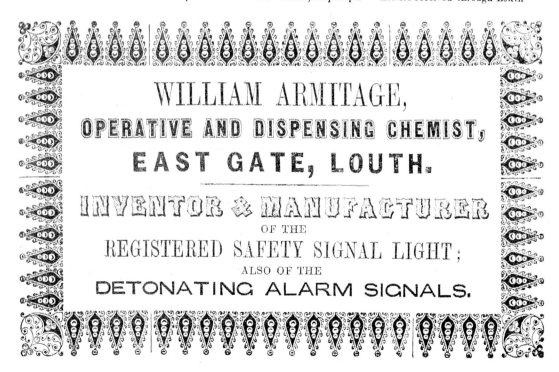

T. COCKING,
NURSERYMAN, SEEDSMAN,
AND FLORIST,

MARKET PLACE, LOUTH

Begs to return his best thanks to the Nobility, Clergy, Gentry, and the Public in general, for the great patronage he has hitherto received, and to acquaint them that he has always on hand a large Stock of

FOREST TREES, EVERGREENS,
FLOWERING SHRUBS,
TRAINED AND OTHER FRUIT TREES,
GREEN-HOUSE AND HALF-HARDY PLANTS,

Suitable for bedding out in Spring; and also a splendid collection of

STANDARD AND DWARF
ROSES, DAHLIAS, DOUBLE HOLLYHOCKS, &C.,

Also, all kinds of

VEGETABLE, FLOWER, AND AGRICULTURAL SEEDS.

T. C. has most particularly to call the attention of his numerous Friends to his ANNUAL IMPORTATION of the most rare and beautiful

DUTCH FLOWER ROOTS,
GERMAN ASTERS, LARKSPURS, STOCKS,
WALL FLOWERS, &c.

Every Article connected with the Nursery and Seed Business, supplied at the shortest notice; and parties ordering by Letter, may depend upon being served with good Articles at low prices: extras put in to compensate for long carriage.

GARDENS & PLEASURE GROUNDS
Tastefully designed, laid out, and planted on the most advantageous terms.

126

Chapter 8
Afterlife of the Panorama

THE LAST TIME the public saw the Panorama in Brown's lifetime was in May 1856 (see the end of Chapter 3). He had been a widower for just over two years and had moved to live on his own in Walkergate (Queen Street; perhaps in a house owned by the Free Methodist church on the north side towards the east end?). He was 68, styled himself as Artist and Reporter and was, as we have seen, still regularly reporting for the *Stamford Mercury*. However, in his last two years he was suffering from advancing cancer, and his last report appeared in December 1858.[1]

Brown died on Friday morning 11 February 1859, aged 70. On the death certificate the cause of death was certified as 'Disease of the Chest', and his unmarried daughter Mary Ann Holland signed as the informant 'present at the death'. She lived at Peckham, Surrey and probably came to look after her father through his last days. (Like her younger brother, she also seemed to have discarded the Christian name Holland, having signed 'M.A.Brown'.) After his death a tumour weighing 14 pounds (!) was found in this chest.[2] In his lifetime as a housepainter, Brown faced the occupational hazard of 'painter's colic', caused by constant exposure to the white lead pigment in the paints he used. Not only that, but he would also mix paints in his shop, using white lead, red lead, linseed oil, turpentine, litharge (lead monoxide used as a drier) and colouring matter.

He was buried on 14 February in the new Cemetery, for which he had campaigned so hard, in Compartment 106, Gravespace 120; there was no gravestone. His burial was conducted by Rev James Kiddall, the Baptist minister, which suggests that towards the end he had joined the Baptist congregation. Indeed, a funeral sermon was preached the following Sunday in the Baptist chapel. The newly established *Louth Advertiser* report described him as 'rather an eccentric character, but of considerable natural talent', and noted that his illustrations of the Pilgrim's Progress 'evinced a large amount of imaginative and manual skill'.[3]

The following week the *Advertiser* gave a fuller appreciation: 'His "Greatest Work" ... was the extensive paintings of Louth and its environs, in the shape of a panorama, 22 feet long, from sketches taken by him from the top of Louth spire when it was scaffolded for repairs some years ago. These views – besides being a faithful representation of the town itself, every house visible from the spire being minutely delineated – comprise an extent of seventy or eighty miles of sea-coast, [a gross exaggeration, thirty-five miles at the most] from Grimsby to Trusthorpe, and the intervening country bestudded with villages and farms ...' It goes on to list his watercolours and lithographs, and noted that 'Mr Brown was also preparing a

Besom hawkers trying for a sale
in Bridge Street.

short time before his decease, to paint several pictorial illustrations of the Fulfilment of the Prophecies of Daniel, he being an assiduous biblical scholar, as well as an artistic genius ... His whole life,' the obituary concluded, 'was one of great industry; and he died, as he had lived, resting for salvation on the merits of the atonement of Christ ...'[4]

The writer of that obituary must have known Brown and had some appreciation of his work, and revealed behind an ordinary life a man of extraordinary imagination and achievement. The obituarist in the *Stamford Mercury* took a more general appreciative line, noting first that the sarcoma (fleshy tumour) 'had been growing upon him for the past two years', and that Brown had been 'one of the most careful and intelligent contributors' to the paper. The obituary speaks of Brown laying aside 'the coarser implements of his business for the more delicate ones of the artist's profession'. It concludes: 'Taking him altogether [he] was a man of no ordinary character, and he has left behind him a fair fame, of which, we believe his veriest antagonist would not wish to deprive him'.[5] The use of 'antagonist' is surely significant. Whether or not Brown knowingly antagonised people, there were those who opposed him, and if it was Henry Boothby (his successor as reporter) who wrote the obituary, he knew who they were. Whatever the reason, it was only the *Advertiser* that mentions the Panorama, and nothing was said, or can be found, about its immediate fate.

What we do have however, three months after his death, is an editorial, signed 'Rip van Winkle', in the *Advertiser* which is another 'freeze-frame' of part of the town, much on the lines of what Brown himself had written fifteen years before, and in a style of which he would have approved.

'The entrance into the town from the Railway Station will be greatly improved by the new stone pavement which is now being laid down in the place of the well-worn asphalted road. The space from the prison corner to the Wellington Hotel is rapidly filling up with middle-class houses, which have been lately much in demand. It is a pity that greater uniformity has not been maintained in the erection of these otherwise ornamental buildings. We question whether any town in Lincolnshire, except Grimsby, has improved so much during the last quarter of a century, as Louth.

'Leaving Ramsgate and passing along Eastgate, what a pleasing transformation we find from the unsightly and protruding long garden wall, into the two beautiful buildings of Roger Sharpley, Esq.; next we meet with the noble edifice, provided as a place of worship by the Free Methodists, at a cost of about four thousand pounds. The scene is certainly marred by the old and dilapidated public house, 'The Woodman', - a century behind the times. In our progress into the interior, we find an anomaly - a Temperance Hotel Beer Shop, which strikes us as having a sign-board too many, and is rather a proof of the march of ingenuity, than of the march of temperance or consistency. Mr. Pearson's splendid mansion [John; miller, corn merchant and baker], formerly a big unsightly warehouse, must be regarded as an excellent metamorphosis, but as a set-off against this gratifying discovery, we are disposed to indulge a feeling of regret that Mr. Ashton's property [William; boot and shoe maker], has not yet met with a spirited and speculative purchaser, as such an exceedingly eligible site, would doubtless be advantageously and profitably occupied by superior houses, or moderately rented shops.

'The new shop fronts of Messrs. Bennett, Holden, Hurley, Haselgrove, Colam, Tidman, and Noble, arrest the attention, but our admiration is excited still more by the magnificent establishment of Mr. Odling. The Auction Mart of Mr. Ryall, and the modern plate glass fronts of Messrs. Kiddall, Wilson, Fanthorpe, and Barret, cannot be passed unheeded. Mr. Morton's beautiful building merits great praise.

Eastgate about 1908.

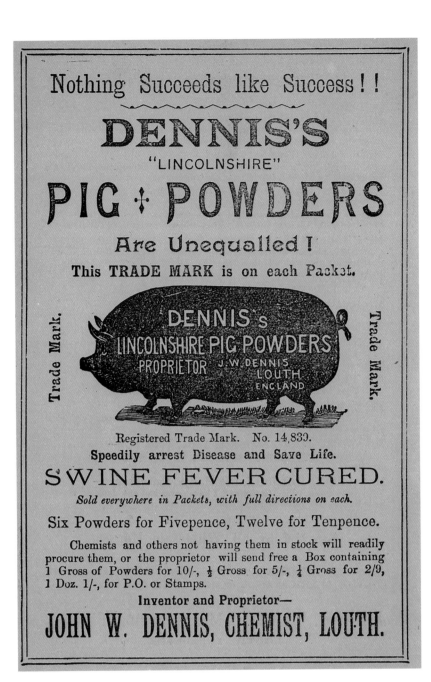

[Using directories we can identify the businesses referred to, giving an idea of the range in the street. William Bennett was a corn and flour dealer, John Holden a grocer and provision dealer, and Richard Hurley a grocer and confectioner. There were two Colams: James, plumber, glazier, painter and gasfitter, and his wife who ran a register office for servants, and Matthias who was a chemist and druggist. George Tidman was a bookseller and stationer; we cannot trace Haselgrove or Noble. The premises of Anselm Odling (see Chapter 4 under Dwellings) had been taken over by 1856 by J W Dennis & Son, chemist, who was to make his name as inventor and manufacturer of Dennis's Lincolnshire Pig Powders; the shop is now occupied by Argos. Elisha Ryall was the auctioneer, William Kiddall was a miller, corn merchant and dealer in linseed cake, Frederick Wilson a tailor and hatter, John Fanthorpe a china, glass and earthenware dealer, Barret & Co were wholesale grocers, and Joseph Morton & Son were iron and brass founders, iron merchants, general furnishing ironmongers and tin plate workers.]

'There is a rumour afloat that the Swan Inn, which protrudes very awkwardly at the opposite corner, is likely to be removed and replaced by first-class shops – the sooner the better in our judgment; this Inn, realising forty pounds a year to its proprietor, occupies abundance of space for three forty-pound shops and a few square yards to spare, wherewith to widen and improve the street.

'Mr. Mawer [Thomas; grocer and provision dealer] must be congratulated on the astonishing improvement made to his establishment, which however is rivalled by the newly-erected premises of Messrs. Swaby [George; tailor and draper] and Snowden [Richard; butcher]. Next strikes our admiring gaze – the Town-hall – the most splendid edifice in the town, except the church, and as a specimen of modern architecture unsurpassed by any public building in Lincolnshire – a wonderful contrast to the 'Pepper Box', as it is contemptuously designated in the market-place of Grimsby.

'Proceeding in our investigations towards the centre part of the town, we find three excellent shops, modernised by the late unfortunate Mr. Armitage, now occupied by Messrs. Walker, Adlard and West, next Mr. Melluish's conspicuous premises. Mr. Catling's very showy banner is in danger of being eclipsed by Mr. Boothby's nearly completed new and handsome shop; yet the Number One Drapery Concern [Eve & Ranshaw], over the way, maintains its respectability and dignity. The shop of Messrs. W. Shepherd, Keith, Oldham and Burton are worthy of note, it is not long since they, at a considerable cost were made to vie with their neighbours. In the market-place, we perceive, that not many years since a row of first-class shops, belonging to Mr. Larder, have been built; a row equally elegant belonging to Mr. Pearson grace another site; but we cannot overlook Mr. Gates's extensive and imposing establishment, or those of Mr. Brotherton and Mr. Askey.

[The readers in 1859 would have known the business of each name, but we have to resort again to directories. William Walker was a chemist and druggist, James Adlard a watchmaker, George West a gunmaker and bellhanger, and James Melluish a leatherseller. William Catling had a fancy repository, and Henry Boothby jnr was a boot and shoe maker (he lived at Holme Cottage on Newbridge Hill and was Brown's successor as local reporter for the *Stamford Mercury*). William Shepherd was a bookseller, printer and stationer, William Keith a brazier, Thomas Oldham a tailor and hatter, and George Burton a tailor and outfitter. Henry Gates was a chemist and druggist and soda water manufacturer, Edmund Brotherton a linen and woollen draper, and William Askey was a silk mercer, hosier, haberdasher and milliner.]

The Market Place Brown knew. This photograph was taken on Tuesday 26 September 1865 – that date chalked on the shutters of Blakelock & Boswell's shop (saddler & harness maker). To the right had been Henry Thompson (furniture broker) and J Thompson (jeweller), and to the left (with blank signboard) the New Reindeer inn (publican Dickinson Lewis). Demolition was about to start to make way for the Market Hall.

'Mr. Jackson's edifice [John and Thomas; printers, booksellers, stationers, bookbinders, publishers, music sellers and patent medicine vendors; now Oxfam] is worthy of the great Metropolis. Nothing has been heard lately of the proposed company, who were to purchase the premises between the Town-hall and the Market-place, for the purpose of erecting in their place a covered Butter-market, and new street; this improvement must sooner or later be added to the list. Few towns of equal importance are destitute both of a covered Butchers Shambles and Butter-market.

[There is an echo of Brown here. At the time of the building of the Corn Exchange (see Chapter 4) he had complained about the lack of covered accommodation for the 'poor butter women'. However, another seven years were to elapse before the Corporation pulled down the properties shown on the Panorama between the Market Place and the Town Hall (including one of the 'great houses' of Louth, formerly occupied by John Naull) to build the Byzantine Gothic Market Hall. It was designed by Louth architects Rogers & Marsden and built in 1866-67 at a cost of £7,000. The iron arch girders of the hall are a smaller version of King's Cross railway station. The wooden gargoyles on the clock tower were carved by T W Wallis.

'King's Cross' girders in the Market Hall.

One of T W Wallis's gargoyles awaiting a repaint, and back in position (with anti-pigeon protection) during the Market Hall restoration in 1995.

The Market Place about 1906.

[Three years earlier a shop which Brown mentioned in his glowing account of improved buildings on the south side of Mercer Row (1841; see Chapter 4) was destroyed by fire. This was the drapery emporium of Sutton & Oldroyd (formerly Sutton & Pettinger). Shortly before 1 am on Saturday 3 January 1863 flames burst from the second storey windows, started by a beam igniting in a flue. Twenty people, including apprentices, who lived at the back of the shop escaped. Neighbouring shops were affected – to the left that of Charles Hargrave, wholesale and retail boot and shoe maker, and stay warehouse (now Light 'N' Shade) and Samuel Preston, printer, bookseller, stationer and bookbinder, dealer in patent medicines and paperhangings, and repository for the Society for the Propogation of Christian Knowledge (formerly Henry Hurton's print works, later Goulding's bookshop, and now Going Places travel shop) – and to the right that of Michael Colbridge, grocer (now The Card Shop) – and even shops on the other side of Mercer Row were charred. The old town fire engine was inadequate and those from Alford, Boston and Grimsby were summoned by telegraph. That from Alford arrived on the mail train at 4 o'clock, and the Boston engine by special express an hour later, but that from Grimsby did not arrive until 8 o'clock, after the front wall of the shop had fallen inwards, burying £10,000 worth of goods.[6] The disaster stimulated the Town Council to establish a proper fire brigade. The shop was entirely rebuilt and is now W Boyes & Co, Depot Store.

The burnt out shell of Sutton & Oldroyd's shop on Mercer Row. (Drawing by T W Wallis).

The inadequate Louth fire engine. It had been bought as long ago as 1681 at a cost of just £18.

[One of Brown's pet hates were the 'disgusting appendages called the Feoffee houses' on the north side of St James's church (see Chapter 4 under 'freeze-frame'). These houses cluttered up the junction of Westgate and Bridge Street, and were not taken down until 1888. The area was levelled, grassed down and enclosed with iron chains (as Brown had advocated) to become the Jubilee Ground in honour of Queen Victoria.[7]]

'Other parts of the town have improved greatly, for instance, Broad Bank is now filled up, quite to the Union-house, with most splendid private residences, but the traffic having chiefly increased on the east side of the town, more capital has been expended there than elsewhere. More than fifty new fronts have been put out in Eastgate in little more than ten years. Before the opening of the Railway, the chief place of resort was Westgate, which on Sabbath evenings was thronged with young people (not to their credit or moral benefit); now, the most popular promenade is in the opposite direction, from the Market-place to Louth Park. Other places of interest and ornament have sprung into existence, within a short period; among the most important are the Cemetery, the Primitive Methodist Chapel, the Baptist School-room, and the Corn Exchange, and we are shortly to have added a Savings Bank; all indicative of public spirit and Christian enterprize. With the advance of morality and religion, population is advancing, education is advancing, arts and sciences are cultivated, peace and order are prevailing, and to crown the whole, a race of sober, thoughtful, pious youths are being trained, who promise to eclipse their ancestors in mental vigour, commercial enterprize, self-respect, and intelligent Christianity.'[8]

A man with a hurdy-gurdy(?) and a monkey on a string entertains children in Westgate.

Although Brown had planned in 1849 to make a pair of engravings of the Panorama dedicated to the nobility, gentry and clergy of the county, and had claimed that they would serve as a 'voucher' for the estates and properties in the town, nothing came of it. Perhaps the nobility, gentry and clergy did not feel they could subscribe to such a religious controversialist. So Brown kept the Panorama at home, added new buildings and showed it for the last time in May 1856. There was, apparently, no attempt or request to put it on permanent display, not even by the Mechanics' Institute, to which Brown owed so much for drawing and other classes and for the inspirational sources of imagery for his other works. A decade after Brown's death, in February 1869 there was a large art exhibition in the Town Hall. By that time the Panorama had disappeared and been forgotten; in any case, perhaps it would not have been regarded as art. Panoramania, it would seem, had died with Brown.

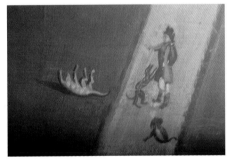

Exercising dogs on the church green.

What happened to the Panorama paintings after Brown's death is a mystery which may never be solved. Indeed, they might never have returned to Louth but for a chance meeting in 1948. That year Wilfred Alex Slack was Mayor of Louth and happened to meet Mrs Whithead, the wife of the vicar of Alford, Rev (later Canon) Whitehead, who said she had two 'pictures' which he ought to see. They belonged to her brother, Commander F A Smyth, who lived in Devon, and she was storing them for him in a cottage in Markby. Mr Slack, accompanied by Ald Maurice Hall and Harold Drinkel went to see the pictures. Painted in oil on linen and mounted on wooden rollers, they were in poor condition, badly torn at the edges, with long and serious cracks in the paint which in some places was peeling off. 'It was immediately obvious', wrote Alex Slack, 'that they were of great local value, giving a detailed representation of mid-19th century Louth'. They had found the Brown Panorama.

The story of how they came to be in a cottage at Markby was that in 1895 the vicar of Sutton on Sea and rector of Hannah with Hagnaby and Markby, Rev Arthur Smyth (related to the Smyths of Elkington, and father of F A Smyth) recognised them in the catalogue of an auctioneer's furniture sale at Sutton on Sea, described as 'maps'. Little interest was shown at the sale and he bought them for five shillings (25p) ! How they came to be in the sale is part of the mystery. Perhaps Brown's son Holland found the two large rolls of canvas on rollers, each nine feet long, just too bulky to take to London with the books and smaller paintings. Could they have been given to one of Brown's grandchildren, that is the children of his son William, because of the double family connection with the Donners of Alford? (See Chapter 5 under His Family). It would explain how the paintings stayed in east Lincolnshire.

Alex Slack quickly realised that the paintings had to be bought for the town and restored. With advice from Sir Geoffrey Harmsworth and F J Cooper, Director of the Usher Gallery in Lincoln, the paintings were skilfully restored by James Bourlet & Sons of London. Cllr Arthur Jaines transported the paintings to and from London without charge. The total cost of the purchase, restoration, framing and glazing was £350. The National Art-Collections Fund made a grant of £100 and Alex Slack raised the balance by public subscription. An anonymous donor sent a blank cheque with instruction to fill in any outstanding amount. The cheque was completed for £14 3s 6d, and in 1949 the paintings were handed over to the Borough Council, who undertook to hang them on the north wall of the Council Chamber, and never to dispose of them.[9] No other town hall in the country has a comparable asset.

Mayor Alex Slack and his wife Margaret in front of the restored and newly hung Panorama in the Council Chamber in 1948. (Courtesy Christopher Slack)

There they hung for another forty years, for much of the time a neglected treasure, their brilliance obscured by a patina of tobacco smoke, finger marks and sellotaped notices and sometimes barricaded with furniture. In the late 1950s, Elizabeth Baxter, the great granddaughter of Brown, visited Louth to see the Panorama as she was gathering material for an intended biography of him.[10] This was never published, but she had his original sketches, which must have come to her through her grandfather Holland/Henry Brown(e). They were to pass to her brother's grandson, Anthony Jarvis, who visited Louth in 1996 and later very kindly lent them for detailed study alongside the Panorama itself.

Not until July and August 1988 was the Panorama finally made visible to the wider world, when it was taken to London for an exhibition 'Prospects of Town and Park' in the Colnaghi Gallery on Old Bond Street, to mark the 85th year of the National Art-Collections Fund. The glass was cleaned and the Panorama photographed professionally, and the panels were reproduced in the exhibition catalogue (one of only seven in colour of the thirty-five in the exhibition). This is the catalogue entry.

WILLIAM BROWN
1788 - 1859
Panorama from the spire of St James Church, Louth, c.1844-55
Oil on linen   183 x 274 cms (72 x 108 ins, each)
TOWN COUNCIL, LOUTH
Acquired in 1949

These fascinating paintings, which together form a complete panorama, provide a detailed representation of the busy market town of Louth and its environs – some fifty towns and villages are shown – in the mid nineteenth century. The right-hand picture shows the view to west and south. The fashionable residential street, Westgate, is on the right; some of the gardens show the influence of J. C. Loudon's advocacy of symmetrical beds, while others retain what he described as 'newt-shaped beds' and beds that twisted 'like eels in misery'. Pupils play in the Grammar School yard; a coach is coming down the London road towards town. The left-hand painting shows the view to the east and north. The commercial centre lies beyond the roof of St James's. Coaches are being made in Esberger's yard; haystacks are to be found in many yards and gardens; the Workhouse of 1837, now the County Hospital, is on the outskirts of town; a water-carrier is filling his cart in the Lud; and a funeral procession is making its way to St Mary's churchyard. Beyond the East Lincolnshire Railway line are the warehouses around the Riverhead; barges are sailing on the canal; Spurn Point Light House and parts of Holderness can be seen; and among the ships on the Humber and North Sea is the Royal Squadron returning from Scotland.

William Brown was born at Malton, Yorkshire, in 1788. From the late 1820s he was resident in Louth and, in addition to his work as an artist, was for many years correspondent to the *Lincoln, Rutland and Stamford Mercury*. In 1844-45, as a result of serious lightning damage, the spire of St James's was restored under the direction of L. N. Cottingham. Brown's preliminary sketches for these paintings were made from the spire, encased in scaffolding, when this restoration was in progress, and 'corrected by later inspection'. On 4 September 1846 the *Mercury* reported that Brown had resumed work on the panorama; it was finally exhibited at the Mansion House in July 1847. In August 1849 an advertisement in the Mercury invited subscriptions of one guinea – one guinea five shillings with key – for a pair of engravings of the painting; the scheme never apparently came to fruition. Brown continued to add to the panorama for some years: he probably anticipated the railway and station of 1848 when the pictures were first shown in 1847; the Corn Exchange of 1853 and the Town Hall of 1854-55 are marked by new paint-work.

These pictures were purchased in 1949 as a result of the efforts of the then Mayor of Louth, Mr W. A. Slack. On seeing them, he realised their importance for Louth, although they were in poor condition, torn at the edges, with serious cracks in the paint and mounted on wooden rollers (dated 1848-53). With the help of the NACF, Mayor Slack raised the money for their purchase, restoration and framing. The pictures now hang in the Council Chamber of the Town Hall, as they have for the past forty years.[11]

The recruiting sergeant steps out of the Wheatsheaf in Westgate.

NATIONAL ART-COLLECTIONS FUND
LOAN EXHIBITION AT COLNAGHI'S

'Prospects of Town and Park'

An exhibition of topographical paintings from Museums & Galleries throughout Great Britain
purchased over the last fifty years with the help of the National Art-Collections Fund

As part of Colnaghi's 1988 sponsorship programme

July 15–August 20   Mon–Fri 10–6   Sat 10–1

COLNAGHI, 14 Old Bond Street, W1X 4JL

'No other townscape in the exhibition matched the obsessive detail' Brown recorded.[12] According to one reviewer (Colin Amery in the *Financial Times*), the Louth Panorama was the star of the show.[13] 'It is a brilliant achievement' he wrote. His comment that it was painted in a 'delightfully primitive style' was meant as a compliment. 'Is it only the artistry, or is it the actual town that, to our modern eyes, looks so totally harmonious in scale?' And he also asks, 'what would a panorama of Louth show today?' The answer is change on the outskirts where the town has spread, but the core is readily recognisable; it still has its harmonious heart of indigenous materials and hierarchy of architectural scale that makes our town so agreeable.

The *Financial Times* gardening correspondent, Robin Lane Fox, also visited the exhibition, and devoted a whole feature to the Panorama – 'Such a couth view of Louth'. He called the paintings 'a pair of landscapes with a message.' 'I cannot think of any other visual elegance', he wrote, 'which is so detailed about such a range of gardens in the 1840s. Here is the entire horticultural hierarchy of a town set before us ... There are formal gardens, symmetrical gardens, gardens in quarters, gardens with cross-belts of gravel, gardens with loops and circles, and just the sort of garden on a slope which would win a modern gold medal for Louth in bloom ...'[14] The *Daily Telegraph* described the Panorama as the 'gem' of the exhibition, 'a pair of minutely detailed paintings which show us what the citizens of Louth got up to on an ordinary day in the 1840s ... we spy on small boys stoning a dog ... an underattended funeral procession ... a woman's knees peek out from the arbour of her Frenchified formal garden, while men labour away at sawmills ...'[15]

To coincide with the exhibition a colour feature under the title 'Aspiring Views' appeared in *Country Life*.[16] A few years later the *Louth Leader* newspaper celebrated with a spread 'Panoramic View of Louth', giving more of its history, and close-ups of detail of the paintings.[17]

Countrywide recognition at last, one thought, but this had results we did not expect. The entry on Brown in *British Landscape Painters* has the left panel reversed, giving a strange looking-glass vision of Louth. Mark Girouard chose to use a detail from each panel of the Panorama as end papers in *The English Town*,[19] but contrived to reverse one of the plates so that the work of a most painstakingly accurate artist moves from fact into fantasy. One would expect that professional printers should be able to tell one side of a transparency from the other, even if the author and proof-reader don't know Louth.

However, the latest, and most prestigious, book to include Brown does get it right. Lionel Lambourne's *Victorian Painting*[20] has a chapter titled 'Virtual Reality': The Panorama, in which the right panel appears. While other nineteenth century panoramas have 'mouldered into dust, there still survives a bird's eye view [of Louth] framed in a time warp on a busy sunny day'. Survives, we would add, perhaps only because a Mayor of Louth met the vicar's wife from Alford in 1948, ninety-two years after Brown last showed his masterpiece Panorama to the public.

Today, at the beginning of a new millennium, with the trend towards globalisation seemingly inexorable, the Panorama stands as a memorial to that love of the local, the immediate environment, from which all other loyalties must grow. In its own way it is a microcosm, not just of Louth or of Lincolnshire, but even of England itself. It is therefore a national treasure, and next to St James's church it is Louth's most precious possession.

William Brown's renowned Panorama looks over the Town Council.

LOUTH TOWN COUNCIL 1991-1992
Cllr Gibson, Mr Cooper (Sergeant)   Cllrs Robertson, Hough
Cllrs Heywood, Hoyle, Shepherd, Finch, Nicholson, Naulls, Cuppleditch, Dean, Thomas,
Cllrs Macdonald, Gathercole, Mrs Sorbie, Mrs Brown, Mrs Grant (Mayor), Mr F P Weir (Town Clerk), Ward, Mrs Bollard, Mrs Ottaway

Footnotes and References

LRSM = Lincoln, Rutland & Stamford Mercury. 2/4 = page 2 column 4.

Chapter 1 Panoramania and the Louth Eye

1. John Harris, Introduction to *Prospects of Town and Park*, P D Colnaghi & Co Ltd, London, 1988, p10.
2. *Louth Herald* 18 July 1847 2/6.
3. *LRSM* 9 July 1847 4/7.
4. *Lincolnshire Chronicle* 25 April 1856 6/2.
5. *LRSM* 6 June 1856 2/4.
6. *Financial Times* 18 July 1988.
7. C Hemming, *British Landscape Painters*, London, 1989, p188.
8. *Financial Times* 6 August 1988.
9. John Harris *op cit* p10.
10. R L Wagner & M W Mikesell (eds) *Readings in Cultural Geography*, p23; quoted in S R Eyre & G R T Jones *An Ecological Basis for Geographical Field Studies*, London, 1966, p17.
11. *Louth Standard* 22 July 1988, p5
12. Ralph Hyde, *Panoramania! The Art and Entertainment of the 'All-Embracing View'*, an exhibition at the Barbican Art Gallery November 1988-January 1989, p28.
13. Ralph Hyde, *Gilded Scenes and Shining Prospects: Panoramic Views of British Towns 1575-1900*, Yale Center for British Art, New Haven, Connecticut, USA, 1985.
14. Ralph Hyde, *Panoramania!* p131.
15. *LRSM* 27 February 1835 3/4.
16. Ralph Hyde, *Panoramania!* p43.
17. Stephen Oettermann, *The Panorama – History of a Mass Medium*, New York, 1997, p7.
18. Stephen Oettermann *op cit*, p8.

Chapter 2 Genesis – the opportunity of the broken spire

1. *LRSM* 19 April 1844 2/3.
2. C J Carter (1784-1851) had been responsible for the rectory (1832), the first Holy Trinity church (1834) and Little Carlton rectory (1843).
3. L N Cottingham (1787-1847) was known for his 'judicious restoration' of Armagh and Hereford cathedrals, the abbey church of St Alban, and the Norman tower at Bury St Edmunds.
4. *LRSM* 19 April 1844 2/3; 7 June 1844 2/5.
5. Captain Allen, William Grant Allison (attorney), Joseph Larder (confectioner), Henry Pye (solicitor), John Booth Sharpley (corn & coal merchant, and leading Wesleyan Methodist), and James William Wilson (solicitor).
6. *LRSM* 19 June 1844 2/4; 5 July 2/4.
7. *LRSM* 24 April 1846 4/2.
8. Pers. comm. Mrs V A Given (great great granddaughter of John Dales), Horton, Northampton. John Dales (1821-1870) married Mary Ann, daughter of master mason Thomas Ablewhite in 1846. He built the Town Hall in 1854 and many other town improvements, and moved to London in the 1860s where he had an architect's practice in Storey's Gate, Westminster.
9. Two long legs with a stay and pulley block.
10. *Autobiography of Thomas Wilkinson Wallis*. Louth, 1899, p65.
11. *LRSM* 30 August 1844 2/4.
12. J M Stratton, *Agricultural Records AD220-1977*, London, 1978, p107.
13. *LRSM* 13 September 1844 2/2.
14. *LRSM* 11 October 1844 3/5.
15. *LRSM* 25 October 1844 2/3.
16. The wild mare in St James is a 'clasp arm' type treadwheel windlass, thought to have been first used in the building of the spire 1501-1515. It is mounted in the top storey of the tower above the bells, the hoisting of which was probably its main subsequent use.
17. *LRSM* 4 October 1844 2/2.
18. Millstone grit is a medium grained grey sandstone from the Pennines, and different from the cream-coloured oolitic Lincolnshire limestone from near Ancaster, of which the spire had been built in 1501-1515.
19. *LRSM* 13 December 1844 2/3.
20. *LRSM* 10 January 1845 2/3.
21. *Illustrated London News* 22 March 1845, pp180-181.
22. William Davis was a carver and gilder, looking glass and picture frame maker and print seller. He probably framed paintings for Brown, and doubtless his shop in Eastgate was near Brown's own premises in Vicker's Lane.
23. *LRSM* 23 August 1844 1/1.
24. *LRSM* 20 December 1844 2/4.
25. *LRSM* 1 August 1845 2/5.

Chapter 3 From Sketchbook to Canvas

1. *Louth and North Lincolnshire Advertiser* 5 March 1859 4/1.
2. C Delano-Smith & R J P Kain, *English Maps: A History*, London, 1999, pp220-221.
3. *LRSM* 17 June 1842 2/4.
4. *Hull Trinity House History of Pilotage and Navigational Aids of the River Humber (1512-1908)*, Driffield, 1871, p36. The Donna Nook beacon was erected in 1835, and the master of the lifeboat stationed there was paid two guineas a year to maintain the beacon.
5. *LRSM* 4 September 1846 2/2.
6. *LRSM* 4 June 1847 4/5.
7. *Louth Herald* 13 July 1847 2/6.
8. *LRSM* 9 July 1847 4/7.
9. *LRSM* 22 December 1848 4/8.
10. *Lincolnshire Chronicle* 9 July 1847 1/2.
11. *LRSM* 6 April 1849 4/3.
12. *LRSM* 17 August 1849 3/5.
13. *LRSM* 11 October 1850 2/3.
14. *LRSM* 24 June 1853 4/1.
15. *Lincolnshire Chronicle* 25 April 1856 6/2; 30 May 1856 8/3-4.
16. *LRSM* 6 June 1856 2/4.

Chapter 4 Recording Public Improvements

1. The self-electing Warden and Six Assistants.
2. *LRSM* 17 February 1837 3/4.
3. *LRSM* 16 June 1837 2/4.
4. *LRSM* 22 March 1839 3/4.
5. *LRSM* 24 May 1839 5/4.
6. *LRSM* 3 July 1840 3/4.
7. *LRSM* 14 June 1839 3/5.
8. *LRSM* 21 June 1839 2/3.
9. *LRSM* 16 August 1839 3/4.
10. *LRSM* 23 August 1839 3/4.
11. *LRSM* 14 August 1840 2/3.
12. G R Willoughby came from York where his father had been surveyor to the Corporation. He married Mrs Beacham, widow of the former landlord of the King's Head, in April 1836, and became landlord of the inn himself while still carrying on his architectural work. He went on to become town surveyor, and was the architect for St Peter's, Raithby 1839, All Saints, Haugham 1840-41, All Saints, Oxcombe 1842, St Andrew's, Claxby by Willoughby 1846, and St Helen's, Biscathorpe 1847.
13. *LRSM* 6 September 1839 3/4.
14. *LRSM* 20 March 1846 4/4.
15. *LRSM* 30 May 1856 2/3.
16. *LRSM* 20 August 1841 3/4.
17. *LRSM* 3 January 1840 2/2.
18. *LRSM* 1 May 1840 3/4.
19. *LRSM* 10 July 1840 3/4.
20. D N Robinson, *The Kidgate Story*, Louth, 1997, pp7-14.
21. *LRSM* 22 October 1841 2/3.
22. *LRSM* 20 October 1854 2/3.
23. D N Robinson, *Eve & Ranshaw Double Century 1781-1981*, Louth, 1981.
24. *LRSM* 3 January 1845 2/3.
25. *LRSM* 29 September 1850 2/2.
26. *LRSM* 26 July 1850 2/6. The short cut was via Northgate, Eve Street and James Street.
27. *LRSM* 13 August 1852 2/3.
28. *LRSM* 2 March 1849 2/2; 11 May 1849 4/3.
29. *LRSM* 3 August 1849 2/2. Pearson Bellamy's son Nicholas Pearson Bellamy was a plumber and brickmaker on Upgate (on the sketches for the Panorama his name is on the roof of No 16). His brickworks were between Priory Road and the railway embankment, and show on the Panorama.
30. *LRSM* 2 September 1853 2/3.

31. *LRSM* 26 April 1850 2/3; 21 June 1850 2/5; 28 June 1850 2/3.
32. *LRSM* 26 September 1851 2/3.
33. *LRSM* 21 August 1857 5/5. For information on mud and stud, see R Cousins, *Lincolnshire Buildings in the Mud and Stud Tradition*, Sleaford, 2000.
34. *LRSM* 13 August 1852 2/4.
35. *LRSM* 4 December 1857. William Tate was partner with Charles Goodwin Smith in Smith & Tate, wholesale grocers, Upgate (next to the Blue Stone tavern). The report includes technical details and analyses about distilling beetroot from a publication of the Central Farmers' Club.
36. Widow of Christopher Byron, yeoman, who was there in the 1820s.
37. *LRSM* 30 April 1858 3/5.
38. *LRSM* 4 June 1858 5/3.
39. *LRSM* 24 December 1858 5/4. (Pearson Bellamy and John Spence Hardy were architects at 30 Broadgate, Lincoln, with a wide reputation in Lincolnshire, the Midlands and Yorkshire.) This was probably the last report Brown submitted as he died a few weeks later.
40. *LRSM* 26 July 1850 2/6.
41. *LRSM* 16 April 1852 2/2.
42. *LRSM* 13 August 1852 2/4.
43. *LRSM* 29 October 1852 2/4.
44. *LRSM* 5 November 1852 2/2.
45. *LRSM* 21 January 1853 4/5.
46. *LRSM* 21 June 1850 2/5.
47. *LRSM* 28 February 1851 2/3.
48. *LRSM* 14 July 1854 2/3.
49. Charles Clark was a builder in Enginegate. His partner was William Crow.
50. *LRSM* 9 July 1852 2/5.
51. *LRSM* 5 November 1852 2/2. Charles Edward Lucas & Brothers were wine & spirit, ale & porter merchants, already in part of the Guildhall. Another part was used as a theatre.
52. *LRSM* 13 May 1853 2/4.
53. *LRSM* 20 May 1853 2/3.
54. *LRSM* 24 June 1853 4/1, 2, 3. The report makes mention of an intended new market place opposite the new Town Hall. This would eventually be the Byzantine Gothic Market Hall of 1866-67.
55. *LRSM* 2 September 1853 2/3.
56. *LRSM* 16 December 1853 2/2.
57. *LRSM* 10 September 1852 2/4; 14 September 1852 2/2; 8 October 1852 1/4.
58. *LRSM* 3 December 1852 2/3. The Guildhall had been built about 1815 (at cost of £1,461) when the old Town Hall and the Butter Cross it stood over in the Market Place were taken down. It had provided shelter for only ten people from 'perpendicular rain', and now the butter women had no covering. – from *Report* [of H M Commissioners] *on the Corporation of Louth*, 1835. Brown had almost certainly read that report.
59. *LRSM* 21 January 1853 4/5.
60. *LRSM* 13 May 1853 2/4. The soft Caen stone was in fact unsuitable for external use, and easily decayed particularly on the exposed upper part. (Report by C F W Haseldine, 1929).
61. *LRSM* 8 July 1853 4/2.
62. *LRSM* 9 December 1853 2/2.
63. Nikolaus Pevsner & John Harris, *The Buildings of England: Lincolnshire*, London, 1964 p304.
64. *LRSM* 13 January 1854 4/6. In fact a dividend of 5% was declared at the first annual meeting – *LRSM* 1 June 1855 2/2.
65. *LRSM* 21 April 1854 2/4.
66. St Mary's church had been finally taken down in 1749.
67. For details of burials and epitaphs see R W Goulding, 'The Epitaphs in St Mary's churchyard', Louth, *Goulding's Almanack*, 1922 (11pp).
68. *LRSM* 22 September 1843 4/5.
69. *LRSM* 3 January 1845 2/3.
70. Wife of James Good, brickmaker of Union-court; she had died in childbirth.
71. *LRSM* 6 June 1845 4/7.
72. *LRSM* 18 December 1848 2/2.
73. *LRSM* 31 August 1849 4/4.
74. *LRSM* 14 May 1852 2/4.
75. *LRSM* 28 May 1852 2/3.
76. *LRSM* 10 September 1852 2/4.
77. *LRSM* 20 May 1853 2/3.
78. *LRSM* 16 December 1853 2/2.
79. *LRSM* 9 June 1854 2/2.
80. *LRSM* 14 July 1854 2/3.
81. *LRSM* 4 August 1854 2/4.
82. William White's *Directory of Lincolnshire* 1856, p250. The members of the Burial Board in 1855 were Rev E R Mantell, J B Sharpley (Mayor & Chairman), William Grant Allison, Samuel Trought, William Thomas Kime, Robert Norfolk, J W Wilson, G R Willoughby and William Ashton, with Christopher Ingoldby jun. as Clerk.
83. *LRSM* 4 May 1855 2/4; 1 June 1855 2/2.
84. *LRSM* 4 January 1856 2/2.

Chapter 5 The man, his family and Methodism

1. Information for Teetotallers: There are in Louth 51 beershops and 26 inns and public houses, together making 77. If we estimate the daily average consumption of one beverage in each house (ale) at 4 gallons per day, it will amount annually to 112,420 gallons, excluding the thousands of gallons of ardent spirits and wines consumed by the town. *LRSM* 18 August 1837 3/4. (The Sale of Beer Act 1830, making beer regulations less strict to combat the high consumption of gin and spirits, led to a growth of beer houses. These did not require a justice licence, but paid 2 guineas excise duty. There were around 20 of these actually listed in Louth. The other thirty odd probably operated on a 'bush licence' on market and fair days.)
2. *LRSM* 17 May 1839 3/4.
3. *LRSM* 18 October 1839 3/4.
4. *LRSM* 1 December 1843 3/5. (The reference to 'the champion' is to the Dymokes of Scrivelsby as King's Champion reversing their horse out of Westminster Hall.)
5. *LRSM* 3 July 1840 3/4. The Park is Louth Park, the butchery is Butcher Market (near Butcher Lane), the churchyard is now the Old Cem, and the church is Holy Trinity (then a chapel of ease).
6. *LRSM* 21 October 1842 2/2. Rev E R Mantell, a high churchman, became Vicar of Louth in 1831.
7. *Lincolnshire Chronicle* 17 March 1854 6/2.
8. *LRSM* 1 December 1843 3/5.
9. *LRSM* 25 April 1845 2/3.
10. Poll Book for the Election of Councillors for the Borough of Louth, 1 November 1841.
11. The Baptist and Wesleyan chapels in Louth, and the Protestant Christian's Memento.
12. A valuation of the messuages, tenements, lands, and property situate in the parish of Louth, 1823.
13. William White's *Directory of Lincolnshire* 1826.
14. This is the only address in a leatherbound notebook of family dates (up to c.1880) from which much of the family history derives. The notebook was kindly lent by Anthony Jarvis, great great grandson of Holland Brown.
15. List of Voters on the question of the Church Rate at Louth, Goulding Collection GL Lout 201, Louth Pamphlets Vol 1. On the Louth Circuit Plan of Wesleyan Preachers' Sabbath Appointments for the first six months of 1835, Brown's address is given as Market Place, of which the Fish Shambles was an extension.
16. A valuation of the messuages, tenements, lands, and property situate in the parish of Louth, 1837.
17. *LRSM* 18 February 1859 (obituary).
18. Minutes of the Board of Guardians, Louth Union, 30 August 1837, Lincolnshire Archives Office PL11/1021.
19. Essay title was 'Human utilization, its nature, elements and promotives'. The prize was £2, and Holland was 17.
20. Brown appears on the Louth Wesleyan Prayer Leaders' Plan, 1850-51.
21. *LRSM* 7 February 1845 2/6. The lecture was followed by a practical session 'of the applicability of the new way of "talking on paper" in all the languages of our babbling earth' (!)
22. D Newton & M Smith, *Stamford Mercury: Three Centuries of Publishing*, Stamford, 1999, p155.
23. Goulding Collection GL Lout 9. Louth Newscuttings & Broadsheets p89.
24. 'The Hortons of Louth', *Methodist Recorder*, Christmas 1903, pp27-31.
25. Rev William Bond (1811-1903), 'Reminiscences of my life', unpub MS, courtesy Eric Bond, great grandson.
26. Rev J Conway Walter, *A History of Horncastle*, Horncastle, 1908, p142.
27. *LRSM* 6 August 1841 3/6.
28. Rev H B Williams, 'The Louth Church Rate Battle of 1834', unpub MS 1998.
29. Author of *Notitiae Ludae*, 1833.
30. *LRSM* 16 May 1834 3/3.
31. *LRSM* 17 October 1834 4/2.
32. Goulding Collection GL Lout 352. Louth Pamphlets Vol 2; and a second enlarged edition GL Lout 287.
33. Goulding Collection GL Lout 252.
34. Goulding Collection GL Lout 287.

35. The annual national meeting of the governing body of the Church, then composed of Ministers only.
36. *LRSM* 29 May 1835 1/1.
37. Perhaps Samuel Taylor's System of Stenography, which was later adapted by Isaac Pitman in 1837.
38. Goulding Collection GL Lout 252. Instituted by John Wesley, the Love Feast was a cherished part of Methodist life, and regarded as a privilege to attend as it was only for those with a Class Ticket of membership. In the early days bread or semi-sweet buns and water (occasionally tea) was shared, but the main part came to be for each to speak freely and plainly of the state of their souls, faults committed and temptations felt since the last meeting.
39. Edward Hackford was a corn miller and flour dealer.
40. *LRSM* 4 September 1835 1/4.
41. W Leary & D N Robinson, *A History of Methodism in Louth*, Louth, 1981.
42. *LRSM* 24 November 1843 3/5.
43. *LRSM* 1 April 1836 4/4.
44. *LRSM* 10 June 1836 3/4. The chapel was built on the site of John Jackson's auction room and the cottage of cabinet-maker George Fell. Most of the trustees were leading tradesmen, but also included a surgeon, Brown's son Francis and his friend George Whelpton. They were: William Brett and his son William, drapers, Mercer Row; George Whelpton, cordwainer, Butchermarket; John Paddison, carpet manufacturer, James Street; John Joseph Moody, tailor & linen draper; Thomas Rayner, tailor; Francis Brown, cordwainer; William Chatterton Blakelock, saddler & harness-maker, Market Place; John Brett,

surgeon, Eastgate; Abraham Gouldsborough Marshall, bookseller, Mercer Row; John Dunstan Naull, ironmonger, Market Place. They set out to raise £1,000 in £1 shares, but had to take out a £400 mortgage, which was still outstanding when the chapel was sold in 1848.
45. *LRSM* 11 June 1841 2/2.
46. *LRSM* 13 August 1841 3/4.
47. *LRSM* 22 December 1843 2/2.
48. *LRSM* 23 February 1844 2/3.
49. *LRSM* 11 April 1845 2/1.
50. *LRSM* 2 April 1847 2/4.
51. *LRSM* 19 January 1849 2/2.
52. *LRSM* 2 April 1847 2/2.
53. *LRSM* 6 October 1848 2/3.
54. *LRSM* 26 July 1850 2/6.
55. *LRSM* 11 October 1850 2/3.
56. *LRSM* 2 April 1852 2/2.
57. Rev P W Robinson, 'Louth and the Rise of Free Methodism', *Journal of Lincolnshire Methodist History Society*, Vol 13 No 1 Autumn 1977, pp2-8.
58. *The Sailor's Yarn, being a true and interesting narrative of the eventful life of John Taylor, Louth, Lincolnshire*, (97pp) 1852. Edwin Squire, like Brown, went to the Free Methodists, and in 1854 began publishing a monthly magazine *The Revivalist*. The issues for 1858-59 recorded crowded revival meetings and services, with testimonies and hundreds of conversions in Louth.
59. *LRSM* 14 July 1854 2/3.
60. *LRSM* 2 January 1857 5/5.

Chapter 6 The Polyopticorama and Brown the artist

1. Goulding Collection, Louth. Miscellaneous Posters. GL 9.
2. *LRSM* 16 May 1834 3/3.
3. *LRSM* 13 February 1835 4/5; R C Russell, (A history of) Louth Mechanics' Institute, unpub MS.
4. *LRSM* 27 February 1835 3/4.
5. *LRSM* 25 September 1835 3/3.
6. *LRSM* 20 May 1836 2/3.
7. William Armitage was at Louth Grammar School 1822-24.
8. *LRSM* 22 April 1836 2/6.
9. *LRSM* 26 August 1836 3/3.
10. *LRSM* 13 September 1844 2/2.
11. *LRSM* 10 January 1840 3/4.
12. *LRSM* 19 March 1841 2/3: 'Mr W. Armitage has ingeniously constructed an apparatus, whereby after a few experiments he has produced several excellent specimens of impressions of seals, coins and engravings'.
13. *LRSM* 7 February 1845 2/6.
14. *LRSM* 23 February 1844 2/3.
15. R W Goulding, Louth Grammar School Boys Part V 1815-1820. *Goulding's Louth Almanack*, 1920, pp125-127.
16. *LRSM* 15 December 1843 2/3.
17. Richard Hubbard (1811-1890), brother of Bennett, was an engraver and lithographic printer, New Street. R W Goulding *op cit* p109.
18. *LRSM* 7 February 1845 2/6.
19. *LRSM* 27 June 1845 4/6.
20. *LRSM* 24 November 1843 3/5.
21. *LRSM* 24 April 1846 4/3.
22. *LRSM* 22 January 1847 2/2.
23. P Smith & M Godsmark, *The Story of Claribel*, Lincoln, 1965, pp37-39.
24. *LRSM* 28 February 1851 2/3.
25. *LRSM* 1 August 1845 2/5; C J Sturman, 'The Mirror with Memory', *Lincolnshire Family Historian* Vol 7 No 4 April 1990, pp107-110.
26. *LRSM* 23 November 1849 4/2.
27. *LRSM* 25 February 1848 2/4; 17 March 1848 4/3; 29 December 1848 2/5; 3 August 1849 2/2.
28. *LRSM* 23 November 1849 4/2; C J Sturman *op cit*; G Webb, 'A Signal Failure', *Lincolnshire Life*, 37, 12, March 1998, p60. Rev John H Beech, Wesleyan Methodist minister then living in Lee Street, published his autobiography in 1884. In it he tells of his 'intimate acquaintance with a clever chemist who had invented railway fog signals ... These are enclosed in tin cases, each of them about twice the size of a crown piece ... The procedure [for drying the signals in the oven] seemed to me so perilous that I remarked that unless some other arrangement were adopted I should not be surprised to read in the Stamford Mercury that an explosion had occurred at the railway signal manufactory, and the owner had been buried in the ruins. Unfortunately the very next day, as I was about to go to the premises, an explosion took place'. *The (Louth) Advertiser* 7 August 1954. There is an original Armitage fog signal in Louth Museum.

29. *Lincolnshire Chronicle* 1 September 1854 5/2.
30. *Lincolnshire Chronicle* 29 September 1854 6/1.
31. *Lincolnshire Chronicle* 11 April 1856 8/1.
32. D Cuppleditch, *Joseph Willey: A Victorian Lincolnshire Photographer*, Louth, 1987.
33. John Dunstan Naull entertained William Cobbett when he visited Louth in 1830 and described the town as lying 'in a deep dell, with beautiful pastures on the surrounding hills'. (W. Cobbett, *Rural Rides*, Vol 11 London, 1886, p321). Naull's house and shop were on the site of the Market Hall (1866-67).
34. *LRSM* 17 June 1842 2/4. The portrait was shown in the shop window of John Brown (no relation to William), gilder on Upgate (his business was bought by Wallis in 1844). The portrait was engraved by David Lucas and 'calculated to transmit the recollection of the living original to the latest memory of the present generation and indelibly to stamp his honest good-humoured qualities upon the minds of the people of Louth, and his friends throughout the kingdom'. (*LRSM* 12 August 1842 2/4). The portrait was given to the Corporation and now hangs in the Town Hall (R W Goulding *op cit* pp108-109).
35. *LRSM* 14 May 1852 2/4; R W Goulding *op cit* p108.
36. *Autobiography of Thomas Wilkinson Wallis*, Louth, 1899, p65.
37. Wallis *op cit* p107.
38. Wallis *op cit* p135.
39. *LRSM* 11 October 1850 2/3.
40. *LRSM* 14 February 1851 2/4.
41. *LRSM* 28 February 1851 2/3.
42. *LRSM* 11 July 1851 2/4.
43. *LRSM* 15 August 1851 4/1.
44. *LRSM* 12 September 1851 2/5; 26 September 1851 4/1.
45. *LRSM* 19 December 1851 2/2.
46. *LRSM* 3 September 1852 2/4.
47. *LRSM* 29 October 1852 2/4. James Fowler had arrived in Louth in 1849 and would design restoration work on St James's church in 1860 and 1866-67 (D Kaye, S Scorer & D N Robinson, *Fowler of Louth*, Louth, 1992).
48. *LRSM* 22 July 1853 2/5.
49. *LRSM* 22 February 1856 2/1.
50. *Louth & North Lincolnshire Advertiser* 26 February 1859 4/3.
51. The Free Evening School was supported entirely by public subscription and opened three nights a week for some 90 adults and 140 youths to be taught the 3Rs. It was so successful that £1,000 was spent on a larger building (now the British Legion Hall) on Northgate in 1863. The School closed in the 1880s.
52. *Louth & North Lincolnshire Advertiser* 5 March 1959 4/1.
53. Tempera is a distemper in which there is no oil. For the Panorama Brown used oil on linen.
54. *LRSM* 28 July 1826 2/7; 11 August 1826 2/4-5. D N Robinson, Ballooning in Lincolnshire, *Lincolnshire Life*, 11, 2/3, 1971, pp24-28, 38-39. See also C J Sturman, Tennyson's Balloon Stanzas reconsidered, *Tennyson Research Bulletin*, 5,1,1987, pp14-18.
55. *LRSM* 17 April 1835 3/3; 20 May 1836 2/3.

Chapter 7 A Window in Time: what the Panorama shows

1. Mrs Jane Loudon (1807-1858), wife of J C Loudon (see below).
2. C J Sturman, A Lincolnshire Hermit: Wolley Jolland (1745-1831) *Georgian Group Report & Journal*, 1987 (1988), pp62-76.
3. B Elliott, *Victorian Gardens*, London, 1986, p16. For background on Victorian gardens see also T Carter, *The Victorian Garden*, London, 1984, and L Flemming & A Gore, *The English Garden*, London, 1979.
4. John Claudius London published *Encyclopaedia of Gardening*, 1822, 1834; *The Suburban Gardener and Villa Companion*, 1836.
5. *LRSM* 22 September 1843 1/5. The advertisement also states that 'the interior of the house is painted and decorated with great taste by London workmen'. The requirement, it would seem, had been beyond the skills of Brown and his fellow housepainters.
6. For the chequered history of Pye as solicitor, County Treasurer, saltmarsh reclaimer and bankrupt, see P Smith & M Godsmark, *The Story of Claribel*, Lincoln, 1965. Claribel was the pen-name of his daughter Charlotte who, aged 16, laid the foundation stone, in July 1847, of the railway station which was to feature on the final version of the Panorama.
7. J Harding and A Taigel, An air of detachment: town gardens in the eighteenth and nineteenth centuries, *Garden History*, 24,2, Winter 1996, pp244-246. C Drake, A study of Bridge Street, Louth in the mid-19th century, unpub MS 1990.
8. F F Goe was a leading citizen, twice Mayor, and a strong supporter of Holy Trinity church. His son, also Field Flowers, was born in 1832 and would have seen the new garden design begin to mature. He became Bishop of Melbourne, Australia (1887-1901).
9. D N Robinson, *The Kidgate Story*, Louth, 1997, p9.
10. For an example of a Lincolnshire nursery and seedsman firm who developed through this period, see D N Robinson, *Double Century: The story of William Crowder & Sons, Nurserymen*, Horncastle, 1998.
11. *LRSM* 11 June 1841 2/2.
12. *LRSM* 6 August 1849 3/6.
13. *Autobiography of Thomas Wilkinson Wallis*, Louth, 1899, p151. The storm occurred on 27 & 28 May 1860; the goods warehouse at the railway station was blown down.
14. D N Robinson, *The Book of Louth*, Buckingham, 1979, pp79-85.
15. There were ten laundresses in Cannon Street Court (now a car park) with only one water tap for twenty houses.
16. A Bates, *Directory of Stage Coach Services 1836*, Newton Abbot, 1969, p80.
17. Bill Howard, *A Church for the Millennium: Holy Trinity Church, Louth – a short history*, Louth, 2000.
18. National Society for the Promotion of the Education of the Poor in the Principles of the Established Church.
19. D Kaye, S Scorer & D N Robinson, *Fowler of Louth: the Life and Works of James Fowler, Louth Architect 1828-1892*, Louth, 1992, pp40-41.
20. D N Robinson, *Orme Almshouses 1885-1985*, Louth, 1985.
21. Bill Painter, *Upon the Parish Rate: The Story of Louth Workhouse and the paupers of East Lindsey*, Louth, 2000.
22. R H Brady came to Louth from Northwich, Cheshire and married Charlotte from Covenham. He employed two journeymen drapers and three apprentices; they lived with the family in Northgate.
23. It must have been unusual for a hawker to have a nameplate. Two of Daniel's sons were also hawkers – Abel and Ephraim, and his other children had Old Testament names – Michala, Salome, Jiriselle and Absalom.
24. D N Robinson, *The Book of Louth*, Louth, 1979, pp63-64.
25. William White, *History, Gazeteer & Directory of Lincolnshire*, 1842, p354.
26. I S Beckwith, *The Louth Riverhead*, Louth, 1976. S M Sizer, *Louth Navigation: A History (1756-1926)*, Louth, 1999.
27. *Louth Industrial Trail*, Louth Teachers' Centre, 1977.
28. H Porter, The Old Paper Mill, Louth, *Lincolnshire Magazine*, 3,12,1938, pp371-372. *LRSM* 20 January 1843.
29. D N Robinson, *Eve & Ranshaw: Double Century 1781-1981*, Louth, 1981.
30. D N Robinson, *The Book of Louth*, Louth, 1979, Chapter: 'Made in Louth', pp135-141.
31. Eleanor Bennett, *Brackenborough: The Story of a Manor*, Louth, 1995, p59.
32. St Adelwold, Alvingham and St Mary, North Cockerington.
33. William Adams Nicholson (1803-1853) established his extensive practice in Lincoln in 1828.
34. See Chapter 4, Note 12.
35. D N Robinson, The Saltfleetby-Theddlethorpe Coastline, *Transactions Lincolnshire Naturalists' Union*, XXI,1, 1984, pp1-12.
36. C J Sturman, The great resort for sea bathing: Saltfleet and the New Inn, *Lincolnshire Past & Present*, 15, 1993, pp11-13.
37. G de Boer, A History of the Spurn Lighthouse, *East Yorkshire Local History Society*, 1968, pp56-59.

Chapter 8 Afterlife of the Panorama

1. *LRSM* 24 December 1858 5/4.
2. D Newton & M Smith, *Stamford Mercury: Three Centuries of Publishing*, Stamford, 1999, p155.
3. *Louth & North Lincolnshire Advertiser* 26 February 1859 4/3.
4. *Louth & North Lincolnshire Advertiser* 5 March 1859 4/1.
5. *LRSM* 18 February 1859 6/2.
6. *Illustrated London News*, 17 January 1863.
7. C Drake, A Study of Bridge Street, Louth in the mid-19th century, unpub MS, 1990.
8. *Louth & North Lincolnshire Advertiser* 14 May 1859. D N Robinson & C J Sturman, Eastgate Revolutionised, *Lincolnshire Past & Present*, 26, 1996, pp17-20.
9. Details of finding, purchasing and restoring the Panorama paintings are from an original copy letter from Alex Slack to the *Louth Standard*, 27 April 1979.
10. Miss Baxter dedicated her book *Brentwood My Heritage* (1953) to 'My ancestor William Brown, Cleric, Artist and Author'. We can only think that 'Cleric' was a misinterpretation of his active Methodism.
11. *Prospects of Town and Park*, P. D. Colnaghi & Co Ltd, London, 1988, pp84-85. Text by Christopher Sturman.
12. *Louth Standard*, 1 April 1988. This feature included a picture of Brown. Also Peter Chapman in the *Grimsby Evening Telegraph*, 4 August 1988, paying tribute to Alex Slack – 'no man was ever more misnamed' – in rescuing the Panorama. There was reference to 'a little-known painted panorama of Louth' in *Panorama*, Newsletter of the International Panorama and Diorama Society, Spring 1999.
13. *Financial Times*, 18 July 1988.
14. *Financial Times*, 6 August 1988.
15. Patricia Morrison in *The Daily Telegraph*, 30 July 1988.
16. Christopher Sturman & John Harris (then Chairman of Colnaghi's), Aspiring Views, *Country Life*, 14 July 1988, pp146-148.
17. Christopher Sturman, Panoramic Views of Louth, *Louth Leader*, 5 January 1994.
18. C. Hemming, *British Landscape Painters*, London, 1989, p188.
19. M Girouard, *The English Town*, London, 1990.
20. Lionel Lambourne, *Victorian Painting*, London, 1999, pp154-155.

Realtime Panorama

During the research for and writing of this book, the Louth Architectural Heritage Foundation was established, in March 1999, as a private limited company. In pursuance of its objects, and with Millennium Festival funding, it set out to re-create in computer virtual reality parts of the town at the time William Brown painted his Panorama of Louth. Work on developing the realtime experience of mid-19th century Louth is still continuing. When completed, computer access will be available in Louth Museum.

Index

LOUTH PANORAMA
1844 - 1856

Left Panel

by William Brown

By permission of Louth Town Council